Transformation of the
German Political Party System

POLICIES AND INSTITUTIONS
Germany, Europe, and Transatlantic Relations
Published in Association with The American Institute for Contemporary German Studies (AICGS), Washington, D.C.
General Editor: **Carl Lankowski**, Research Director of the AICGS

Volume 1
GERMAN UNIVERSITIES PAST AND FUTURE: CRISIS OR RENEWAL?
Edited by Mitchell G. Ash

Volume 2
TRANSFORMATION OF THE GERMAN POLITICAL PARTY SYSTEM: INSTITUTIONAL CRISIS OR DEMOCRATIC RENEWAL?
Edited by Christopher S. Allen

Volume 3
THE GERMAN SKILLS MACHINE: SUSTAINING COMPARATIVE ADVANTAGE IN A GLOBAL ECONOMY
Edited by Pepper D. Culpepper and David Finegold

Volume 4
BREAKDOWN, BREAKUP, BREAKTHROUGH: GERMANY'S DIFFICULT PASSAGE TO MODERNITY
Edited by Carl Lankowski

Volume 5
POWER SHIFT IN GERMANY: THE 1998 ELECTION AND THE END OF THE KOHL ERA
Edited by David P. Conradt, Gerald R. Kleinfeld, and Christian Søe

Transformation of the German Political Party System

Institutional Crisis or Democratic Renewal?

Edited by
Christopher S. Allen

Berghahn Books
New York • Oxford

First published in 1999 by
Berghahn Books

© 1999 Christopher S. Allen

All rights reserved.
No part of this publication may be reproduced
in any form or by any means
without the written permission of Berghahn Books.

Library of Congress Cataloging-in-Publication Data

Transformation of the German political party system : institutional
crisis or democratic renewal? / edited by Christopher S. Allen.
      p.   cm. (Policies and institutions ; v. 2)
   Papers of two workshops held at University of California,
Berkeley and at the American Institute of Contemporary German
Studies, Washington, DC.
   Includes bibliographical references.
   ISBN 1-57181-127-3 (alk. paper)
   1. Political parties—Germany—Congresses. 2. Comparative
government—Congresses. 3. Political science—Germany—
Congresses. 4. Germany—Politics and government—20th century—
Congresses. I. Allen, Christopher S. II. Series.
JN3971.A979 T72   1999   99-13734
324.243'009'049—dc21   CIP

British Library Cataloguing in Publication Data

A catalogue record for this book is available
from the British Library.

For Katherine

Contents

List of Tables	ix
Contributors	x
Introduction	xi
Chapter 1: Germany and the Comparative Political Party Experience: Sclerotic or Dynamic Institutions? *Christopher S. Allen*	1
Chapter 2: The Evolution and Transformation of the German Party System *Hans-Georg Betz*	30
Chapter 3: The German Party State: A Reassessment *Michaela W. Richter*	62
Chapter 4: Unification and the Changing Fortunes of Germany's Parties of the Far Right *John Leslie*	99
Chapter 5: Green Trumps Red? Political Identity and Left-wing Politics in United Germany *Andrei S. Markovits and Stephen J. Silvia*	133

Chapter 6: The Major Parties:
Dealignment and Realignment in
Post-Cold War Germany
  Henry Kreikenbom — 160

Chapter 7: Agents of Democratization and
Unification: Political Parties in the
New German States
  Ann L. Phillips — 179

Chapter 8: Institutional Elasticity in a
Changing Political Order: The Eastern
German Nonprofit Sector and Its
Contribution to Political Integration
  Wolfgang Seibel — 207

Bibliography — 234

Index — 262

LIST OF TABLES

Table 4-1   Immigration into the Federal Republic during the 1980s

Table 6-1   Age Structure and Party Identification in the GDR

Table 6-2   Occupation/Education and Party Identification in eastern Germany

Table 6-3   Volkskammer Voting Results by Denomination, 1990 and 1994

Table 6-4   Strength of Party Identification, East and West

Table 6-5   1994 Bundestag Election Results, West and East

Table 7-1   Party Membership in the New German States

Contributors

Christopher S. Allen: University of Georgia

Hans-Georg Betz: KOC University

Henry Kreikenbom: Universität Jena

John Leslie: University of California, Berkeley

Andrei S. Markovits: University of Michigan, Ann Arbor

Ann L. Phillips: The American University

Michaela W. Richter: The College of Staten Island, CUNY

Stephen J. Silvia: The American University

Wolfgang Seibel: Universität Konstanz

INTRODUCTION

The primary purpose of *Transformation of the German Political Party System* is to go beyond conventional treatments of German political parties that tend to provide quick snapshots of the state of the polity in a given election year. Rather, the contributors to this volume analyze underlying patterns of continuity and change in reconciling popular demands and system requirements. While ostensibly about German political parties, several authors also place the German experience in a comparative and historical framework. The volume evaluates the performance of the German parties and party system in dealing with the problems of integration and legitimation that are common to all industrialized democracies, and in so doing, presents a sharp analysis of the effects and incompleteness of German unification amidst continuing Europeanization. Specifically, it deals with the pressures on the German political party system deriving from a devolution of state power downward to citizens' initiatives as well as upward with respect to regional and European integration.

In characterizing and evaluating the political party system of a developed nation state in an edited volume, we made several conscious choices to elaborate both continuities and changes in the Federal Republic of Germany (FRG). We identified four essential tasks to perform. First, we wanted to situate the German political party system within the context of party systems in other developed countries (Allen). In some respects there are powerful similarities between Germany and its allies, yet on other dimensions we found significant differences. As comparativists, we believe strongly in a core maxim of the subdiscipline, namely to understand what, why, and how we are comparing. Second, we rejected the notion that the story of the German political party system began only with the founding of the Federal Republic immediately after World War II. In two historically-focused chapters (Betz and Richter) we address the deeply-rooted institutional continuities of the German political parties, their constituencies, cleavages, and roles as broad-based membership organizations. Third, we also wanted to capture the significant changes that have transpired in the German political party structure, namely the formation of new political parties within the past two decades (Markovits/Silvia and Leslie). In a fundamental sense, the capacity of a party system to respond to, if not incorporate, new social forces and party groupings within a country's institutional structure provide important clues to its health as a democratic polity. Fourth, we wanted to offer an evaluation of Germany's greatest modern experiment, namely the incorporation of the former German Democratic Republic (GDR) into the Federal Republic (Kreikenbom, Phillips, and Seibel). Specifically, we wanted to evaluate how political parties and interest groups in all of a united Germany affected the performance of the German party system.

Christopher S. Allen's chapter, "Germany and the Comparative Political Party Experience: Sclerotic or Dynamic Institutions?" is explicitly comparative, situating the German party system in the context of party systems in other industrialized democracies. It takes a four part perspective that looks comparatively at parties and party systems in the U.S., U.K., France, and Italy to corroborate the claims of whether the German parties are in crisis or not. In the process it identifies different institutional "pathologies" in each of the four countries' party systems. It also briefly examines some of the literature on political parties to verify exactly what parties are and what they are supposed to do in a democratic polity and suggests that Germany has developed a party system characterized by dynamic stability at three levels: macro institutional, party systemic, and intra-party. Finally, using a new institutionalist perspective, Allen suggests that characterizing parties as rigid or sclerotic often misses the internal dynamics of these unique collective political institutions.

Hans-Georg Betz's chapter establishes an important historical foundation in arguing that despite a partial erosion in the 1980s and 1990s, German parties have been able to maintain core constituencies while appealing to emerging new social groups. He suggests the key to party durability has been an ability to manage changes in party cleavages in different eras. Germany's postwar pattern of religious and class cleavages was increasingly overlain by cleavages that emerged within the middle class beginning in the 1970s. Their political expression first favored the Social Democratic Party of Germany (SPD) in the 1970s, then the Christian Democratic Union (CDU) in the 1980s. The Greens and the Party of Democratic Socialism (PDS), the former East German Communists, now are the dominant institutional expressions of this cleavage. In short, this is a story of change within institutional continuity.

Michaela W. Richter's reassessment builds on Betz's foundation in analyzing the fascinating process by which the party state emerged at the founding of the Federal Republic. Overcoming both Allied and domestic opposition to strong parties in the wake of Weimar, the unlikely coalition of Christian Democrat Konrad Adenauer and Social Democrat Kurt Schumacher, leaders of their respective parties in the British Zone in 1946, helped to grant political parties a privileged position in the democratic FRG. In the process, the party state helped establish representative government, but whether this once vibrant party state has proven a capable actor during the process of unification requires closer scrutiny. Richter suggests two potential paths: an uncritical acceptance of the party state theory as a legitimating formula or a reinvigoration of the parties as dynamic membership organizations. The former would erode the party state while supposedly paying homage to it while the latter would invigorate German democracy.

John Leslie examines a troubling new and old phenomenon in his chapter on the changing fortunes of Germany's far right parties. The legal and institutional parameters of parliamentary democracy in the old FRG shaped the electoral chances of far right parties and there is a question whether and how the environment has changed with unification, specifically in terms of the external constraints imposed on these parties. Given this focus, the chapter neither devotes much space to the internal organization and development of far right parties themselves nor does it compare specific events in Germany with similar developments elsewhere in Europe. Instead, the first section considers the prevailing West German parliamentary conditions which shaped the emergence of far right parties in the late 1980s. A second section regards the changes in the political environment accompanying unity which explain developments after Fall 1991, particularly the emergence of xenophobic violence. A final section explores the extent to which, despite the transformations wrought by unification, the relatively restrictive constraints faced by far right parties have remained intact. In doing so, it asks whether the turbulence of unity, rather than assisting parties of the far right, has undermined their electoral chances.

The chapter by Andrei S. Markovits and Stephen J. Silvia focuses on the problems confronting the Alliance Greens that have prompted periodic outbreaks of identity crises in the party and on the German left. They first assess the Alliance Greens as a political party, in particular its relationship with the two other left-of-center political parties, the SPD and the PDS, and with the constituent parties of former Chancellor Helmut Kohl's conservative coalition, the Free Democratic Party (FDP), CDU and Christian Social Union (CSU). The discussion concentrates on the Alliance Greens as a political party in the changed topography of Germany's party landscape. The second section looks at the impact of the Alliance Greens as a movement on the content and discourse of contemporary German politics, assessing the trajectory of the Alliance Greens as an innovative force in German politics. The chapter concludes with a discussion of policy, which attains particular salience in light of the Alliance Greens' emergence as another significant electoral force in the Federal Republic and as the junior coalition partner in the first "Red-Green" government elected in 1998. In other words, the importance of Green policy positions grows with the entry of the Alliance Greens into the inner sanctum of German politics at the national level.

Henry Kreikenbom's consideration of de-alignment and re-alignment begins with Lipset and Rokkan's powerful cleavage theory. He evaluates its impact in a Germany where a new cleavage has been created by the economic and social processes of modern industrial society and the three party system broken open by the Greens. Kreikenbom investigates whether the de-alignment process has been accompanied by the creation of a new coalition of voters and parties or whether this process has lead to a party system based on a rational party orientation of voters. A further cleavage has developed among eastern Germans along the ideological dimension of a socialist rather than a western affinity. To analyze this phenomenon, Kreikenbom combines aggregate and individual data analysis complemented by qualitative interviews. He describes the process of de-alignment and realignment in West Germany based on empirical data for the period up to 1989 and then addresses the cleavage structure in the GDR and in the new states (Länder). Last, he addresses possible future developments in the coalitions between voters and parties in a united Germany as determined by the cleavages.

In "Agents of Democratization and Unification," Ann L. Phillips uses the prism of structure-agency theory to investigate the role German political parties play in the democratic life of the unified FRG. This model is particularly salient given the sister party phenomenon of western German parties extending their reach eastward to encompass the bloc parties of the former GDR. This chapter assesses the transformation of parties as institutions through changes in party leadership, membership, organization and program, evaluating parties as they perform traditional functions and activities. It is the structure-agency dilemma that animates attempted fusion of the sister parties. Phillips concludes the democratization of the parties has generally been successful, but that their efficacy as agents of democracy is weak. Both cultural and contextual differences undercut the ability of western German structures and institutions to take root in the five new states of eastern Germany.

Finally, Wolfgang Seibel departs from a primary focus on political parties, preferring to examine the role that nonprofit organizations play. He suggests they play an essential role in underpinning German parties and the party system, for while parties and interest groups secure political legitimacy as input factors of political systems, nonprofit institutions mobilize political support through both input and output functions. In terms of output, nonprofit institutions provide quasi-public goods, in terms of input, they organize civil society through voluntarism and network structures. Nonprofit institutions are an integral part of the German polity and are essential to political integration. Thus there are important reasons to examine societal continuities and discontinuities again relative to the role of nonprofit institutions after the recent dramatic political changes in Germany. In short, the nonprofit sector may be conceived of as both a determined and a determinant factor of political integration and political stability. On the one hand, the nonprofit sector is dependent on the resource mobilization capacity of civil society. The degree of social networking and voluntarism is crucial to the nonprofit sector's viability and vitality. On the other hand, nonprofit institutions, once they exist, represent a resource of social order building and political integration in itself.

This volume originated from two workshops, one on each of the American coasts, that were part of a project cosponsored by the Center for German and European Studies at the University of California at Berkeley, and Johns Hopkins University's American Institute of Contemporary German Studies in Washington, DC. Special thanks go to Beverly Crawford at Berkeley and Jackson Janes and Carl Lankowski in Washington for providing the resources to assemble our contributors for two stimulating and productive sessions. Needless to say, the additional contributions of the German Marshall Fund were most helpful in providing support for these two events.

I would also like to thank all of my fellow contributors to this volume as well as various discussants at the conferences (especially Peter Merkl, Alex Stone, and Uli Weber) for their comments and suggestions on individual chapters and on the volume as a whole. It was – and is – a distinct pleasure to work with such a fine community of scholars.

Finally, I would like to thank three individuals at Berghahn who have been of immeasurable assistance in the preparation of this volume. First, I very much appreciate the work of John Bendix. Nominally he was the superb copy-editor, but his contribution to the final volume far exceeds that function. John used his expertise on German political parties to ask insightful queries, recommend additional crucial sources, and suggest significant rewording of portions of two chapters. Second, Janine Treves's role in making the trains run on time is essential for any author or editor who may have a less rigorous temporal sense. She provided most helpful suggestions, advice, and encouragement in this writer's pulling together of the contributions. Finally, I would like to salute Marion Berghahn for her continued unflagging support for the social science community whose primary research focuses on German (and European)/American comparisons.

Christopher S. Allen
Athens, GA
March 1999

Chapter 1

GERMANY AND THE COMPARATIVE POLITICAL PARTY EXPERIENCE
Sclerotic or Dynamic Institutions?

Christopher S. Allen

Introduction

The popular perception in the late 1990s regarding political parties in developed political systems suggests there has been a great diminution of their strength and viability. This assessment has also been made of one of the pillars of a strong party system, the Federal Republic of Germany, and quick observation of German politics suggests that its party system might be suffering the same erosion as in other countries. Numerous indicators would seem to confirm this:

1. German voter turnout, despite a small increase in the 1994 and 1998 federal elections back to more than 80 percent remains considerably below the prevailing patterns for the Federal Republic since its founding.

Until the 1990 election, German voter turnout had always been above 80 percent in all elections except the first one in 1949.
2. The upheavals brought on by unification and the lagging integration of the five new Länder have eroded some of the old parties, created new ones, and caused new cleavages in apparently strong ones.
3. Several smaller parties have now displaced the comfortable "two-and-a-half" party system that had dominated the Federal Republic's politics for thirty years from 1953 to 1983.
4. The continued precariousness of the FDP – as it regularly struggles with the five percent electoral hurdle – suggests a crucial stabilizing balance wheel of the German system could depart, leaving a political vacuum in the center of the ideological spectrum.
5. The anti-party sentiment of the 1990s has profoundly affected the two major parties. The SPD still searches for a focus and its governing constituency despite leading the new coalition; while the CDU/CSU's departure from power in 1998 shows all the signs of a party that was in power too long and had exhausted its mandate and its vision for German politics.

Thus, can we conclude that Germany's party system is in crisis? Not necessarily. Several indicators suggest a more cautious conclusion. Observers of German politics are well aware of the predilection in German political discourse to stress that whatever appears to be the momentary issue of concern is a crisis (Markovits and Allen, 1984). A quick glance at literature on crisis during the past twenty years (Dyson, 1984; Streeck, 1984) juxtaposed with German economic and political performance suggests that German crises are often exaggerated and are of a kind that in other countries would hardly be represented as crises at all.

To examine German political parties properly requires a different and comparative viewpoint. Such an approach is necessary to determine if German parties are eroding like many elsewhere, or if German parties and the party system are special and have maintained greater comparative continuity and durability than the conventional wisdom on political parties would suggest. This chapter challenges many of the dominant explanations of political party and party system behavior in democratic states and hypothesizes that there is a theoretically important institutional explanation for the comparatively more stable German political parties and party system.
   This chapter takes a four-part perspective that: (1) looks comparatively at parties and party systems in the U.S., U.K., France and Italy to corroborate the claims of whether the German parties are in crisis or not, in the process identifying different institutional shortcomings in each of the four countries' party systems; (2) examines briefly some of the core literature on political parties to verify exactly what parties are and what they are supposed to do in a democratic polity; (3) suggests that Germany has developed a party system characterized by dynamic stability at three levels: macro-institutional, party-systemic, and intra-party; and (4) using a new institutionalist perspective, suggests that characterizing collective institutions such as parties as rigid or sclerotic often misses the internal dynamics of these unique collective political institutions.

The Crisis of Political Parties in Developed States

In virtually all developed political systems, political parties as dominant institutions have seen their monopoly on political discourse challenged (Ziegler, 1993). One obvious form this challenge has taken is the role of television in allowing candidates to go directly to voters (and party members) and make direct appeals without the mediating influence of political parties

(Gans, 1993). The personalization of the Tony Blair candidacy in Britain in 1997 and the direct election of Prime Minister Benjamin Netanyahu in Israel are two such examples. A second form is the role of independently wealthy candidates who try to bypass the party system altogether, or at least use parties as a flag of convenience for their candidacy. The most obvious examples of the latter phenomenon are Ross Perot in 1992 and Steven Forbes in 1996. But this tendency is not confined to the United States, witness the phenomenon of Italy's Silvio Berlusconi in 1994 who formed a "political party" Forza Italia (based on a soccer stadium chant) three months before running for and winning the office of Prime Minister. A third form might be the general decline of faith in political institutions that has affected all industrialized nations in the late twentieth century (Dogan, 1988).

The following section takes a two-pronged comparative overview of party systems both across four different advanced industrialized states (the U.S., U.K., France and Italy) and over time – to examine their respective "states of health." Before we can begin to analyze whether the German party system is in crisis at the end of the 1990s, we need a cross-national and longitudinal comparative benchmark to understand how political parties have evolved since the mid-twentieth century. The argument made here is that each of these four countries has a different institutional shortcoming that partially undermines its political parties and its party system in ways that make the German system seem robust by comparison.

The United States: Presidentialism and Primaries

The dominant characterization of the American polity is that of a two-party, presidential system. Yet depending on how political parties are actually defined, it may actually be a no party system.

When one reflects upon and examines developments in American political parties during the past forty years, some striking changes become evident. As recently as the 1960s primary elections were held only in a handful of states with candidates selected either by party caucuses or conventions. Some observers praise the shift away from this old system; they argue that it is more democratic because the selection of candidates is taken out of smoke-filled rooms and put "in the hands of the people, where it belongs" (Aldrich, 1995; Leonard, 1991). To support this interpretation however, depends on how one defines the term "democratic" (Pateman, 1970). Is the issue one of choice or one of participation?

What is the difference between a primary election where individual voters choose one candidate from among as many as five or six (or more) compared with a system where caucus or convention among party members performs candidate selection? Both, after all, perform the same function, namely to select candidates. But before answering this question, one needs to define exactly what being a "member" of a party entails.

> American political parties do not recruit energetically prospective members of their party. There is no reason for them to do so. If all it takes for someone to become a Democrat is self-declaration (a notoriously weak commitment), why bother spending money on such party "members?" ... Why waste money trying to increase party membership, when the goal is to persuade voters to identify with a candidate when they step into the voting booth? (Ziegler, 1993: 49)

This is not as easy to answer as one might imagine. Informal surveys of most Americans about where they can find their local Democratic or Republican headquarters or party office generally elicit blank stares and confusion. If they do respond, generally it is to name the storefront where an individual candidate's campaign office is located. When asked to identify where the party's office is located, they are generally stumped.

The problem is that the combination of presidentialism and the reliance on paid media in the form of millions of dollars of campaign advertising have dramatically eroded the core functions of what political parties used to do. This has meant the idea of "membership" in a party, where individuals physically associate with like-minded citizens and are tied to a common set of political beliefs has virtually disappeared (Wattenberg, 1994). When individual candidates can and do run either outside the party system or with scant attention to the party as an organization, then the idea of the political party as an organization to which one "belongs" has lost all substantive meaning. To many Americans, belonging to a political party means nothing more than being on a list that allows them to vote for either Democrats or Republicans in primary elections. Yet even that minimal distinction has even less salience today, since recent changes in electoral laws in many states allow independent voters (i.e. non-members of either party) to vote in either of the two primary elections. And in some states, such as California in 1996, referenda have passed that allow any voter registered in any party to vote in either of the two primaries!

When one follows the evolution from caucus/convention to primary election, the original purpose of the primary was to have a different way for party members to select their candidates for a general election. If virtually anyone can choose a party's candidate for a general election as is the case with the current U.S. primary system then the idea of a party as a coherent political organization has lost all meaning. So from the point of view of the chapter's central concern, the U.S. faces an atrophy of both the political parties themselves, as well as the party system as a whole.

Great Britain: Single Member Districts

Britain has long enjoyed a privileged status as both the ancestor of all parliaments and as the locus for the formation of the modern, mass-based democratic political party (Belchem, 1991). Yet this much more structured system with its organizationally robust parties also finds itself burdened with an institutional shortcoming that tends to undermine the efficacy of the party system.

The problem the British party system faces is different from that of the "party-less" U.S. The U.K. electoral system based on single member districts and a "first past the post" winner take all mandate may produce a clear winning party. However, it also finds it difficult to find compromise across parties or societal consensus when one governing party reverses the policies of the departing government (Hart, 1992). The British majoritarian system tends to produce governing parties that may enjoy a majority of the seats but attain only a plurality of the votes, creating a problem for representation. The essence of the problem is that Britain's three-party system does not fit well with an electoral format in which single member district, "first-past-the-post" rules invariably allow representation of only two nationwide parties.

For all the acclaim that former Conservative Prime Minister Margaret Thatcher received with her "landslide" victories in the 1979, 1983 and 1987 Parliamentary elections, her Conservative Party never received more than 42 percent of the popular vote. Even Tony Blair's Labour "landslide" in 1997 produced only a popular vote plurality of 45 percent. In fact, in no British general election since 1935 has the party winning the majority of the seats received 50 percent of the votes (Crepaz, 1996). So how did Thatcher's Tories in 1979, 1983 and 1987 and Blair's Laborites in 1997 receive a huge majority of the seats? In many electoral constituencies both Labour and Conservatives win candidate races with 40 or 45 percent of the vote, yet win 100 percent of the seat. This was as true for the Tories during the Thatcher/Major years as it was for Blair and the Labour Party in 1997. The Liberal Democrats, on the other hand, win few constituencies outright, while frequently finishing second in both Labour and Tory strongholds. The voting pattern over the most recent eighteen-year cycle confirms this.

This system produces exaggerated majorities not based on the popular vote electoral strength, but on peculiarities of the distribution of support for the parties in different parts of the U.K. The Tories' primary strength is in the south and west of England, the areas most benefiting from Conservative Party policies in the 1980s, where they regularly finished first in many constituencies. They didn't need to win a majority of the vote to win the seat, only a plurality. The Labour Party, on the other hand, finds most of its support in the industrial districts in the Midlands, as well as in Wales and in Scotland. In many of these areas, Labour finished first in a plurality and won the seat. More than geographic considerations, these voting patterns also reflect a concentrated electorate and the stability of class and occupational voting patterns by demographic groups that Tories and Labour were able to exploit.

The problem for the Liberals was that they finished second in many of these constituencies won by either Tory or Labour, but seldom finished first. In the South and West, it was Labour that often finished third, while in the North, Wales and Scotland, the Tories brought up the rear.

Beyond an apparent unfairness of this system, there are also more serious policy consequences. This exaggerated majoritarian system also produces wide policy swings between the two dominant parties. Many observers of the post-World War II period characterized British economic policy as "stop-go" because of the contrasting policy preferences of the Conservative and Labour parties (Hall, 1986). Labour was in power from 1945 to 1951, Conservatives from 1951 to 1964, Labour from 1964 to 1970, Conservatives from 1970 to 1974, Labour from 1974 to 1979, and Conservatives from 1979 until 1997 when Tony Blair's Labour Party was elected. During each of these single-party majority periods, British economic policy has swung widely. While many other Western European countries enjoyed relatively consistent economic policies and growth, British economic performance since the 1950s has lagged seriously behind that of other major industrialized countries, despite recent improvements.

While other structural factors certainly contributed to the comparatively poor British economic performance (Kemp, 1985), many analysts suggest that the wide swings in economic policy produced by the exaggerated results of the electoral system also bear major responsibility.

Although the British party system contains three major parties, the electoral mechanism makes it functionally a two party system. The long-standing conflict between Labour and Conservatives is exacerbated by the virtual impossibility of a coalition government in which the Liberals might take part. The only way the third party Liberals might enter the governing equation is in the case of a hung parliament in which neither of the two large parties was able to gain a majority. The closest that Britain came to such an event occurred in the first (spring) election of 1974.

The price of admission that the Liberals would charge either the Tories or Labour would be to change the electoral system to proportional representation. By allowing the percentage of the votes to equal the percentage of the seats, proportional representation helps provides a configuration of parties that institutionalizes a wide spectrum of opinion necessary for political discourse. Contrasted with the single member district ("first past the post") system of the U.S. and U.K. and the low threshold system of Italy, proportional representation helps reinforce a system that has a diversity of political opinion and stable majorities. In other words, the choice of a proportional representation electoral system has the effect of reinforcing the strength of parties as institutions, and invigorating them in the process. Such a change would more adequately produce a correspondence between the Liberals' percentage of the votes and the percentage of the seats in Parliament. For the last two decades of the twentieth century, the Liberals have tried various organizational forms to find an electoral breakthrough. For a short time they allied with a small group of right wing Labourites who were called the Social Democrats and called themselves the Liberal Alliance. The party remains firmly in third place behind the Labour and Conservative parties.

The persistent problem that troubles the relationship between the two large parties is that both emphasize defense in a very narrow sense and never seem to move toward a party system that produces anything other than a zero-sum outcome. In the mid-1990s, the Tory hegemony neared the end of its eighteen-year rule. Yet the Labour Party under the leadership of the more moderate Tony Blair won a huge legislative majority, and despite claims of moderation may overturn many of the economic policies of Thatcher and her successor John Major. Viewed through the prism of stability and continuity, the British electoral system seems again to produce a sub-optimal outcome for the party system by lurching in the opposite policy direction while still freezing out the third party (the Liberals). Thus, Britain's problem is less the parties themselves but a party and electoral system that is biased toward two parties producing inflexibility both within the polity and in U.K. public policy.

Despite taking advantage of the electoral system, Prime Minister Blair has started to discuss a series of constitutional and electoral reforms (Brazier, 1998). From reforming the House of Lords, to granting regional autonomy to Wales and Scotland, to considering proportional representation, the Blair government seems aware of many of the shortcomings of the British system. Whether such changes actually take place remain uncertain in such a tradition-bound nation.

France: Mixing Presidents, Parliaments, and Electoral Systems

The French party system from the late 1980s to the late 1990s experienced numerous crises and upheavals. On the left, these included the virtual disappearance of the Communist Party, hitherto one of the most durable Communist parties in Western Europe. It also saw the weakening of the Socialists from a party that obtained over 30 percent of the vote in the 1981 elections to one which had less than half that support at the end of President François Mitterrand's second term. But the Socialists also managed a remarkable resurgence in 1997 by winning the National Assembly elections. On the right, there was continued feuding after 1995 between the Gaullists and Republicans, even thought they had captured both the Presidency and a majority in the National Assembly (only to lose the National Assembly to the left two years later). Further right was the continued presence of the neo-Fascist Front National, led by the demagogue Jean-Marie Le Pen did not help matters (Keeler and Schain, 1996). This is clearly a case of both parties and a party system in disarray.

There are several proximate causes of the volatility of the French party system. First, the French fifth Republic's constitutional provision mandates a mixed system combining a strong directly elected President who enjoys powers greater than the U.S. President with a parliamentary body (the National Assembly). Second, France has changed its electoral systems twice in two years for no more valid reasons than political expedience. Third, there is a cavalier provision that allows the President (elected for 7 year terms) to dissolve the National Assembly and call for new elections with few constraints.

It was not always so in France. Both the Third Republic (1870-1940) and the Fourth Republic (1944-1958) were multiparty parliamentary systems with a ceremonial President as head of state. Why was this system changed with the Fifth Republic in 1958? In a word: de Gaulle (Macridis and Brown, 1976) The dominant figure of mid-twentieth century French politics, Charles de Gaulle, agreed to be called out of retirement only if the country changed to a strong presidential system. The Fourth Republic, a multiparty parliamentary system, was plagued by unstable coalitions in which no one party or group of parties could remain in power very long. This example would seem to militate against a parliamentary system with multiple parties and justify de Gaulle's insistence in a strong executive. But contributing to instability in French politics during the Fourth Republic was a factor that also was evident in Italy. Both countries had large Communist parties in their parliaments that received substantial percentages of the vote: 20-25 percent in France and often over 30 percent in Italy. In the midst of the Cold War, these parties were estranged from Social Democratic parties to their immediate right, and were seen as unsuitable coalition candidates by centrist and right wing parties. If other political parties had treated Communist parties as at least a potential ally, rather than ruling them out *a priori* from any possible governing coalition, then the parliamentary systems in both countries might have performed more effectively. This, however, was not to be.

When de Gaulle became President of the Fifth Republic in 1958, he tried to institutionalize this divide between the Communists and Socialists by changing from an electoral system of proportional representation used in the Fourth Republic to a single member district system with a runoff election (Beckwith, 1992). Under this system, only those candidates receiving 12.5 percent of the vote on the first round of voting could stand in the second. In practice, this led many parties to try to form electoral blocs in which parties not receiving the minimum threshold in the first round of voting would encourage their members to vote for the candidate of a party whose views were similar to theirs in the second round. This system virtually guaranteed a permanent majority for the French right, as the Gaullists were almost always able to strike electoral deals with the Republicans and other parties of the center-right. In fact, de Gaulle specifically designed this system to prevent the left from gaining power or influence. As long as the Communist and Socialist parties remained divided by the Cold War, they were also shut out of political power. For it was difficult for a left wing candidate who failed to attain the 12.5 percent of the vote in the first round of the parliamentary elections to encourage supporters to vote for the other left wing party.

When the May 1968 demonstrations initiated the end of de Gaulle's presidency, they also forced the Communists and Socialists to find new possibilities for political cooperation. The Vietnam war and the removal of the deep Cold War gulfs that separated Communists from Socialists in Western Europe made possible a "Common Program" uniting French Communist and Socialist Parties by 1972 (Ross, 1982). This pact allowed them to agree on many issues (while still disagreeing on others) but more important, it meant they could now support each other's candidates in the second round in every French election.

While de Gaulle was likely turning in his grave at the thought of the left actually obtaining power, the Communist and Socialists were growing in strength and came close to majorities in the 1973 and 1978 National Assembly elections, as well as in the 1974 Presidential elections. By 1981, this "Common Program" electoral alliance enabled François Mitterrand to attain the Presidency, and under the Fifth Republic's constitutional provisions, allowed him to call for new National Assembly elections that produced a left wing majority, the best showing for the French left in fifty years (Daley, 1995). Yet within two years the left coalition was eroding, largely around economic policy, and began to produce several institutional pathologies that undermined the party system.

When the Communists chose to resign from government, after provocation from Mitterrand, it also changed the electoral logic of the "Common Program," namely the pledge on the part of Communist and Socialist candidates to support each other in the second round of the election. This became an immediate problem for President Mitterrand, for though presidential terms last for seven years; National Assembly terms only lasted for five. The next scheduled Assembly election was set for 1986, and Mitterrand calculated that he could not win without the Communists. His "solution" to this problem was to change the electoral system back to proportional representation (Beckwith, 1992), calculating that a PR system would at least produce a PS plurality that would at least allow him to get much of his program through. This calculation failed on two counts: (1) not only did the Socialists not get a plurality, the Gaullists and Republicans received a majority and (2) the proportional representation system together with the rapid erosion of electoral support for the Communists allowed the neo-Fascist Front National party to gain seats in the National Assembly.

Mitterrand's (and the right's) solution this time was to change the electoral system again, this time back to the two ballot runoff system! This was fine with the right, since the two parties benefited directly, and it would cut off the options for the Front National since no party would ally with them, and they rarely if ever could attain 12.5 percent of the vote on their own. It also meant that the Gaullists and Republicans wouldn't have another competitor to their right. Mitterrand also benefited since he no longer could count on Communist support anyway, and hoped that some of the populist voters, who had left the Communists and voted for the far right, might now reconsider and be disposed to vote for the Socialists.

Over and above all of these electoral shenanigans was the constitutional tension between a strong President and the National Assembly. Mitterrand clearly took advantage of this tension by choosing a "Rose Garden" electoral strategy for the 1988 Presidential election, by using the office of the Presidency to run explicitly above the parties and portray his opponents as squabbling politicians. Like de Gaulle, Mitterrand used the institutional power of the French presidency to frustrate his opponents for years. Yet while this tactic enabled Mitterrand to gain re-election, it also served to undermine political parties in general, and the Socialist party in particular. Even after 1995, with the right controlling the presidency, tensions between

Gaullist President Jacques Chirac and his Republican allies remained high, and grew higher still after 1997 when the Socialists retained control of the National Assembly once again. In essence, presidentialism has diminished a core purpose of political parties in France, namely the representation of political ideologies and group interests. The changes to the electoral system Mitterrand undertook out of political expediency have helped undermine the party system and added to French political cynicism, which has hardly been a scarce commodity.

Italy: Multiple Parties, Low Thresholds

Italy seems to be the embodiment of political party chaos. Until the dramatic election of 1996, Italy had a technocrat Prime Minister with an "all technocrat" government for over a year. Many of the political parties that still remain after the huge party shakeup of the early 1990s, some of them renamed, are on the sidelines. The last non-technocrat government was comprised of an unlikely coalition of neo-fascists, Northern separatists, and Italy's combination of Ross Perot, Ted Turner, and Rupert Murdoch, namely Silvio Berlusconi.

The problem with Italy's parties and party system since the end of World War II, a period that has seen over fifty governments, is that its proportional representation electoral system has had too low a threshold for representation (Morlino, 1984). Any party that received 1.5 percent of the vote was able to attain seats in Parliament. Not surprisingly, there have regularly been more than ten different political parties.

As in France, Italy had excluded its Communist Party from any possibility of belonging to a government coalition. This exclusion also applied, until recently, to the Neo-Fascists. With the Communists receiving as much as 34 percent of the popular vote (1976) and the Neo-Fascists regularly receiving 5-6 percent of the vote, up to 40 percent of the members of parliament were ruled persona non grata in terms of participating in government. The remaining six to eight elected parties in Parliament would then have to form a coalition representing over 50 percent of the deputies to form a government, but only be able to consider 60 percent of those holding seats! It is no wonder that there have been so many governments in Italy since World War II. Not only has the low threshold allowed many minor parties to attain seats and make coalitions harder, but the ruling out of Communists and Neo-Fascists from consideration, has also exacerbated the problem. All the more mysterious, that is, if Cold War considerations weren't involved, was that this ban on Communist participation in national government took place when Communists ran most northern cities and regional governments. They administrations saw far fewer of the scandals that beset most of the governing parties (Christian Democrats, Socialists, Republicans, etc.).

Finally in the 1990s, the Italians realized that this combination of a multiplicity of parties and low thresholds was not functional for the political system in general, and the party system in particular. The primary catalysts for these fundamental changes were the end of the Cold War and the massive political scandals. The former caused the Communist Party to reassess their role in Italian politics, eventually inducing it to change its name to the Party of the Democratic Left; and the latter literally decimated the Christian Democrats and Socialists. But unfortunately for the parties as institutions, they were the wrong kind of changes. Starting in the Italian Senate, electoral rules following the British system of "first past the post" were introduced (Gilbert, 1994). Fully in effect first during the 1996 Parliamentary elections, this change has started to produce two different blocs, as all single member electoral systems do. The first bloc was the winning "Olive Tree" coalition comprised of the Party of the Democratic Left (ex-Communists), the Greens, some technocrats, and a few stray ex-Christian Democrats). The second was the losing coalition comprised of Berlusconi's Forza Italia and the Neo-Fascists). The regional separatist Northern League declined to participate in either coalition. This electoral reform is an attempt to force a bipolar division on a society and a polity with multiple ideological and regional cleavages. It is unlikely that solutions such as this will produce either a healthy polity or party system in Italy. In fact, the Olive Tree coalition has only a plurality, and depends on its support from the Communist Refounding party, comprised of those leftists who thought that the Party of the Democratic Left was too moderate. In the first few years following the ascension to power of the "Olive Tree" coalition's leader, Romano Prodi, the pressures on the government from the left created additional government crises. The most serious of these saw Prodi's resignation in favor of the ex-Communist Massimo d'Alema, who headed a minority government.

When we step back and look at the shortcomings of the party systems in Britain, France and Italy, such an exercise places the German political party system in a useful comparative perspective. Germans might prefer to question the functioning of their political institutions. However, when viewed comparatively, we can quite legitimately say "Crisis? What crisis?" when we look at the German political party system.

What Do Political Parties and Party Systems Do?

Before turning to the German political party system, we need to reiterate what parties and party systems are supposed to do (Lipset and Rokkan, 1967; Duverger, 1972; Lijphart, 1994). The modern foundational works in comparative politics literature suggest that the primary task of political parties is to institutionalize political representation and to provide a vehicle for the discussion and transmission of political discourse.

A look at this literature allows us to understand some of the basic factors, features, and roles of parties and party systems in any democratic polity. This literature helps us clarify several issues.

The first issue that this literature helps us to understand is the relationship between a party's voters and its members. As we have seen in the U.S. case, this issue can be very confusing, though it need not be if one understands that political parties in most democratic countries are organizations to which individuals belong and in which they physically participate. In most countries where membership is important, there is a clear distinction between these two categories of party adherents. Voters are individuals who prefer specific parties (and their candidates) at elections, but often have no more active support for such parties than to have a general belief in the goals and programs of the party. Members, on the other hand, are individuals who take a more active and involved role in the workings of the party as an organizational entity. Among the tasks members do and voters don't is to attend meetings, organize party functions, participate in internal party debates, and select candidates who will stand for office on the party's label. In recent years, both the level and intensity of party membership in many countries' political parties have allegedly declined. Some of this apparent decline can be attributed to an overemphasis on the personality of some candidates, other sources of political information (i.e. television), or a cynicism toward parties due to either political scandals or seemingly intractable public policy problems. Yet a recent study argues that the "decline of parties" debate has been overstated relative to the entire twentieth century, and not the idealized "golden age" of parties in the fifteen years after World War II (Scarrow, 1998). The debate on party decline notwithstanding, the distinction between voters and members outside the U.S. remains significant and is an important criterion to understand how parties are changing and evolving.

The second issue is whether parties serve as arenas for deliberative discussion. One of the key indicators about whether parties themselves, and perhaps legislative bodies as well, are organizations where debate can lead to the resolution of issues is the presence (or absence) of initiative and referenda. If a polity or sub-unit thereof, regularly has a large number of initiative petitions or referenda, this is generally a measure of the ineffectiveness of either the parties, the legislative body, or both.[1] As a vehicle for expressing popular opinion, a referendum can be quite effective. However, it is limited in what it actually produces since it is, in essence, only a snapshot of the electorate at a single moment in time. Referenda also only permit yes/no options, and there are numerical barriers in submitting names, there are numerous issues of wording, as well as turnout problems. Even more important is how comparatively rare they are in national politics around the world (Butler and Ranney, 1994). They generally result from individual leaders (de Gaulle), via constitutional mandates (Switzerland), and amendment processes (U.S. states). In general, however, we can best characterize the modern practice of referenda as more like a plebiscite.

On the other hand, the virtue of a deliberative body such as a party organization is that members establish a dialogue (a motion picture instead of just a snapshot, so to speak) and can resolve complicated issues that would limit the effect of a one-time referendum. But what causes what? Do weak parties lead to more referenda, or do referenda weaken parties? The answer to this chicken or egg problem is both; they are mutually reinforcing. However, if there are organizationally strong and coherent political parties, one also tends to find responsible and effective legislative bodies, thereby obviating the need for turning to referenda to solve day-to-day political problems, clearly a task for which they are not particularly well-suited.

This literature sheds light on a third issue, namely the relationship between citizens and the legislatures that represent them. One of the primary functions that political parties have

1. We are not referring here to occasional referenda for major national questions, but as regular device to address rudimentary public policy issues. The former are essential for sampling widespread public opinion on an issue that can be addressed in a yes/no format. Public policy issues that require deliberation and nuance are ill suited for referenda.

historically performed is to serve as a mediating institution, or glue that solidifies this relationship. Political parties have played a two-way function acting as the body where specific political and ideological positions are determined, largely through the input of party members and voters and acting as the collective voice of their supporters while engaging in legislative business (Duverger, 1972). However, the specific nature of this representation depends greatly on the electoral system that produces representatives to legislative bodies. Single member district (or "first past the post") systems are in effect in most Anglo-American polities, while proportional representation (percentage of the popular vote equals percentage of the legislative seats) are in effect in most other democracies.

Single member district systems claim to offer "better" representation to constituents since all voters can easily identify who their own representative is. In proportional representation systems, parties construct lists of candidates for a wider electoral area than the more narrowly defined single member districts in Anglo-American systems (Rae, 1967). Adherents of single member districts generally fault proportional representation systems for shortchanging this representative function. However, this issue is not so simple. If a liberal Democrat lived in former U.S. House Speaker Newt Gingrich's district, who was that person's "representative?" By the same token, if conservative Republicans from Vermont look to the legislator who "represents" them, all they see is the independent socialist Bernard Sanders, the state's lone member of Congress. The issue of representation in proportional representation systems may at first appear to be problematic, but it need not be. It depends much more on how the parties select candidates who will appear on the party's list. Clearly if representing geographical areas or specific groups is important for the party, then it is in the party's interest to construct a list of candidates that represent the interests (geographical, ideological, etc.) of the region where the election takes place. In this instance, adherents of proportional representation could argue that a multi-party PR-based list system could provide far more extensive representation for all citizens in a polity than the supposedly more representative single member district system. The issue is the nature of the representation of citizens in their country's legislative body. And the electoral system can have a profound effect on the parties that take part in this process.

Last, the classic literature on political parties must confront the dilemma of how new media technology might erode the functions that political parties have traditionally performed (Gans, 1993). The most obvious threat to political parties is paid television advertising, as outlined in the U.S. example above. Using television to bypass political parties inevitably weakens them. But new media technology is far more than television, as the Internet has shown. Some observers have argued that this new generation of technology will democratize the process by moving from the one-way medium of television to a much more interactive Internet. Some speak of voting at home or of instant referenda.

There are several problems with this interpretation. Interactive technology clearly allows individuals to bypass the parties as institutions, but if they do, what are the implications for democratic politics (Fletcher, 1997)? What definition of democracy are we using, an individual one emphasizing discrete iterative choices or a collective one emphasizing deliberation and reason? It seems this individualizing mechanism of interactive technology destroys the sense of collective participation, the capacity to think, reason, and discuss issues among various groups of people, that has been at the heart of modern political parties for over a century. If this participatory function disappears so too does the logic and rationale for political parties as institutions. Moreover, the new "techno-democracy" does not insure universal access. If one wished to participate in political party activities in the past, there was no barrier to entry, other than finding the spare time to exercise one's rights as a citizen inside any one of several political parties. However, access to the new media technology is very dependent on one's capacity as a consumer, in the sense of being able to afford the hardware. Some individuals might be able to practice democracy this way, but not all. In this case, there is a clear difference between being a citizen versus being a consumer! What kind of democracy would we have then?

The Dynamic Stability of German Political Parties

The remaining two sections of the chapter use an "historical new institionalist" perspective (March and Olsen, 1989; Steinmo, Thelen and Longstreth, 1992) to examine the German parties and party system both practically and theoretically. Briefly, this approach suggests that institutions are not some mysterious black box into which inputs flow and from which outputs emerge, but are instead active collective entities, embodied by actors who both contribute to and benefit from these institutions. Building on the work of the companion chapters in this volume, this perspective permits the following section to suggest that Germany has developed, whether by design, accident or a combination of both – a party system characterized by a "dynamic stability" at three levels: macro-institutional, party systemic, and intra-party. Clearly there is turmoil in the German party system, some of which is similar to some of the pathologies affecting the party systems outlined above, but there is clearly more institutional continuity, or dynamics of change, in Germany than either sclerosis or disintegration.

The Macro Institutional Level

Political parties in Germany occupy a privileged position within the political system. Unlike the U.S. Constitution in which parties are not mentioned, the German Basic Law gives them an institutional presence and legitimacy at a fundamental political level. From 1945 to the founding of the Federal Republic in

1949, there was considerable debate about how to best insure a democratic polity (Richter, this volume). Many occupation officials, particularly the Americans and the French, wanted to diminish the role of political parties and give greater power to the executive branch (the Minister-Presidents of what would later become the Länder). The reason for stressing the authority of the executive sprang both from a desire to minimize internal conflict in the wake of the Third Reich and from an alleged need for practical, impartial solutions. Such an executive-based institutional choice would have undercut the role of political parties as a dominant pillar of the new Federal Republic. German democracy, however, took another path.

The driving force behind establishing a place for political parties was the unlikely duo of Konrad Adenauer, the founder of the CDU and later the first Chancellor, and Kurt Schumacher the leader of the SPD. These two party founders argued that parties, as institutions, played a crucial role for the development of democracy in Germany. Precisely because there were crucial issues to address, both Adenauer and Schumacher argued that democracy depended on a reasoned discourse between opposing views that should be encompassed within a coherent organizational form. In the absence of political parties as coherent institutions, Schumacher argued, all that would remain would be "the chaotic clash of opinions and feelings." What parties offered was a structured presentation of platforms and programs that would aggregate the interests of members and voters and offer clear platforms upon which policy could be based. In addition, Schumacher, whose SPD lagged behind the more dominant CDU/CSU, stressed the importance of establishing an opposition party: without it a democracy could not really function.

As a result of this farsighted effort by two otherwise sharp rivals, Article 21 of the Basic Law established the constitutionality of political parties as the major institutions through which democratic participation and representation was to take place. In other words, the Federal Republic's founders, later reinforced by the Supreme Court, created a "Democratic Party State" in which the vehicles for political expression in the Federal Republic were the parties themselves. Rather than castigating the political parties as "factions," as was the case in the U.S., the Federal Republic allowed political parties an institutional presence and permanence that has been rarely duplicated in other democratic states.

The Party-Systemic Level

At the level of the party system, proportional representation, and particularly the 5 percent electoral threshold for representation in Germany, has proven essential for a dynamically stable political party system (Taagepera and Shugart, 1989). At the founding of the Federal Republic in the late 1940s, American occupation authorities, in particular, wanted to dissuade the Germans from replicating the pure proportional representation system in force under the Weimar Republic. This preference was not surprising since Weimar institutions and practices were suspect due to its collapse to the Nazis after only fifteen years. In addition, neither American nor British authorities had practical experience with proportional representation as an electoral mechanism and naturally preferred the single member district system. German party officials chose to accede to some of these demands by Occupation authorities while safeguarding the essence of the more broadly representative proportional representation system.

The new German electoral system proved to be an inventive synthesis. It combined the British and American tradition of a single legislator representing one district, and the more common method in continental Europe of proportional representation in which a group of party members represent a given region depending on the percentage of the party's vote in that region. This unusual combination resulted from a compromise between the British and American preference for single member districts and the prevailing German practice of multi-party representation. Single-member district voting systems tend to produce a two-party system and Germany wanted to insure that all major parties were represented, not just two. In practice, the German hybrid system, known as personalized proportional representation, requires citizens to cast two votes on each ballot. The first is cast for an individual member of a political party, who is usually, but not always, from the district; and the second for a list of national/regional candidates grouped by party affiliation. Thus, this system has the effect of personalizing list voting because voters have their "own" representative but also can choose among several parties. To insure that only major parties are represented, only those that get 5 percent of the national vote or have three candidates that win individual seats directly gain representation in the Bundestag.

Allocation of seats by party in the Bundestag however, functions more like proportional representation. Specifically the percentage of total seats won per party corresponds strongly with the party's percentage of the popular vote. For example, if a party's candidate wins a seat as an individual member, the candidate's party gains one less candidate from the list. In practice, the SPD and CDU, the two large parties win most of the district seats, since the district vote is winner take all. The smaller parties' representatives, on the other hand, are almost always elected via the party lists. Thus, the list system creates stronger, more coherent parties. Furthermore, the substantial, direct financial subsidies awarded to all parties that elect members to the Bundestag are also a significant factor (Conradt, 1996). In 1993, the German parties received $450 million directly from the state. This supported all electoral activities as well as their party-affiliated foundations that support broad educational and cultural activities.

The Intra-party Level

Unlike many parties in other comparable democracies, the German political parties remain functioning organizations in which members participate in party life and debate. This is a third level that contributes to German parties' dynamic stability.

To be sure, the number of Germans who actually belong to political parties has declined in recent years. In the mid-1980s, both the SPD and CDU/CSU had almost a million members each and even the smaller Greens and FDP parties had nearly 100,000 members each. Figures a decade later show a drop in all parties' membership from between 10 percent to as much as 30 percent (Römer, 1988). Nonetheless, by any international comparison, the German political parties retain a large organizational membership. Their continued role as membership organizations with an active presence as collective institutions have helped ward off the cult of personality that has afflicted politics in many other countries. A focus on personality profiles of party leaders elsewhere has eroded many political parties in the process.

Despite the relative decline of membership in the past decade, the continued presence of substantial numbers of party members produced several benefits in terms of institutional continuity. Among these are: a dues structure that further augments party finances, and a base of party workers who can be mobilized for electoral campaigns. Most important are the active groups of individuals who generate and reinforce the institutional memory of the parties. This last point is particularly important since each of the parties has faced sharper cleavages among their memberships since unification as well as with the development of European integration. The CDU/CSU confronts religious, regional and state vs. market issues, the SPD faces tension between its working class and professional class constituencies, the FDP between its "social" and "free market" wings, the PDS on regional or left issues, and the Greens along many dimensions. While such cleavages could divide some parties, they also force the parties as institutions to debate what they are and what they stand for within an organizational structure that frames the conflicts and encourages dialogue.

New Institutionalism and the Dynamics of Change

Various forms of rigidity have profoundly and adversely affected parties in other countries, as we have seen from our brief comparative overview of the U.S., UK, France and Italy. For various political, institutional and constitutional reasons, these parties and party systems have eroded as organizations. This has not been the case in Germany.

The chapter argues that compared to other industrialized democracies German political parties have proven to be durable as collective actors. As dynamic institutions, these parties have produced and maintained an evolutionary system while still providing effective representation of interests. Moreover, the system dynamics have produced sufficient space or cushion necessary that have hitherto prevented sclerosis or disintegration at an institutional level. The new institutionalist approach suggest that institutions like political parties need not be seen as static black boxes but rather as agents that shape and direct outcomes in a much more dynamic way (March and Olsen, 1989). Precisely because the political parties' institutional patterns have proved more encompassing, durable and effective over time, we suggest a "historical" or "structural" institutionalist approach adds a second layer to this analysis of the German political parties (Steinmo, Thelen and Longstreth, 1992). The combination of the parties' constitutionally privileged position, their reinforcement by the party system, and the sense of collective participation enhanced the organizational structure of their membership represent characteristics many countries' voters and politicians long for.

Is this relatively dynamic German party system immune from threat or possible change? Hardly. In fact, this system depends for its continuity on avoiding several specific kinds of problems. Among the events that could undermine the "dynamic stability" of the German party system are:

1. A sharp economic recession. The inability of the German polity to bridge the economic divide between eastern and western Germany could undermine the parties as effective organs for the representation of interests. Some of the tension between sister parties in the Federal Republic would deepen, with more severe economic consequences.
2. A failure to maintain a proportional representation system with a 5 percent threshold, or to move toward a direct election of the Chancellor, as Israel has done for the election of its prime minister for the 1996 election. Such a personalization of the executive would come at the direct expense of the parties as organizations.
3. The erosion of parties as membership organizations and as physical places for debate and discussion. A primary system would be a disaster in this respect.
4. An introduction of political advertising that would erode or eliminate one of the key reasons for the parties' existence. The new privately owned cable networks in Germany have both the capacity and interest to use such an "American" format.
5. The ruling out of certain parties that have achieved representation in the Bundestag from participating in governing coalitions. Clearly most democratic parties would look askance at considering an alliance with a far-right or neo-Fascist party, much as the French right has disdained alliances with Le Pen's Front National due to their attacks against democratic practices. But what about the PDS? Like the former Communist Party in Italy, will they be consigned to regional government coalitions only and be denied from participating in a governing national coalition? Such a choice by the major parties could increase instability in the German party system.

All or most of these changes or threats to the parties as institutions might produce some of the characteristics that embody the conventional wisdom regarding German parties stated at the outset. However, based on the mutually reinforcing nature of the parties as organizations and as part of a collective institutionalization of democratic practice, this political party system will likely remain more durable and viable than its detractors will surmise.

Chapter 2

THE EVOLUTION AND TRANSFORMATION OF THE GERMAN PARTY SYSTEM

Hans-Georg Betz

For much of the post-1945 period, the German electorate was one of the most predictable and the German party system one of the most stable of the advanced West European democracies. Although in the 1970s and 1980s, growing electoral volatility, an increase in unconventional political behavior, and the defection of significant portions of the electorate to newly emerging parties posed a serious challenge to the established political parties, these developments stopped short of bringing about a fundamental change in the party system. On the contrary, available evidence suggests that despite a significant increase in partisan dealignment, the traditional sociodemographic bases of political support continued to play a crucial role in defining partisan preferences.

Given the profound socioeconomic and sociocultural transformation of German society during the past three decades, the resilience of both the established parties and the party system was remarkable. In the early 1980s, there were widespread expectations that the shift from industrial to postindustrial society throughout Western Europe would engender new lines of conflict between the "proponents of the established industrial order" and the "supporters of New Politics goals." (Dalton, Flanagan, and Beck, 1984: 456) In the face of a dramatic rise in education levels and the diffusion of postmaterialist values among young voters, generational turnover was expected to expedite the erosion of traditional lines of conflict while bolstering a "secular realignment in voting patterns" (Flanagan and Dalton, 1984: 11). At the same time, growing social tensions created by technological change and fundamental shifts in employment patterns were expected to create new lines of conflict between "modernization winners" and "modernization losers."

The actual development of the German party system fell considerably short of these expectations. From 1961 until the early 1980s, German politics was dominated by a three-party system that included two mass people's parties (the center-right CDU/CSU and the center-left SPD) and the small liberal Free Democrats (FDP). In 1983, the Greens became the first new party since the early 1950s to gain Bundestag representation. Although the emergence of the Greens marked a significant turning point in German politics, the party's immediate impact on the distribution of support for the established parties remained rather limited: in 1987, the CDU/CSU gained 44.3 percent of the vote, as compared to 45.3 in 1961; the SPD gained 37.0 percent, as compared to 36.2 percent; and the FDP gained 9.1 percent, as compared to 12.8 percent in 1961 (Smith, 1992: 77).

It was not until the late 1980s that Germany, like other advanced West European democracies, saw the rise of a radical populist right. Its main proponents, the Republikaner, appealed to a combination of latent sentiments of political disenchantment among the West German public, growing animosities toward immigrants and refugees, and diffuse socioeconomic anxieties. Yet despite significant gains in regional and European elections, the party consistently failed to overcome Germany's 5 percent hurdle in Bundestag elections. Unlike other Western European countries, the German party system proved remarkably resistant to the radical right wing challenge.

The resilience of the German party system became even more evident in the elections immediately following German unification. In the first all-German election in 1990, the three established parties attained a combined total of 88.3 percent of the vote, about 2 percent less than they had received in 1987. "This was a minimal decline considering that in 1990 several 'indigenous' East German parties were also in contention, and it is all the more striking bearing in mind the addition of a large, new and relatively 'untied' electorate (about one fifth of the whole) which had suddenly been grafted onto a competitive party system (Smith, 1992: 78). In fact, the established parties' dominance became even more pronounced considering that the (West German) Greens failed to meet the 5 percent mark. The outcome of the second post unification election in 1994 appeared to confirm this picture of stability. Despite significant gains by the Greens in the western part of Germany, equally significant gains of the Party of Democratic Socialism (PDS) in the East, and not negligible gains by marginal parties, the traditional parties still managed to muster 84.7 percent of the vote.

The relative stability of the German party system in the early 1990s was particularly remarkable when compared to developments in other countries, such as the complete collapse of the Italian party system, the rapid decline of the two Austrian *Volksparteien* (ÖVP and SPÖ), or the growing fragmentation of the French party system in the early 1990s. However, appearances can be deceiving. On the surface, the German party system appeared to have remained relatively unchanged when compared to the 1960s: the share of the vote gained by the established *Volksparteien* in 1994 was almost identical with the share they won in 1961. Underneath, however, there had been significant changes in the social composition of their electorates. These changes have been the result of a combination of secular sociostructural and sociocultural changes that have been transforming German society and politics over the past several decades, as Germany gradually moved from a predominantly industrial to an increasingly postindustrial society. As a result, the major parties have come under increasing electoral pressure, while the small FDP has seen its support base severely reduced.

This chapter offers a survey of the evolution and transformation of the social base of the major German parties and the German party system. Specifically, I will show that the particular configuration of the German party system has been shaped by sociocultural milieus whose origins lie to a large extent in Imperial Germany. Although as a result of dictatorship and war these traditional milieus have lost much of their cohesion, the party system of the Federal Republic was largely built around major sociostructural cleavages which have endured until today. In the final sections of this chapter, I will explore the effect of both the emergence of postindustrial society and of unification on the German party system.

The Origins of the German Party System

It is generally accepted that Western European parties and party systems have their origins in a set of historic conflicts which gradually congealed into major sociopolitical cleavages, defined as enduring coalitions between a population group and a political party which is constantly invoked and reinforced through elections (Pappi, 1986b: 17). These cleavages are the result of two successive revolutions in the formation and development of modern European states, the national and the industrial revolution (Lipset and Rokkan, 1967). The process of nation-building gave rise to two social cleavages. The first cleavage revolved around a center-periphery conflict between the dominant culture of the nation-building elites and an array of ethnic or linguistic minorities in the peripheral areas of the newly emerging nation-state. The second cleavage centered on a church-state conflict which tended to pit the modernizing central government, often in alliance with the national Protestant Church, against a Catholic Church that sought to preserve its established privileges. The industrial revolution generated two more cleavages. The first cleavage revolved around a rural-urban conflict that matched the landed elite against the rising class of industrial entrepreneurs in a conflict over the maintenance of acquired status as opposed to the recognition of achievement. The second cleavage involved the rising industrial working class in its struggle against the propertied bourgeoisie over working conditions, working class organization, and compensation. The degree to which these lines of conflicts gave rise to conflicting parties depended both on the timing and character of these revolutions as well as on the extent to which the resulting conflicts led to mass mobilization by elites.

Compared to its western neighbors, Germany was relatively late in developing political parties. Two developments had a decisive effect on the creation of lasting socioeconomic and sociocultural cleavages and their translation into political parties: national unification and rapid industrialization. Both contributed to the rapid "political mobilization of increasingly broader sectors of the population" following unification, facilitated by relatively liberal electoral laws (Ritter, 1990: 32). Unification was largely enacted from above by the Prussian political and military elite who, together with the Protestant Church, were the main supporters and beneficiaries of the creation of a unified German nation.

The main loser was the Catholic Church (Stürmer, 1983: 197). Not only did German unification reflect the victory of the exclusionary protestant conception of the Reich over the Pan-German conception espoused by Catholic Vienna, it also meant that with the exclusion of the German parts of Austria the Catholics were in a minority position in the new Germany despite the fact that Catholics accounted for nearly one third of the population (Dahrendorf, 1967: 111). But it was not until Bismarck launched the church-state struggle known as the *Kulturkampf* (1871-1879) that the latent Protestant-Catholic conflict turned into an enduring religious cleavage from which the catholic Center Party drew its strength at the polls.

A second cleavage engendered by unification pitted the dominant Prussian national culture against several regional and ethnic minorities. These cultures were mostly situated on the periphery of the German Empire and had populations that were often predominantly Catholic (e.g. Poles, Alsace-Lorraineans) (Berghahn, 1994: 215). Given the relatively small size of regional and ethnic minorities, however, this conflict never reached politically significant dimensions (Lepsius, 1973a: 66).

The third cleavage shaping the German party system was the result of the rapid growth of the working class in the wake of the industrial revolution in Germany (Claggett et al., 1982). It led to the second major wave of political mobilization, this time in response to Bismarck's repressive measures against the trade unions and working class political organizations enshrined in the anti-Socialist laws enacted from 1878 to 1890. Intended to curtail the rise of the Social Democrats, these measures provoked the formation of a major and enduring cleavage that underpinned the SPD's steady rise as a major mass party.

National unification in Germany thus gave rise to discrete subcultures organized around distinct socioeconomic or sociocultural cleavages whose origins largely antedated unification and industrialization. Lepsius (1973a) has distinguished four "social-moral milieus" consisting of the Catholic, conservative, bourgeois-Protestant, and socialist subcultures; Rohe (1992: 92-97) has preferred to divide the political landscape of the German Empire into three sociostructural groups (Catholic, socialist, and national). What informs both conceptions is the notion of distinct sociocultural communities that derived their cohesion as much from the negative demarcation from each other as from shared historical memories and emotions that underlay the structure of the German party system (Bendikat, 1989: 485; Rohe, 1992: 21). As Karl Schmitt has put it: "Each party was rooted in its own more-or-less closed subsociety, each of which had all the essential characteristics of a subculture ... and was structurally differentiated to an extent which ensured its cohesion and survival as an independent unit. Consequently, the existence of the parties was bound up with their respective subsocieties or subcultures. In short: it was not individuals who elected parties but subcultures" (1990: 182).

Gerhard Ritter, in his studies of the social bases of the political parties, has shown to what degree communal ties informed voting behavior in Imperial Germany. Thus, between 1874 and 1887, the Center Party won on average two-thirds of the vote in constituencies with clear Catholic majorities as compared to fewer than 2 percent in those districts with Protestant majorities. While the end of the *Kulturkampf* and gradual secularization in the wake of industrialization and urbanization led to the slow disintegration of the Catholic milieu, the Center Party managed to retain much of its appeal in predominantly Catholic areas.

Similarly, the rise of the Social Democrats in the 1880s and 1890s was intimately tied to the rapid expansion of the number of urban, industrial workers. Thus of the 110 seats the SPD captured in 1912, they won 106 of them in the 195 electoral districts in which the absolute majority of the population gained their living from industry, trade or commerce. A further three seats it won in the forty-nine districts where a relative majority earned their living from industry, trade or commerce. But the SPD won none in the remaining 104 constituencies where an absolute majority earned their living from agriculture (Ritter, 1990: 335-38).

Unlike the Center Party or the Social Democrats, the liberals and conservatives appealed to heterogeneous social groups with relatively weak links to the political parties. There was a good reason why the Protestant middle and upper classes were much less organized as a population group than the Catholics or workers: "there was no need for separate organizations because they were the 'nation'" (Pappi and Terway, 1982: 181). This was particularly precarious for the liberals whose initial broad support base of large industrialists, the petty bourgeoisie, farmers, artisans, and workers gradually eroded (Sheehan, 1976; Winkler, 1978). Against that, the conservatives managed to hold on to their strongholds in the east-Elbian agrarian regions in Prussia and Mecklenburg. However, even if the national *Lager*, compared to its Catholic and socialist counterparts, lacked organizational and ideological cohesion, the liberals and conservatives managed to preserve a considerable base of support that was held together by common religious and loose ideological convictions as well as a shared aversion to national "particularists, blacks, and reds" (Rohe, 1982: 348; Rohe, 1992: 66).

As a result of the persistence of these distinct *Lager*, the German party system distinguished itself by its "remarkable stability and linear development" that lasted well into the late 1920s (Lepsius, 1973a: 62). In terms of the "fragmentation along ideological, regional, religious, and class lines" the electoral patterns of 1928 bore "marked similarity to the pattern of a generation earlier" (Loewenberg, 1971: 265). However, given the stability of the German party system despite World War I and the ensuing political turmoil that characterized much of the Weimar Republic, what explains the explosive growth of the National Socialists between 1928 and 1933? As Jürgen Falter (1988; 1990) has persuasively shown, the rise of the Nazis was the result of a combination of factors. On the one hand, the Nazis benefited from a dramatic erosion of electoral support for both the conservatives and liberals, particularly among the traditional petty bourgeoisie and segments of the new middle class, resulting in the near collapse of the traditional national *Lager* (Winkler, 1976; Childers, 1991). In addition, particularly in the early 1930s, the Nazis managed to mobilize newly eligible voters and previous non-voters. Finally, whereas both Catholic and communist voters remained relatively immune to the Nazi temptation, the party successfully appealed to a considerable number of Social Democratic supporters. As a result, working class voters consistently represented a significant part of the National Socialist German Workers Party (NSDAP, or Nazi) electorate (Falter, 1990: 78).

The rise of the Nazis thus cannot be reduced to a single cause. Rather it was the result of a combination of developments, including dealignment processes among middle class voters, the mobilization of new electorates, and a general increase in the number of protest voters. Given the heterogeneity of the Nazi support base, it is not surprising that some observers have characterized the NSDAP as a "catch-all party of protest" or the "first German Volkspartei"(Falter, 1988: 57). It is a moot question whether and to what degree Nazi voters might have developed lasting ties to the NSDAP had the party permitted democratic elections to be held. As soon as they seized power, the Nazis almost immediately abolished the democratic system by outlawing the remaining parties which had not yet, like the Center party, dissolved themselves (Jesse, 1992). This marked the end of the traditional German party system which had survived for more than half a century.

The Revival of the German Party System

The end of World War II, the complete collapse of the Nazi regime, and the revelations about the extent of its crimes marked a decisive turning point in German political history. For the political parties, as for German society in general, 1945 meant a radical break with the past without a clear notion of where the future might lead. There are good reasons to support this interpretation. Perhaps most important, twelve years of Nazi dictatorship had fundamentally transformed German society.

The Nazis "completed for Germany the social revolution that was lost in the faultings of Imperial Germany and again held up by the contradictions of the Weimar Republic" (Dahrendorf, 1967: 381). This was particularly pronounced in the case of the traditional ruling elites whose ranks had been severely decimated by the combination of dictatorship and war. The loss of the eastern territories, together with the Soviet occupation of large parts of Prussia, deprived the remnants of the former elite of their traditional base of social and political power. Their involvement with the Nazi regime and its aggressive policies of genocidal expansionism further discredited both traditional nationalism and conservatism and prevented the revival of the national *Lager*.

What was equally important was that the loss of the eastern territories, combined with the division of what was left of the Reich, put an end to the traditional preponderant position of Protestantism in Germany. In the Federal Republic, Catholics and Protestants were roughly at par. This not only opened up new perspectives for the Catholic part of the population but also led to the gradual erosion of the traditional Catholic milieu. Finally, there was the impact of the occupying powers, whose insistence on democratic organization and public accountability for party funding "found its way into the German constitution and became the basis for outlawing both the Communists and a radical right-wing party" (Loewenberg, 1971: 269).

Despite fundamental changes in the social structure and political foundations of postwar Germany, there were remarkable continuities between the party system of the Federal Republic and that which had existed until 1933. In fact, the first general election in 1949 displayed many characteristics reminiscent of a previous era and was thus as much the "last election of the Weimar period" as it represented the first election of the Federal Republic. It was not until the general election of 1953 that a new party system gradually took form (Falter, 1981). However, even if the traditional milieus had disappeared or were experiencing gradual erosion, the new German party system was still built on major social cleavages whose origins predated the founding of the Federal Republic. The two major cleavages underlying the new German party system were class and religious denomination.

The Endurance of Religion and Class in West German Politics

Given the fundamental change in the balance between the two major denominations, the persistence of religion as a major cleavage is perhaps surprising. It is even more remarkable given the transformation of the political expression of this cleavage. One of the most significant political innovations of the postwar period was the founding of the Christian Democratic Union and its Bavarian sister party, the CSU. Both parties represented prototypes of *Volksparteien* or catch-all mass parties, a "loose conservative coalition under a nonsectarian Christian label," which stood in sharp contrast to their predecessors, the Center Party and the Bavarian People's Party (BVP) (Chandler, 1988: 61). Unlike the BVP, the CDU/CSU made a conscious effort to break out of the confines of the traditional Catholic milieu and, at least in theory, appeal not only to both denominations but to all social strata.

In practice, however, the Christian Democrats to a large extent did assume the legacy of the Center Party without which, in many regions, they would have been unable to survive as a significant political force. Moreover, the extensive support of the Catholic Church in the first national election showed that the majority of the Catholic clergy regarded the CDU/CSU as the party representing their particular interests (Hoffman, 1993). Similar strong links between the CDU/CSU and the Protestant churches were never established (Pappi and Mnich, 1992). As a result, Catholics in general were significantly more likely to vote for the CDU/CSU than Protestant voters. In the early elections in the history of the Federal Republic, the CDU/CSU share of the Catholic vote was "surprisingly close to those of the Center Party. The catholics' prewar united front had been preserved. The CDU/CSU had indeed inherited the political loyalties of the catholic voters" (Schmitt, 1990: 191).

This should not be interpreted as a resurgence of the old cleavage pattern, however. In reality, what emerged was a new cleavage that no longer ran between the two large denominations but separated practicing Catholics and Protestants from the secularized parts of the population (Wolf, 1996). As Franz Urban Pappi (1985) has shown, religiosity cannot be defined the same way for both denominations. Given the formal links between the Union and the Catholic Church, what predisposed Catholic voters to support the CDU/CSU were above all formal expressions of religiosity such as regular church attendance. For Protestant voters, whose institutions lacked formal ties to the CDU/CSU, it was as much individual religious convictions as affiliation with a church that made them more likely than nominal Protestants to vote for the Union. The new religious cleavage thus gave rise to at least two distinct voting patters. First, Catholic voters were generally significantly more likely to vote for the Union than were Protestant voters and second, religious voters of both denominations were significantly more likely to vote CDU/CSU than were nominal members of both denominations or secularized voters.

Data from the 1950s and 1960s, when West German society was still relatively unaffected by secularization, clearly show that the CDU/CSU could rely on the relatively stable support of about two-thirds of the Catholic electorate. Among Protestant voters, CDU/CSU support only reached a little more than a third by 1969 (Pappi, 1973: 199). The reverse was true for the SPD and the FDP; both received a disproportionate share of the Protestant vote. The FDP stood clearly on the secular side of the religious conflict, which might explain why the FDP did particularly well among religious Protestants in predominantly Catholic areas with strong Center Party traditions. In these regions, the party still retained some of its traditional identity as "an anti-clerical force against the Catholic Church."

Against what one might expect, religious differences have remained the most enduring cleavage in German society (Baker, Dalton and Hildebrandt, 1981; Pappi, 1986b; Pappi and Mnich, 1992). As Karl Schmitt (1990: 199) has shown, in the 1980s the Catholic and Protestant share of the CDU/CSU vote remained virtually the same: 59 percent in 1987 as compared to 62 percent in 1953 in the case of the Catholic vote, 37 percent as compared to 36 percent in the case of the Protestant vote. The reverse has been true for the SPD and, to a lesser degree, for the FDP, both of which lost some Protestant support while gaining support from Catholics and non-denominational voters.

Given the relatively rapid process of sociocultural modernization and secularization that characterized German society starting in the late 1960s, the stability of the religious cleavage might come as a surprise. After all, there was a significant decline in religiosity starting in the 1960s. Thus the proportion of Catholics with strong religious ties (measured in terms of regular church attendance) fell from 60 percent in 1953 to 40 percent in the mid-1970s, and then to 30 percent in 1990. At the same time, the proportion of Protestants with strong religious ties, always substantially lower than for Catholics, dropped from 19 to 7 percent (Forschungsgruppe Wahlen, 1994a: 639).

Such evidence suggests that the picture of cleavage stability needs to be somewhat modified. The relative stability of the religious cleavage should not detract from the fact that the composition of the CDU/CSU electorate has significantly changed since the 1950s. In 1953, about three-quarters of the CDU/CSU electorate were practicing Christians (i.e., attending church services at least once a week), but by the early 1980s, this group accounted for less than a third of this electorate. At the same time, electoral support among voters with strong religious ties remained consistently high in both denominations (Kaack, 1971; Berger et al., 1977; Rohe, 1992). Thus in 1990, 78 percent of catholics and 65 percent of non-Catholics with strong religious ties voted for the CDU/CSU (Forschungsgruppe Wahlen, 1994a: 648).

Despite these trends, the CDU and CSU have remained fundamentally confessional or, perhaps more accurately, Catholic parties (Veen, Hoffmann, and Gluchowski, 1994). What has been crucial for this development is the decision of the CDU/CSU leaders in 1945 to found an interconfessional party. This enabled the party to limit the potential losses of support that might have resulted from secularization. In this way, the CDU/CSU has managed to secure the loyalty of those Catholics who have maintained their ties with the traditional milieu while making it possible for "a large proportion of other Catholics to loosen their religious ties without abandoning their traditional party affiliation." Paradoxically, the continuation of confessionally-bound voting behavior has thus been the result of the "deconfessionalization" (Schmitt, 1990:200) of the CDU/CSU. At the same time, the SPD maintained its lead among secular voters. In 1990, 37 percent of Catholics and 44 percent of non-Catholics without religious ties voted for the Social Democrats (Forschungsgruppe Wahlen, 1994a: 648).

If religion has remained an enduring cleavage in postwar German politics, the second important sociostructural determinant of voting behavior, social class, has seen significant modifications. Like the religious cleavage, the class cleavage reflects more than one line of conflict. The most basic one is obviously the classic conflict between capital and labor or, in more contemporary terms, between manual workers and the middle class. However, as Franz Urban Pappi has pointed out, operationalizing the class cleavage in these terms is quite misleading. The middle class variable includes not only the classic groups of capitalists and petty bourgeoisie, but also white collar employees and civil servants whose interests are presumably rather different from those of the former (Pappi, 1979). In order to alleviate the resulting conceptual problems, Pappi proposed to restrict the middle class variable to the self-employed, who presumably come closest to fighting "a surrogate battle on election days for the bourgeoisie." (Pappi and Terway, 1982: 179).

A comparison of the voting behavior of manual workers and the self-employed supports Pappi's thesis of the continued stability of the traditional class cleavage (Pappi, 1986b). As late as 1987, an overwhelming majority of the self-employed intended to support the CDU/CSU (70 percent) or FDP (8 percent), whereas more than 50 percent of blue collar workers said they intended to vote for the Social Democrats (Feist and Krieger, 1987: 38). Additional evidence suggests that the main line of conflict ran less between the SPD and the CDU/CSU, than between the SPD and the FDP. Not only did the FDP's electorate contain a disproportionately large number of self-employed voters in its ranks; the party also had consistently less appeal to manual workers than the CDU (Pappi and Terway, 1982: 133). Although the FDP lost a considerable proportion of its support among the self-employed to the CDU/CSU when it formed a coalition with the SPD, this loss was only temporary. After switching back to the CDU/CSU in 1982, the FDP recovered much of its previous losses among the self-employed (Veen, Hoffmann, and Gluchowski, 1994).

Though there is evidence for the notion that traditional class cleavages persisted well into the 1980s, class cleavages have been changing under the impact of the socioeconomic transformations of the past several decades. Between 1950 and 1991, the size of the working class declined from 51 to a little less than 39 percent of the (west) German population. At the same time, the proportion of the self-employed fell from about 28 to 9.5 percent (ForschungsgruppeWahlen, 1994: 638; Schäfers, 1995: 192). Given the SPD's disproportionate support from blue collar workers, one might expect these trends to have led to a significant decline of the Social Democrats' electoral fortunes.

Instead, the party experienced steady gains in the 1960s until it became the largest party in the 1972 Bundestag election.

The key to resolving this paradox has been the changing electoral behavior among segments of white collar employees and civil servants, in what has come to be known as the "new middle class." As Russell Dalton and others have shown, the success of the Social Democrats in the 1960s was largely the result of their growing appeal to this new middle class, a growing number of whom abandoned the white collar and civil service habit of supporting the CDU (Baker, Dalton and Hildebrandt, 1981; Dalton, Flanagan and Beck, 1984: 127). Between 1961 and 1972, the proportion of SPD supporters among the new middle class voters increased from 30 to 50 percent, about the same amount as the CDU lost among these strata. It is significant that the surge in new middle class support was roughly as strong among Catholics as it was among Protestants (Pappi, 1973).

The growing appeal of the SPD among new middle class voters was not primarily the result of growing class consciousness among white collar employees and/or civil servants suddenly discovering their proletarian status (Pappi, 1977). Rather, it was the result of secularization processes, which manifested themselves first among the new middle class and led its members to act as "the forerunner of general secularisation." This explains why a growing number, after rejecting the traditional, religiously-inspired positions of the CDU on the role of the churches in public life, or on divorce and abortion, were increasingly attracted to the reform program espoused by the social-liberal coalition (Pappi, 1986b). Ironically enough, the SPD's steady rise thus occurred at a time when the position of its traditional core clientele was more and more weakened. The result was increasing tensions between the traditional working class SPD and the emerging "teachers SPD" (Rohe, 1992: 176-77).

Although the growing electoral importance of the new middle class had no direct effect on the older class cleavages, it posed a challenge to both major parties, thus changing the logic of party competition. The CDU, in particular, was forced to rethink its positions and modernize its program. As a result, the Christian Democrats gradually managed to recover a significant number of white collar employees and civil servants, and were able to increase their support among new middle class voters from 37 to 47 percent between 1980 and 1987. At the same time, the SPD saw its share of the new middle class vote plummet from 50 percent to 37 percent (Conradt and Dalton, 1988).

Given the decline of both the traditional working class and the proportion of the self-employed among the general population, one might question the continued usefulness of defining the class cleavage in terms of a conflict between these two groups. A more appropriate measure might be union membership, especially if it can be shown that for the SPD, union membership serves a function similar to that of church attendance for the CDU/CSU.

Few would challenge the observation that despite significant changes in the social composition of its support base, the SPD has remained "the primary party for blue-collar workers and especially for trade union families" (Chandler, 1988: 70). Although the trade unions, after they had been allowed to reorganize after the war, were officially supposed to maintain a neutral stance, in practice they were always closer to the SPD than to the parties of the center-right. Using data from the early 1960s, Klaus Liepelt was the first to demonstrate that union membership was by far the most important sociostructural variable explaining SPD support (Liepelt, 1971: 189). Aside from medium-term fluctuations, union membership has remained a constant and stable predictor of electoral behavior. Between 1953 and 1983, the proportion of union members voting SPD declined from 55 to 53 percent. As late as 1990, almost half of union members (in the west) still retained their loyalty to the Social Democrats (Klingemann, 1985: 259; Jung and Roth, 1992: 213).

Data from the 1990 Bundestag election suggest that the predictive power of union membership holds equally true for workers and white collar employees and civil servants. Thus in 1990, in the western part of Germany, more than half (52 percent) of unionized manual workers and a little less than half (47 percent) of unionized white-collar employees voted SPD, against only 39 percent of non-unionized workers and a mere 27 percent of white collar employees and civil servants (Forschungsgruppe Wahlen, 1994a: 645). The data also suggest that one reason for the Social Democrats' declining fortunes in the 1980s was their lack of appeal among the non-unionized new middle class, a near two-thirds majority of whom consistently voted for the center-right parties (Feist and Liepelt, 1987: 285).

The changes in voting patterns, while supporting the notion that class has remained of enduring importance in postwar German politics, also imply alterations in the nature of the class cleavage. If in the early years of the Federal Republic, the main class cleavage was between manual workers and the self-employed, in the late 1980s class conflict appears to have become both more diffuse and more clearly defined. For example, the revival of union membership, albeit with new types of workers, as the most significant predictor of SPD support, marks a revival and redefinition of traditional cleavage politics, similar to the significance of church ties for the CDU (Pappi, 1986a: 382). This speaks not only for the resilience of older cleavage patterns, it also indicates that the strategy of the two major parties to emancipate themselves from their traditional milieus and promote themselves as *Volksparteien* has reached a point of exhaustion.

Postindustrialism, Globalization, and the Transformation of the German Party System

The major parties' fading appeal outside of their traditional constituencies is but one indicator of more profound changes in the German party system. Other indicators have been increasing electoral volatility, declining voter turnout, and a growing fragmentation of the party system. Perhaps the most significant result of these developments was the emergence and rise of the Greens in the early 1980s. This was followed by the emergence of a number of protest parties, the most important of which was the radical right wing populist Republikaner. A lesser sign of party system fragmentation has been the establishment of the PDS in the east German Länder.

Some scholars have interpreted these developments as symptoms of growing voter alienation from, and public resentment of, the established political parties (Rieger, 1990). A number of surveys support this suggestion, for instance those measuring confidence in the major sociopolitical institutions. Thus within little more than ten years, there has been a dramatic decline in public trust in political parties, with the percentage of German citizens expressing confidence in political parties falling from 43 percent (1980) to 21 percent (1991) (Wiesendahl, 1992: 4). However, they fail to explain what has caused this sharp rise in political alienation.

An alternative explanation sees the fragmentation of the party system as a political response to fundamental sociostructural changes in German society in the last two decades, the result of a combination of external and domestic developments affecting all advanced Western democracies (Castells, 1996). Domestically, the most important has been the expansion of mass higher education starting in the late 1960s that has led to dramatic shifts in the educational structure of West German society. Whereas in the early 1950s, the vast majority of West German youth was enrolled in primary education, by the late 1980s, more than two-thirds were enrolled in secondary-level schools. One of the most important results of this development was a significant devaluation of lower-level degrees (Geißler, 1996: 253-59).

Closely connected to this development in education has been the expansion of an array of public and private sector administrative, technical and professional positions. Many of them are located in the service sector, most notably in professional, business, financial, social, community, or personal services. There has been a significant change in the production process as well. In the 1980s, the once dominant large-scale, geographically highly concentrated production of standardized products has given way to relatively small-scale, flexible, and spatially diffused manufacturing of specialized products.

The domestic structural transformation of advanced industrial societies has been further intensified by external changes. Among the most important developments have been technological innovations, especially in the field of information and communication, and the increase in competitive pressures engendered by the integration and internationalization of goods, services, and capital markets. According to recent World Bank estimates, during the past two decades, merchandise exports have increased from 11 to 18 percent of global output. At the same time, financial deregulation and the abolition of capital controls led to a dramatic increase in financial transactions. In 1992, daily foreign exchange trading amounted to roughly $880 billion, a more than forty-fold increase compared to 1982. In the same year, the combined total volume of trade in foreign exchange, government bonds, and equities amounted to more than $400 trillion (Boyer and Drache, 1996).

Technological innovation, economic globalization, and the shift to postindustrial employment structures have significant implications for the structure of advanced industrial societies. The expansion of the service sector has given rise to new social strata with distinct values and life styles. Given that many positions in the service sector involve analyzing information as well as interacting with clients and coworkers, these positions tend to require high levels of education, and/or social and communicative skills. The result has been the rise of a "new knowledge class" of "symbolic specialists" who have seen a steady increase in their ranks (Reich, 1991). The situation is similar with respect to the rise of flexible specialization and global competition. In its wake, demand for "fordist" mass production workers has rapidly declined in favor of a highly qualified, "polyvalent" workforce. As newly industrializing countries increase their production of tradable manufactures, cost competition increasingly forces manufacturers in advanced industrial countries to "slice up the value added chain" by relocating the lower-skill parts of the production process to low-wage countries while maintaining only those parts at home that are relatively intensive in the use of highly skilled labor (Krugman, 1995: 333). In both cases, routine production and clerical as well as less educated and experienced workers are increasingly faced with stagnant or even declining incomes, the threat of redundancy, and the prospect of structural and long-term unemployment.

In the short and perhaps even intermediate term, the combination of expanding postindustrial employment structures and intensified global economic competition thus has a significant impact on life chances in advanced industrial societies. At least until older generations of workers with generally lower skill levels have retired and new generations have adapted themselves to the exigencies of the global information economy, economic and social modernization invariably leads to social disruptions. In an increasingly skill-intensive labor market, education becomes the key to individual success. Additional factors are age and increasingly gender, given the relative decline in traditional male-dominated industrial jobs and the rapid increase in postindustrial positions requiring analytical, communicative, and social and interpersonal skills, which are either gender-neutral or "female-biased" (Economist, 28 September, 1996: 23-26).

One might assume that the profound sociostructural changes engendered by the combination of expanding postindustrialism and intensified global competition would create new lines of political conflict. Much of the comparative literature on both left-libertarian and radical right-wing populist parties suggests that the emergence and success of these parties in the 1980s and early 1990s is largely the result of their ability to appeal to these new sociostructural cleavages (Kitschelt, 1990; Betz,

1994). The supporters of the Greens do share a distinct social profile, and what differentiates them most clearly from the supporters of other parties is the combination of age and education. The lower the age and the higher the educational level, the more likely he or she will vote for the Greens (Bürklin and Dalton, 1994: 275). Thus in 1990, more than 25 percent of 18 to 34-year-old West Germans with at least a secondary degree *(Abitur)* voted for the Greens, but among those in the same age group with not more than basic, primary education, only 6 percent did. Given their relatively young age it is hardly surprising that a significant number of Green voters are not yet part of the labor force. In 1990, almost one out of every five Green voters was a student *(in Ausbildung)*. It is not unusual that the party has persistently attained some of its highest results in university towns such as Tübingen or those districts in large cities dominated by universities, such as the inner city district of Munich. Among those employed, a considerable portion of Green supporters and sympathizers hold higher-level positions in the postindustrial sector of the economy (Schmitt-Beck, 1994).

Their distinct social profile, their origins in their struggle against nuclear power, and the mobilization of many young Germans into new social movements, lend support to the notion that the Greens represent a new milieu party (Veen and Hoffmann, 1992). In the past, this milieu was largely grounded in the networks and communities of the alternative movement, but as the Greens became more successful, the milieu became increasingly amorphous. It did not lose its most distinct characteristics, and the Greens increasingly established themselves in the late 1980s as the representatives of a highly educated, urban segment of the new postindustrial service class. By 1989, almost half of employed Green supporters held positions in the public sector, with a further quarter employed in the private service sector (Feist and Liepelt, 1987: 284; Bauer and Schmitt, 1990: 20).

One of the most significant signs of the transformation of the Greens has been the party's growing appeal to younger women.

Whereas in the early 1980s male voters were slightly more likely than women to vote for the Greens, the situation had reversed itself by the late 1980s. The party's appeal has been particularly pronounced among highly educated younger women. In 1987, almost a third of women, but only slightly more than a fifth of men, who had an *Abitur* said they intended to vote for the Greens (Molitor, 1992: 138-41; Schmitt-Beck, 1994: 210-11). In addition, the Greens did particularly well among women without church or union affiliations. The growing support among better educated younger women correlates nicely with the growth in female enrollment in higher education in Germany. In 1960, the percentage of 18-year-old males enrolled in university preparatory high schools (*Gymnasium*) was significantly higher than that of young women (10.4 vs. 6.3 percent), by the mid-1980s female enrollment had not only caught up with male enrollment, but was about to surpass it. By 1992, almost 25 percent of 18-year-old women, but only slightly more than a fifth of young males, were enrolled in secondary schools (Schäfers, 1995: 159).

Although it would be an exaggeration to claim that the Greens are a women's party, the appellation does capture important trends in electoral behavior. For a growing number of women, increasing educational opportunities and the postindustrial labor market lead to an emancipation from traditional institutional ties and behavioral patterns. This newly found freedom, in turn, finds its expression in support for left-libertarian parties, perhaps the most significant indication that the Greens represent a new postindustrial cleavage in German politics.

If the Greens form one side of a new cleavage in German politics, the other side has remained largely vacant. Unlike in Austria, Belgium, or France, in Germany radical right wing populist parties have enjoyed only limited success. The sudden rise of the Republikaner in the late 1980s, followed by their equally rapid collapse in the early 1990s, is one case in point. Other protest parties such the right-wing extremist German People's

Union (DVU), the right-wing populist Stattpartei, or the right wing populist Federation of Free Citizens have not fared much better (Hoffmann, 1995). However, the failure of right-wing protest parties to establish themselves in the German party system should not be taken as an indication of the fundamental lack of a potential right wing electorate. The dramatic upsurge of support for the National Democratic Party (NPD) in the 1960s, the sizable gains of the Republikaner and the DVU in regional elections in the late 1980s and early1990s as well as a number of empirical studies on the radical right wing potential suggest just the opposite (Falter, 1994).

Superficially, the upsurge of right wing protest in the late 1980s might be dismissed as a postmodern pastiche of the 1960s. However, a closer comparison between the rise of the NPD in the 1960s and that of the Republikaner in the late 1980s reveals fundamental differences between the two phenomena. The NPD was in many ways a last attempt to reassemble the traditional nationalist *Lager*, drawing much of its early support from former right-wing supporters of the FDP and a number of right wing nationalist parties. Generally, the party attained its highest results in those areas, "in which, during the most crisis-laden time of the Weimar Republic, the NSDAP achieved its greatest electoral victories" (Nagle, 1970: 147-155). Unlike the established parties, the NPD lacked a clear social profile (Liepelt, 1967). It did attract disproportionate support from the generation of older, particularly male, voters who had spent their formative years during the Third Reich, as well as from the traditional old middle class, and unskilled and semi-skilled workers. However, their numbers were not significant enough to contradict the general conclusion that, if anything, the NPD was more of a catch-all party of protest than a class or interest party (Nagle, 1970: 161).

Support for the radical populist right in the late 1980s and early 1990s by contrast was much more clearly concentrated in certain population groups. At the height of their electoral success,

Republikaner supporters distinguished themselves in terms of gender, age, and education. Those generally most likely to sympathize with the party were younger men with relatively low levels of formal education and blue collar status. This was confirmed by the national election of 1990, where heavy losses left the party with little more than their core constituency. In this election, the party received its largest support among two groups: young men aged 18 to 24 (3.9 percent) and blue collar workers (3.6 percent).

Local studies point in the same direction, whether of the Republikaner in Frankfurt (Hennig, 1991), Berlin (Schmollinger, 1989), or Hamburg (Jagodzinski, Friedrichs and Dalmer, 1995) or of the DVU in Bremen (Dinse, 1992). The far right did particularly well in working class areas where a relatively large proportion of the population had little more than basic education and which distinguished themselves by a generally low quality of housing. As studies of the Republikaner successes in the 1992 Baden-Württemberg election show, the party did disproportionately well in regions with high levels of industrialization and low levels of affluence (Feist, 1992; Falter, 1994).

Such distinct social characteristics suggest that the far right managed to exploit the new sociopolitical conflicts engendered by social and economic modernization, at least for a time. As elsewhere in Western Europe, the far right in Germany benefited from the confluence of several developments. There was growing apprehension among the least educated and skilled about mass unemployment and socioeconomic marginalization as a result of sluggish growth, government budgetary constraints, and rapid technological innovation. There was also growing anxiety over the continued viability of the welfare state as it confronted a growing number of immigrants and refugees making claims on the system. Most important politically, there was growing disenchantment with the established parties of the left for adopting a postmaterialist or left-libertarian agenda in an attempt to attract the expanding new middle class and in the process abandoning its traditional role as an advocate of the underprivileged social strata (Kitschelt, 1994; Padgett and Paterson, 1994; Kitschelt, 1995). As a result, the SPD lost a considerable number of its working class constituencies to the far right parties, which in turn increasingly presented themselves as vehicles for working class protest. Thus in the 1996 state election in Baden-Württemberg, four out of ten Republikaner voters (the party received 9.1 percent of the vote) but only three out of ten SPD voters were blue-collar workers (Forschungsgruppe Wahlen, 1996: 20).

The near-collapse of the far right parties in the early 1990s (save for Baden-Württemberg) means neither that these conflicts have diminished nor that the right wing electorate has disappeared. In fact, one study of non-voters suggests, former radical right-wing voters may have joined the growing ranks of those citizens who no longer participate in the political process (Falter and Schumann, 1994).

The Impact of Unification on the German Party System

A great deal has been written about the importance of unification for German postwar history, but less on its effect on the German party system. In 1990, that effect appeared minimal and the first post unification Bundestag election saw the party system largely unchanged. Most notable were the failures of the West German Greens to surmount the 5 percent hurdle and the election of the PDS to the Bundestag. However, whereas few observers were prepared to write off the Greens as a significant political factor, most considered the PDS a short-lived protest phenomenon unlikely to survive once the socioeconomic situation in the former GDR had stabilized (Smith, 1992: 100).

By the end of the decade, the impact of unification on the German party system appeared to have been more profound than had been anticipated. Perhaps the most important development was the emergence of the PDS as a significant actor both regionally and nationally. Not only did the party recover a significant following in the eastern part of Germany, but by winning four direct seats the party also managed to regain representation in the Bundestag in 1994 and repeated this electoral success in 1998. Other changes to the party system were less conspicuous, involving modifications in the composition of the social base of the major parties.

By the late 1980s both major parties had fairly distinct social profiles. Among CDU/CSU voters, Catholics and members of the middle class predominated; among SPD voters it was manual workers and unionized new middle class voters. The first post unification election in 1990 led to several "anomalies in eastern German voting behavior when compared to that of the West" (Dalton and Bürklin, 1995: 79). This was hardly surprising. Unification could be expected to modify the prevailing sociocultural balance for two reasons (Rohe, 1992: 183-85). First, the eastern part of Germany had traditionally been predominantly Protestant. Although more than forty-five years of communist dictatorship had significantly eroded religious loyalties, the fundamental imbalance between the confessions remained. In 1990, roughly a quarter of the population said they were members of the Protestant churches, but only 6 percent considered themselves as belonging to the Catholic Church (Statistisches Bundesamt, 1994: 554). Two-thirds of the population said they had no religious affiliation. Second, the occupational structure in the east German Länder differed considerably from that in the West. This was particularly pronounced with respect to the percentage of manual workers and the self-employed among the active population. In 1993, manual workers made up a little more than 42 percent of the active population, while the self-employed accounted for less than 7 percent (Statistisches Bundesamt, 1994: 86-87).

West German experience suggested that the predominance of Protestant, non-religious, and working class voters in the east should have significantly favored the Social Democrats. Instead, the 1990 election saw not only a striking reversal of class voting patterns but also a significant departure from traditional confessional voting patterns in the eastern Länder. The eastern CDU won a majority of the working class vote as well as a majority among both Catholics and Protestants and a third of non-religious voters (Gibowski and Kaase, 1991). Despite the fact that in 1994, the CDU ceded a significant portion of its support among both blue collar workers and the non-religious to the SPD and especially the PDS, this did not fundamentally change the prevailing pattern. As a result, it has been argued that what emerged from the two post unification elections were two distinct electorates. Its most striking evidence has been the religious composition of the electoral base of the CDU. In 1994 in the west, more than half of the CDU voters were Catholics, 29 percent were Protestants, and only 8 percent nonreligious, whereas in the east, 52 percent of the CDU's electorate were without religious affiliation (Dalton and Bürklin, 1995: 92).

However, an alternative interpretation suggests the differences between east and west might not be as significant as this comparison implies (Rohe, 1992: 186-87). If one assumes some degree of equivalence between non-religious voters in the east and voters without strong religious ties in the west, the differences between the two electorates become considerably smaller (Weßels, 1994: 150). The heavy CDU losses among non-religious voters in 1994 were perhaps the most important indication of the potential reassertion of the established postwar religious cleavage in post-unification Germany (Jung and Roth, 1994). Despite the fact that in 1994 the CDU was still the strongest party among blue collar workers, the heavy defection to left-wing parties suggests that there is "a gradual convergence between East and West" (Gibowski, 1995: 123-24). The 1998 elections continued this defection.

The first three post-unification elections did confirm one important pre-unification trend in electoral behavior. In 1990,

1994 and 1998, significantly more women then men voted for the Greens. Unlike in the past, these differences were no longer confined to certain age groups, even if the Greens continued to achieve their best results among younger voters. However, post election surveys after 1994 also showed that the Green gains among women were largely confined to the west. In the east, it was the PDS that proved particularly attractive to younger women and the PDS explicitly targeted young women in several of their 1998 campaign advertisements.

This raises a number of intriguing questions about the nature of the SED successor party. At the time of its emergence in the Volkskammer election of March of 1990, the PDS relied largely on support from the members of the old GDR elite, in other words those holding high positions in the state administration, judiciary, the party apparatus, the media, science and education as well as their families. At 31 percent, the proportion of PDS voters among these groups was almost twice as high as the party's overall share of the vote, and it was particularly pronounced in (East) Berlin where half of all members of the socialist "intelligentsia" voted PDS (Roth, 1990). Given that these groups were the main losers in the unification process, the future of the PDS appeared rather dim.

The party's success in subsequent regional and national elections, however, indicated that the party was succeeding in gradually expanding its social base. By 1994, electoral support had reached proportions that suggested that the PDS was close to becoming an East German regional *Volkspartei*. The party's electoral base remained distinctive, for despite its radical left-wing self-understanding and pretensions, the party's appeal has been weak among manual workers, as has been its attraction to the self-employed and to farmers.

Yet, the PDS has done particularly well among white-collar employees and civil servants with higher levels of education, and among younger voters, achieving some of its best results in 1994 in urban areas with relatively low levels of unemployment and relatively high levels of administrative sector employees (Falter and Klein, 1994: 28; Schultze, 1995: 343-44). Although the party still represents a significant portion of those social groups that lost out during unification, it has also managed to claim representation of a new stratum of highly educated urban professionals, predominantly in the public sector, with relatively high levels of income (Klein and Caballero, 1996). The party's electoral base thus shows a striking resemblance with that of the Greens. This might explain in part why Alliance 90/The Greens have so far failed to establish themselves in the eastern Länder (Betz and Welsh, 1995).

Conclusion

One of the main characteristics of the German party system has been its stability and relative resilience to socioeconomic change. Until the end of the Weimar Republic, the German party system was largely grounded in distinct sociocultural milieus whose continued cohesion assured the system's stability. The rise of the Nazis in the late 1920s was largely a result of the collapse of large parts of the traditional nationalist *Lager*, which left a void that the Nazis were quick to fill. The social revolution brought about by Nazi dictatorship and total war not only destroyed the old elites, but also severely weakened the traditional sociocultural structures. As a result, the postwar party system was spared a return to the fragmentation of the Weimar period. Instead, what emerged within a decade was a stable two-and-a-half party system that lasted until the early 1980s. The success of the parties in this system was partly due to their ability to revive the traditional sociostructural alliances but it was also partly due to a conscious strategy to reach out beyond the closely circumscribed confines of the older cleavage patterns.

The CDU/CSU's dominant position in the immediate postwar period, and particularly the SPD's growing appeal to the rising new middle class in the late 1960s and early 1970s provided the most striking evidence of the success of this catch-all strategy. The declining ability of both major parties in the 1980s to appeal to heterogeneous constituencies with increasingly disparate interests serves as a reminder of its limits. Their sensitivity to the socioeconomic and sociocultural shocks of the past two decades suggests that the emergence of the *Volkspartei* was to a large degree a function of a combination of mass affluence and societal political consensus. Once confronted with the postmaterialist demands of a rising postindustrial service class and the no less vocal materialist demands of manual workers increasingly anxious over mass unemployment, the SPD's constituency gradually disintegrated. The rise and establishment of the Greens in the German party system was the logical consequence of the SPD's inability to resolve its sociostructural dilemma. As a result, the SPD's social base was increasingly reduced to its traditional core constituencies. The rise of the far right in the late 1980s and their sporadic successes in the early 1990s was an indication that similar developments were occurring on the right.

In some important ways, the past decade thus has seen somewhat of a return to the traditional patterns of political support. The rise of the Greens as a distinct milieu party and their increasingly successful strategy to replace the FDP as an "ecological civil rights party" is one more evidence of this trend. Ironically enough, the Greens might be the first successful attempt since 1945 to revive, if only in terms of its earlier size, the traditional liberal *Lager*. Even the establishment of the PDS as a major party in the eastern *Länder* was largely the result of its ability to appeal to a distinct subculture (Schultze, 1995).

The rise of the Greens in the early 1980s, the emergence of the far right in the late 1980s, and the rapid establishment of the PDS in the eastern Länder together with the near-collapse of the FDP in the early 1990s are among the most important symptoms of a major transformation of the German party system. Although less pronounced than in Austria, these changes are indications of a bifurcation of the German party system into two distinct systems, each following their own logic. Where the old system was largely grounded in the experience and social structure shaped by postwar economic growth and the expansion of the welfare state, the new system is grounded in the experience and social structure shaped by the rise of postindustrialism, global economic integration, and mass unemployment. The old system is still largely informed by membership in traditional institutions; the new system is largely informed by the contextualized identities of age, education, and gender. This proposition lends support both to those who have stressed the resilience of the traditional cleavage patterns and to those who have argued that political behavior is increasingly shaped by newly evolving milieus, lifestyles, and taste cultures (Vester et al., 1993; Schultze, 1993). To what degree they will shape the future of the German party system depends as much on sociostructural developments as it depends on the ability of the political parties to adapt themselves to them.

Chapter 3

THE GERMAN PARTY STATE
A Reassessment

*Michaela W. Richter**

Introduction

Few cases demonstrate more dramatically the critical role parties can play both in the destruction and in the construction of democratic systems than does Germany in the past two centuries (Palma, 1990; Pridham, 1990). In Imperial Germany, conservative constitutional and legal theories hostile to parties retarded the development of parliamentary democracy (*Geschichtliche Grundbegriffe* 4: 677-733; Faul, 1964). In the Weimar Republic, the persistence of this anti-party tradition, a polarized party system and the sorry political record of the Weimar parties created the conditions requisite for mass and elite support of the NSDAP's anti-democratic one-party Führer state (Bracher, 1955; Matthias

---

* The author would like to gratefully acknowledge the support of the College of Staten Island, CUNY through its scholar incentive program and other assistance.

and Mersey, 1960; Nipperdey, 1980). Against this background, there was little reason at the end of World War II to believe a stable democracy based on competitive parties could ever take root in Germany.

Yet to a degree unimaginable at its creation in 1949, the Federal Republic did become a successful democracy. This chapter argues that the principal reason that "Bonn did not become Weimar" was because of its distinctive form of democracy in which political parties enjoy a privileged position that was both unprecedented in German history and unique among Western democracies. Hence the now generally accepted designation of the Federal Republic as a "democratic party state." Its defining features first emerged during the Occupation. They were the products of deliberate strategies for overcoming Germany's anti-party legacy, both by ending the old dualism separating parties from the state and by making democratic parties into the designated agents for shaping the public will. As subsequently legitimated and strengthened by the Federal Constitutional Court and reinforced by a stable party system, the democratic party state not only provided effective governance but facilitated the emergence of a democratic political culture.

The democratic party state first demonstrated its adaptability and strength in the face of economic downturns. Then, during the 1970s and 1980s, it overcame forces and currents of opinion highly critical of the party state and its principal parties. Electoral disaffection, protest voting, and the end of the two-and-a-half party hegemony produced repeated assertions that the party state was in crisis. Yet on the eve of unification in 1989, the party state and constituent parties remained strong and securely in place.

Unification was to prove by far the greatest test for the party state. Faced once again with the task of managing the democratic transformation of a society long under totalitarian rule, the Federal Republic's founding parties responded by expanding the West German party state and party system eastward. This decision has raised the question whether transplanting West Germany's distinctive democratic model can succeed under altogether different conditions in the former East Germany. The possible failure of the party state there might destabilize the all-German party and political systems, and renewed evidence of political and electoral strains have occasioned portentous announcements yet again of a "party crisis" and even of a "crisis of German democracy" (Ehrhart and Sandschneider; 1994; Hoffmann et al., 1994; Jaschke, 1992; Padgett and Paterson, 1994; Rattinger, 1993; Rieger, 1994).

Against such diagnoses, I argue that despite the enormous and difficult challenges presented by this second democratic transformation unification represents, the achievements of the party state are considerable. In fact, unification has demonstrated once again the capacity for effective, consensual governance by the Federal Republic's main parties, as well as the integrative capacities of its party state. After seven years, there are few grounds to fear either for the survival of democracy in a united Germany, or for its distinctive party state.

The first section of this chapter examines the origins of the party state during the occupation, with special attention paid to the part played by Kurt Schumacher and Konrad Adenauer. Next I turn to the role of the Federal Constitutional Court and the tripartite party system in consolidating and expanding the party state. The third section treats characteristics of the party state as it has evolved in practice, and the consequent criticisms raised against it during the decade prior to unification. The final two sections assess the performance and consequences of the party state and party system since unification, the first of which traces the Federal Republic's eastward expansion and the second of which analyzes its consequences and the future implications of unification, both negative and positive, for Germany's parties and party state.

The Occupation and the Origins of the Democratic Party State

Most analysts have attributed the Federal Republic's success to the postwar division of Germany, its prolonged economic boom, generational change, and external constraints. In fact, even during the Occupation, Konrad Adenauer and Kurt Schumacher had adopted strategies to secure a dominant position for political parties in both state and society. They were to prevail despite the resistance of the Western Allies, elements of the German elites, and the mass public.

The military defeat and collapse of the Third Reich ostensibly provided preconditions far more favorable to democratic party government than had accompanied the formation of the Weimar Republic. Although its critics had dismissed Weimar as a mere "party state," a key weakness of that democracy had been its failure to create responsible party government and thus to supplant both the ideal of an autonomous nonpartisan state and the elites who were strongly committed to the older, authoritarian state tradition (Smith, 1982a: 66). The army and civil service, together the most prestigious and powerful opponents of democracy in the Empire and the Weimar Republic, had their moral authority and power undermined through collaboration with the Third Reich, military defeat and occupation. After 1945, they were in no position to challenge the reestablishment of political parties and parliamentary democracy.

Political parties, by contrast, having been banned within months of the Nazi seizure of power, were untainted by ties to the Nazi regime. Moreover, the shared experiences of persecution, exile, or concentration camps during the Third Reich, had not only undermined the *Lager* mentality characteristic of political leaders in the Empire and Weimar Republic but had also created a common elite consensus for a democratic, constitutional order for the first time in German history.

Nonetheless, in 1945 it was by no means self-evident that political parties could assert themselves as legitimate political actors, much less as founders of a new, viable party-based democracy. Major obstacles had to be overcome: the reluctance of the three Western occupying military governments to give governing responsibilities to the newly formed political parties, persistent anti-party attitudes among some German public officials and politicians, and a population indifferent or hostile to political parties.

Germany's democratization was initiated by the occupying forces. As a central component of this project, the closing communiqué of the Potsdam Conference called for the rapid return of political parties. The Soviet Military Government was the first to take this step in June 1945, followed by the Western Allies (Staritz, 1987), who by December 1945, had licensed the same four parties recognized in the Soviet zone: the Social Democratic Party, the Communist Party, the Christian Democratic Union and the Liberal Democratic Party (which in the West would eventually rename itself the Free Democratic Party.

In the three Western zones, Allied policies sought to ensure a party system free of the flaws which, in the Allied view, had undermined the Weimar Republic, namely excessive fragmentation, the presence of extremist parties, and highly centralized party organizations. In their effort to restructure the German party system, the Allied military governments adopted roughly analogous strategies. To reduce party fragmentation, they limited the number of licensed parties. To minimize extremist tendencies, prior Allied approval was required for party membership, programs, organizational rules, and finances. The American and British military governments allowed small nationalist and regional parties to form, but only permitted them to operate in a few localities. In the case of the Communist party, all allied governments sought to limit its expansion in their zones. To encourage grassroots democracy, Allied policies tried to strengthen local party members and branches vis-à-vis Land or zonal organizations (Rogers, 1995; Smith, 1974).

Not all these objectives were met, most notably in trying to ensure transparency in financing and strong local organizations. On the other hand, the net effect of Allied policies was to give the SPD, CDU/CSU, and FDP a political and electoral edge which they never lost even after the end of the occupation. To this extent, Allied policies laid the foundation for the Federal Republic's stable system of centrist, democratic parties.

Yet having restored political parties and competitive elections, the Allies were none too eager to hand over real power to party politicians. Given the enormous tasks confronting them, the Allies wanted problems dealt with efficiently, without lengthy partisan debates or attacks by a parliamentary opposition on occupational authority and policies. To the Allies, political parties were to serve as lightning rods for popular grievances before these could turn into direct challenges to the military governments (Klein, 1990). Given a choice, Allied governments clearly preferred to work with "nonpolitical" German administrators and "nonpartisan" minister presidents. Active measures were taken to reduce partisan challenges to occupational administrations. Throughout the Occupation the Western Allies insisted on all-party governments or grand coalitions within their respective zones. Parity among parties on key bodies became the rule, with elements of corporatist representation built into governing bodies. Party influence on public policies was also reduced by limiting the powers of elected bodies.

The Allied ambivalence about the restoration of partisan politics was widely shared on the German side. During World War II, the traumatic memories of Weimar party conflicts colored all constitutional plans for a future German democracy on the part of German political exiles or resistance figures. The draft constitutions of that time, whether Social Democratic, liberal or conservative (Benz, 1979), generally reflected a desire to curtail the "influence of parties in general and party bureaucracies in particular" (Mommsen, 1987: 575). Indeed, the Allies came under considerable pressures from German officials to delay licensing of political parties for fear that partisan politics might complicate their already difficult tasks (Rogers, 1990).

In an unusual reversal, after 1945 civil servants abandoned their traditional anti-party stance and actually supported a more direct role for political parties in zonal governance. They did so in part to have political cover for unpopular decisions, (*Parl. Rat.*, v. 1: 963; for the British zone, Ebsworth, 1960: 146) but also to avoid charges of collaboration, a particularly sensitive issue for the French military government (Rogers, 1990). Instead, the strongest opposition to the reinsertion of parties into political life came from the minister presidents of the Länder, especially in the American zone. Like the Allies, their key concern was to provide efficient government without partisan conflict and wrangling. But their attitudes towards political parties continued traditional prejudices.

As in the older theory of state, these German officials distinguished between a "higher form of politics" and "partisan politics" (*Parl. Rat.*,v. 2: 59). They also subscribed to the negative view of parties as "partial spokesmen for the interests of different groups" (Foelz-Schroeter, 1974: 227), and hence incapable of those "common efforts" by which "... the German nation and the German people [can] be guided towards a normal, healthy life" (Klein, 1990:59).

More positively, the South German minister presidents discovered a new form of democracy in the Länderrat, the federal council of states created in the American zone to coordinate policies across Land lines. Its superiority to the traditional parliamentary version, they argued, lay in its two central principles: "federalism and coordination – both true children of the democratic spirit" (*Parl. Rat.*,v. 1: 80). Federalism was seen as limiting the power of central party organizations. Without strong autonomy for the Länder, centralized parties "would easily override Länder parliaments and run everything to the smallest detail" (Klein, 1990: 344). Coordination was made necessary by the fact that all minister presidents had to consent to Länderrat policies. For such unanimity to be achieved, "all opinions and positions must be thrashed out until a single view emerges." The need to forge a "common will" was seen as preferable to majority rule, in which "superior numbers ... can simply cut off or ignore the opinions ... of the minority" (*Parl. Rat.*, v. 1: 996).

In stark contrast to the Weimar Republic, the minister presidents did not form the core of a conservative opposition to democracy. Nonetheless, in their yearning for nonpartisan governance and clear distaste for the conflicts and competition that are at the heart of pluralistic democracy, their views reflect the legacy of conservative anti-party thinking. The persistence of such conceptions was all the more worrisome in the absence of any democratic ground swell on the part of the population at large.

Public opinion polls after 1945 revealed that the German people, after thirteen years of totalitarian rule, were singularly ill-prepared for the democratic experiment. The OMGUS surveys conducted by the American military government between 1946 and 1949 showed little popular support for democracy and virtually no popular interest in politics. Few citizens bothered to participate in elections and constitutional referenda, and most people expressed either indifference or hostility to political parties (Meritt and Merritt, 1970).

No political leaders did more to break down this new anti-party front than Kurt Schumacher and Konrad Adenauer. By 1946, they were the undisputed leaders, respectively, of the SPD and CDU in the British zone. From their perspective, both Allied efforts to minimize partisan politics and the call for nonpartisan politics among important German public officials signaled the revival of the very hostility towards party government which had destroyed the Weimar Republic. Despite other differences, they concurred in the belief that constructing a democratic Germany required not nonpartisan bodies or officials but political parties with alternative and competing conceptions of public policy (Pütz, 1975).

To Adenauer and Schumacher, the creation of institutions which excluded or neutralized political parties only served to weaken democratic forces. Among the most important of these institutions were the British Zonal Council, in which parties shared representation with interest groups and minister presidents; the Länderrat in the American zone, which excluded parties altogether, and the original model of the Bizonal Economic Council, which was to be administered by experts. In Schumacher's view, such nonpolitical bodies had traditionally served as "the breeding ground of German nationalism and militarism" (1985: 370). In Adenauer's view, they threatened to revive the authoritarian "*Führer* principle," in which the Länder chiefs, surrounded by large coteries of civil servants, feel free to act and do as they please" (*Parl. Rat.* v. 1: 1137).

Schumacher and Adenauer were convinced that democracy in Germany could become viable only if strong, competitive and responsible parties were to exert the leadership and direction hitherto associated with the state. Their efforts towards this end laid the foundations for the Federal Republic's democratic party state, a version of democracy quite different from that envisioned by the Allies and by other Germans.

Working against both Allied and German anti-party tendencies, Schumacher and Adenauer pursued a broad and largely successful strategy to secure the primacy of political parties. First, their joint efforts ultimately transformed both the British Zonal Council and the Bizonal Economic Council into exclusively party dominated bodies. Second, they systematically imposed on their own parties organizational features that Allied and German critics had condemned in the Weimar parties, but which Adenauer and Schumacher saw as vital for effective party government. Thus both insisted that all elected public officials, including minister presidents, must adhere to party decisions. Schumacher and Adenauer asserted full control over the local party organizations and party functionaries, and both pushed for absolute party discipline in Länder parliaments, bizonal structures and most importantly, in the Parliamentary Council.[1] Third, both leaders worked against all Allied measures designed to keep parties out of the state and society. Ignoring repeated Allied pressures to create a nonpartisan civil service, Schumacher and Adenauer, intent on recruiting civil servants to a future democratic state, encouraged them to join and participate in their parties. They also established "party book" appointments in local and Land administrations, and, contrary to Allied expectations, successfully secured a party presence in the key agencies of the Bizonal Economic Council as well as in the media (especially radio).

Finally, Schumacher and Adenauer consistently undermined efforts by the Allies and the minister presidents to manage the political reconstruction of Germany without the participation of the major licensed parties. The combined opposition of these two leaders torpedoed the 1946 Bremen Conference called by the minister presidents (with the encouragement of the American and British military governments) to draw up plans for a future government. Schumacher and Adenauer, backed by the French military government, also forced the conveners of the 1947 Minister Presidents Conference to limit its agenda to purely economic issues. When, following the London Conference of 1948, the Allies called upon the minister presidents to lay the constitutional foundations for a separate West German state, Schumacher and Adenauer were quick to seize control of this process. They played a central role in drafting the German reply to the Allied proposals (the Frankfurt Documents) and ultimately won key concessions from the Allies. These two leaders then made sure that the Parliamentary Council, which was to draft the Basic Law, was essentially an "assembly of party men" (Otto, 1971: 41).

1. For Adenauer's efforts to control the CDU within and outside the British zone see Pütz (1975:87-98). In demanding strict party discipline in the Parliamentary Council, Schumacher insisted that there is "no direct connection between delegates and voters, but a very strong one between delegates and the party…"(1985:637).

Nonetheless, in the course of drafting the Basic Law, proponents and opponents of strong party government were ultimately forced to reconcile their differences. In the end, the Basic Law made significant concessions to political parties and party government, but also included provisions designed to check their power.

Foremost among the favorable provisions in the Basic Law was Article 21 that gave constitutional recognition to political parties. The framers of the Basic Law also rejected extraparliamentary devices to curb the power of parties. Despite the experiences of the Weimar Republic, there was still considerable support within the Parliamentary Council for a strong, independent presidency and for direct forms of participation.[2] But the Parliamentary Council decided to strengthen the Chancellor rather than the federal president. It also rejected all plebiscitary mechanisms, about which both Schumacher and Adenauer also had reservations (Jung, 1993: 30) as too dangerous, given the political immaturity of the population and potential abuse of plebiscites by the Communists.

Yet the Basic Law also reflects continued misgivings about political parties. This emerges most clearly in those sections of Article 21, which require political parties to share the task of forming the public will with others (not specified). Political parties are further required to have a democratic program and organization, to make the sources of their financing public, and to uphold the constitutional order or else risk proscription. Moreover, several provisions in the Basic Law were clearly designed to counterbalance the popularly elected and party-dominated Bundestag.

The Parliamentary Council established a strong check against the parliament through the creation of a Federal Constitutional

---

2. The FDP's Dr. Becker advocated a powerful federal president for two reasons. A strong authority figure could "cultivate in [the German population] a better impression of democracy than is afforded by ... recurrent government crises of parliamentary regimes." Such a leader would also be able to act in a crisis, when multi-party coalitions might lack the will to do so (Golay, 1958:125).

Court with the power of judicial review. The Basic Law also incorporated the principle of the independent mandate perceived by its FDP champions as a necessary defense against excessive party domination of members of parliament.[3] Given the Allied stipulation of a federal form of government, a second chamber of parliament had to be established. Because it was seen as a counterweight to the party-dominated lower house, the SPD originally opposed any such body. On the other hand, key elements of the CDU and FDP preferred a Senate of notables as a counterweight to the lower house. At the insistence of the Allies, the second chamber finally adopted was the Bundesrat to represent the Länder governments. This was a victory for the southern German delegates, who had all along favored the Bundesrat as the most effective "bulwark" against the partisan lower house (Parl. Rat, v. 2: 132-46).

In the end, the Basic Law successfully balanced the two contending conceptions about the place of political parties in the new democratic order. Although it incorporated Allied ideas and influences, "no less important for its form and content were the lessons drawn by Germany's newly constituted social and political forces" (Löwenthal, 1979: 14). The particular synthesis thus arrived at created a shared commitment to the new constitutional order absent in the Weimar Republic.

The Consolidation of the Democratic Party State

Although the Basic Law gave political parties a formal constitutional status, it did not register the pervasive influence of the

3. The SPD held that since members of the parliament were elected through their party, they should vote with it. Some members of the Parliamentary Council also felt that the independent mandate should be dropped because it no longer reflected reality. Eventually a less emphatic version of the Weimar Constitution's provision was accepted. (For the debate over Article 38, see Parl. Rat, v.3:105 et seq.)

parties in both state and society which Schumacher and Adenauer had secured for them during the occupation. As in the Weimar Republic, therefore, the constitutional form did not reflect political practices. This gap between constitutional ambiguity and political reality was ultimately closed by the Federal Constitutional Court. It not only introduced the concept of the democratic party state, but played a pivotal role in its consolidation and expansion. The Court's contribution was both theoretical and practical.

Especially under the influence of Justice Gerhard Leibholz, the Federal Constitutional Court developed a distinctive constitutional theory that shaped both its own decisions and how the main parties came to define their place in the Federal Republic. Central to this constitutional theory was Leibholz's thesis that universal suffrage, political democratization, the emergence of mass parties and their participation in government have transformed the classical parliamentary system of representation into what he called the "democratic party state" of today (1958: 93).

As the sole means through which mature citizens can articulate and express their interests, reach political decisions, and produce state policy, parties alone give meaning to the ideals of democracy. Thus to Leibholz, party competition in modern democracies are a "rationalized version of plebiscitary democracy," making irrelevant other forms of direct democracy such as referenda or initiatives. Finally, parties give civil society its political character and enable it to shape and control state action. Hence, according to Leibholz, in the democratic party state, the dualism of state and society disappears (1958: 74-106; for critiques see Dyson,1977; Saage, 1983: 156-80).

To Leibholz and the Federal Constitutional Court, Article 21, by acknowledging the constitutional role of parties, "in effect legalized the modern democratic party state" in the Federal Republic (Liebholz, 1958: 123). By giving political parties a constitutional function to perform, the Basic Law had also fundamentally transformed their status and character. As "integral components of the constitutionally ordered political life," political parties "... are no longer merely political and sociological ... organizations." Instead the Court has variously defined them as "constitutionally relevant organizations"; as "constitutionally necessary instruments for the formation of the political will of the people"; and even as a constitutional institution *(Verfassungsorgan)*.[4]

Armed with this new and powerful constitutional doctrine, the Federal Constitutional Court has in practice greatly enhanced the political and electoral positions of the established parties. Thus the Court has recognized the constitutional status of the parliamentary parties as well as their right to enforce party discipline.[5] It has upheld public service laws that encouraged the "participation of parties within the system of state institutions" and the concomitant right of civil servants to be active in parties and to pursue a parliamentary career. It thus acknowledged Leibholz's contention that the democratic party state had made irrelevant the traditional boundary between state and parties. Since 1958, the Court has approved state financing of the parties, and though it has periodically altered the methods and scope of funding (most recently in 1992), it has remained committed to the principle of state support for political parties.[6]

Equally important, the Federal Constitutional Court's rulings have shown a clear bias in favor of the large *Volksparteien*.

---

4. The relevant cases are 1 BVerfGE 223-225; 2 BVerfGE 11; 4 BVerfGE 30, 149; 6 BVerfGE 91; 20 BVerfGE 10; 35 BVerfGE 30.
5. This seems to run counter to Article 38 which guarantees the autonomy of Bundestag deputies. Rather than resolving the tension between that article and the doctrine of the democratic party state, the Federal Constitutional Court has confined itself to concrete issues arising out of specific cases. The result has been a body of contradictory rulings. For details see Abelein (1977).
6. See cases 8 BVerfGE 51; 44 BVerfGE 125; 52 BverfGE 83.

The Court has consistently maintained that the goal of elections is "not only to assert the political will of voters as individuals" but also to "form a government capable of acting." This requires "clear parliamentary majorities conscious of their responsibilities to the public weal" and these can only be formed by the *Volksparteien*.

Thus despite its occasional support for small contenders (such as the separate 5 percent clause for the first all-German federal election), the Court has consistently given precedence to the need for stable government over the constitutional principle of equal chances for competing parties.[7] By using the principle of "militant democracy" to ban political groups and parties which violate "the basic democratic order," the Federal Constitutional Court has further reinforced the political and electoral hegemony of the principal founding parties.[8] Such Court rulings have not only limited the number of competitors, but have also forced new opposition or protest parties like the Greens, PDS, and Republikaner to adapt their programs, appeals and tactics to the ground rules set by the Basic Law and the parties which had drafted it.

The Federal Constitutional Court's constitutional theory and practical support for the Federal Republic's principal parties legitimated political parties to an extent inconceivable during the Empire or the Weimar Republic (Kommers, 1989). In so doing, the Court helped supplant the pejorative sense in which the con-

---

7. In support of the larger parties, the Court has consistently backed the 5 percent threshold for federal as well as local, state, and European elections. It has also supported more broadcast time and public funds for the larger parties. To help smaller parties, the Court has supported proportional representation, invalidated signature quotas for entering elections, provided access (though at lower levels) for small parties to public funding and to the public media (Rinck, 1966).
8. Both concepts were first articulated by the Federal Constitutional Court in its 1952 decision to ban the right wing Socialist Reich Party (SRP) and in the 1956 ban of the KPD (Kommers, 1989:224-28).

cept of a "party state" had been used in the Weimar Republic with a positive one which, in turn, facilitated the acceptance of the democratic party state among both elites and mass publics.

No less critical to the development of the Federal Republic's distinctive form of democracy was the "post-war conversion from polarized pluralism to a stable party concentration of the center" (Smith, 1982b: 66). The emergence of the Federal Republic's distinctive tripartite party structure can be seen as both the product of the democratic party state and as a source of its solidity and strength.

The three principal licensed parties, SPD, CDU/CSU, and FDP, together received four-fifths of the vote already in 1949. By 1957, only these three parties remained, and this stable three-party structure lasted until 1983 when the Greens first entered the Bundestag. Coalition governments were still necessary, but with only three parties, forming coalitions was simpler and more predictable than in the Weimar Republic.

No less striking was the concentration of all three parties at the center. One reason was the FDP's crucial role in creating a ruling majority coalition, which prevented either of the main parties from veering too far to the right or left. Reinforcing this pattern was the erosion of pre-war sociopolitical cleavages. Confronted with new electoral conditions, the two principal parties rejected polarizing ideological and sectarian appeals, instead choosing centrist, integrative, vote-maximizing catch-all strategies (Kirschheimer, 1966).

The successful economic and political performance of the new democratic party state created, for the first time in German history, a political culture highly supportive of competitive political parties as agents of the public will and of elective government by parties. This cultural transformation clearly benefited the three parties most associated with it and reinforced the Federal Republic's stable tripartite party system. In turn, from the 1950s to 1983, the grip on the party system by the two *Volksparteien* and their junior partners (FDP and CSU) facilitated those collaborative agreements for sharing power and positions now considered as emblematic of the party state. In effect, until the appearance of the citizen movements in the mid-1970s, there was no one to challenge the unprecedented powers and privileges which the Federal Republic's founding parties had acquired for themselves.

The Party State and Its Critics

As it has evolved in practice, the Federal Republic's party state is marked by several features. To begin with, political parties have firmly established themselves as the exclusive representatives of the public will. They have successfully defeated all forms of direct participation, refused electoral participation to citizen movements, and neutralized such nonparty competitors as local voter associations or city hall parties (Guggenberger and Maier, 1994). Reformist initiatives within the Bundestag to weaken party control over deputies' votes and to restore the independence of deputies in line with Article 38 have similarly failed (Hamm-Brücher, 1993).

A second feature of the party state is its politicization of governmental institutions originally conceived as nonpartisan. Contrary to the intentions of the Parliamentary Council, the Bundesrat has become an extension of party politics (Dyson, 1977: 15-20). Opposition parties use it to block or reshape the policies of the governing parties or else to force them into a quasi grand coalition. Ambitious Land politicians from all parties manipulate it to advance their own political careers.[9]

Just as the *Bundesrat* has been "integrated" into the party state, so has communal government. Traditionally, government

---

9. According to one observer, the greater the successes of minister presidents in pushing their Land's economic and financial interests, the "better the chances of their party in the next state or federal elections and the better their personal chances of becoming their party's candidate for the chancellorship" (Thaissen, 1994).

at this level was based on expertise and competence rather than party affiliations. Local mayors and councilors were customarily elected to their unpaid positions by nonpartisan voter associations. Increasingly, however, the main political parties seized control over the distribution of communal jobs, projects, publicly-funded activities, paid consultancies, and positions on communal supervisory boards of public and private institutions. These patronage positions are usually divided among local party leaders through reciprocal quota agreements unaffected by electoral outcomes (for a critical view of this practice, see Scheuch and Scheuch, 1992).

The judicial branch too has come under increasing party influence. Nominees for the Federal Constitutional Court are selected by a special Bundestag committee with a careful eye for maintaining a party balance among the justices in both chambers.[10] The politicization of the judiciary extends as well to lower federal, as well as to Länder courts. Similar party considerations also play a role in appointments to other federal bodies, including the various security agencies.[11]

The third and most striking feature of the party state has been the virtual fusion of political parties with the state apparatus. This is exemplified by the proliferation of both political civil servants and parliamentary state secretaries. The former are permanent civil servants who are meant to carry out the political objectives and views of the government. This group includes

---

10. For details on the 1992 appointments to the Federal Constitutional Court (including an interview with Hans-Joachim Vogel, the head of the Bundestag Committee involved in the selection of justices) see *die tageszeitung*, 9 September 1995. For the judiciary in general, see "Diener zweier Mächte" *die tageszeitung*, 27 July, 1992.
11. It is customary for the SPD and CDU to hold the presidency of the security agencies. Thus, if a person close to the CDU is appointed president of the Office for the Protection of the Constitution, then the SPD expects someone close to it to head the BND or vice versa. For maneuverings to this effect, see *Der Spiegel* 8 (1995), 16.

state secretaries, and ministerial directors (heads of ministerial departments as well as assistant heads) and press officers. By now there are some 170 positions classified as political civil servants (*Die Zeit*, 24 January, 1994). Most are chosen because of their membership in or closeness to the governing parties, though already by 1972 more than half the senior officials at the federal level were members of one or the other major party.

The number of parliamentary secretaries, first introduced in 1967, has risen from the original seven to thirty-three in 1992. Originally intended to give promising Bundestag deputies governmental experience, these positions have since become largely a source of patronage for the governing parties. Although they do not carry civil service status, they are generously remunerated.[12] Party book civil service appointments are just as pronounced at the Land and local level. During the 1970s, over 85 percent of the state secretaries in SPD governed Länder were SPD members and in CDU-governed Länder, the figure was 70.1 percent (Steinkemper, 1974: 47).

A fourth feature of the Federal Republic's party state is the etatization of the main parties. This has several dimensions. The first is the exceptionally close relationship between the political parties and the civil service, a trend initiated by Adenauer and Schumacher. The strategy also benefited civil servants since "membership in a licensed party was the most tangible sign of democratic reliability for candidates for the public service" (Dyson, 1977: 22). Subsequently, party membership proved invaluable to career advancement. The result has been an extraordinary prominence of civil servants within the main parties (including the Greens), among both members

---

12. These positions are normally distributed by the governing parties according to customary quota rules. Thus, in appointing parliamentary secretaries, Chancellor Kohl has considered such criteria as party loyalty and service, but also geography (North and South, East or West), gender (women), intra-party factions, and the interests of his coalition partners (*Der Spiegel*, 47 (1992), 21-22).

and elected deputies. Although civil servants make up only 5 percent of the population, they form 10 percent of the SPD, 12.4 percent of the CDU, 14 percent of the FDP and 17 percent of the Greens members. At the federal level, some 15 percent of senior civil servants have had political careers (Lorig, 1994). By the mid-1970s, 49 percent of Bundestag members were permanent civil servants (Dyson, 1982: 86).

The etatization of the main parties is manifested by the spectacular increase in their public financing. Since 1958, when the Federal Constitutional Court first made them eligible for public support, political parties are funded at the level of major state activities. Despite various efforts by the Federal Constitutional Court to curtail public contributions to the parties, most recently in 1992, funding continues to increase. The strict ceiling of DM 230 Million for all federal parties imposed by the Court in 1992 was soon undermined by the Bonn parties (Kaltefleiter and Naßmacher, 1994: 253). By 1994 the main parties had managed to push up federal funding to DM 352 Million. To this must be added public financing of the party foundations (DM 630 Million), moneys given to the federal and Länder parliamentary parties (about DM 230 Million) and to party youth organizations (DM 10 Million). Further moneys to deputies, including salaries, pensions, "transitional income" after the loss of a mandate, reimbursements for performing various public functions, travel expenditures and other benefits.[13]

The etatization has also affected the self-perceptions of political parties. As the founders of the Bonn Republic's distinctive form of democracy, the older parties see themselves as representing and maintaining the interests of the democratic state rather than those of the citizen. The "coincidence" of state

13. For these figures, see *Der Spiegel* 48, (1994), 21-22; on the amounts received by the party foundations see *Der Spiegel* 52 (1994), 26-29; for recent figures on expenditures for parliamentarians and former officeholders, see *Der Spiegel*, 14 (1997), 22-27. For more details on public financing of political parties see Volkmann (1992) and Armin (1995).

and party outlooks may be seen as well in the preference among the established parties for an administrative style of politics which values above all "official expertise and technical competence" (Dyson, 1977: 20). Avoiding partisan conflicts, once an ideal of the state's representatives, has now been adopted by the leadership of the main parties, which leads to the preference for constructive rather than adversarial opposition. Public rhetoric notwithstanding, in opposition, the principal parties seek mutual accommodation rather than confrontation.[14]

A final feature of the party state is the increasing permeation of society by parties. The centrality of political parties as articulators, aggregators, and shapers of the public will has been facilitated through generously funded party foundations. Party quotas in public broadcasting and television has given parties a position within the media likened to that of a "spider in the net of political communication" (Alemann, 1992: 89).[15]

Party patronage also dominates key appointments to every social institution that has public status and receives public funding. This includes public law institutions, non-governmental welfare, charitable or service organizations, public works, universities, theaters, and opera houses. Many of these have supervisory boards to which party members are appointed on the basis of prior quota agreements, as are representatives of interest and social groups. Parties are present as well in all major interest groups and in leisure associations from sports clubs to

---

14. The concept of opposition adopted by the main parties was articulated most succinctly by Kurt Schumacher: "The essence of opposition," he declared, "is the permanent attempt to force the positive creative will of the opposition in concrete instances and with concrete propositions on the government and its parties" (quoted in Smith, 1982b:66). Inter-party cooperation and bargaining are also encouraged by such institutional mechanisms as federalism and the required involvement of opposition parties in the working committees of the Bundestag (Hereth, 1969).
15. On the relationship of parties and media see Kleinsteuber (1982) and Humphreys (1994).

gardening clubs. For the major parties these associations have become an important pre-political arena crucial to party mobilization and recruitment. Increasingly, party representatives have even made inroads into private business enterprises, especially those eager for public contracts. Well-paid appointments of politicians to boards of directors or supervisory councils have become common practice. This pervasive and complex entanglement of public and private interests, reinforced by party-book administrations, has been dubbed pejoratively *Filzokratie* (Dyson, 1977: 38), a term implying corruption and nepotism.

But the ever-expanding reach of the parties within and beyond the state has not gone unchallenged. Indeed, by the late 1970s, it seemed that the greater the hold gained by the parties over state and society, the more they lost support among voters. Party memberships, levels of party identification, support for the principal Bonn parties, and voting turnout all began to decline, while volatility in voting and ballot-splitting increased (Schultze, 1987). Public opinion surveys revealed a pervasive disaffection with the character and performance of the main political parties. About three-quarters of those questioned expressed such negative views, despite their overall satisfaction with democracy (Küchler, 1982).

The popular anti-party mood was nowhere more obvious than in the extraordinary proliferation of citizen action groups. By the early 1980s, it was estimated there were 50,000 such groups, able to mobilize more people than all the political parties put together (Kempf, 1984). With the sudden entry of a new protest party, the Greens, into local, Land and (since 1983) federal parliaments, the tripartite monopoly was broken. For much of the 1980s, the cumulative impact of all these changes led many prominent analysts and commentators to declare the existence of a "party crisis" (Raschke, 1982; Scholz, 1983; Frotscher, 1985; Krokow and Lösche, 1986; Stolleis, Schäfer, and Rhinow, 1986; Haungs and Jesse, 1987; Stöss, 1990).

Although some traced the roots of these strains in West Germany's electoral politics to the post-materialist revolution, much of the party crisis literature in the 1980s attributed disaffection to the democratic party state and the main parties which sustained it. Condemnations of the party state center on the negative consequences the close relationship between the main parties and the state allegedly have had on the constitutional system, on society, and on the parties themselves.

The influence of parties on appointments is said to have undermined the Basic Law's governing principles, such as the separation of powers and the independence of parliamentary mandates (Hamm-Brücher, 1991; Hennis, 1992). From the perspective of critics, as parties are pushing themselves ever deeper into social spheres, they are "strangling" civil society (Raschke, 1982: 17). Moreover, the ever-expanding party patronage reveal parties as more interested in sharing the spoils of the party state through secretive accommodations of mutual interests than in addressing the problems and needs of the citizenry. In this view, the undesirable intimacy among the established parties, the state bureaucracy, public institutions and private interests, have reinforced public impressions of an all-powerful, increasingly corrupt "cartel of power" (Raschke, 1982: 12) closed to ordinary citizens and immune to reform through conventional electoral politics (Katz and Mair, 1995). According to such critics, voters who feel unrepresented by the main parties can express their political will only outside conventional politics either by embracing citizen movements, new protest parties or, increasingly, by not voting.

In 1989, on the eve of unification, voter behavior continued to suggest major strains in the West German party system. In the West Berlin municipal election of December 1988, nearly a quarter of voters supported protest parties of the left (the "alternative" alliance GAL) and the right (the Republikaner). This was followed by a strong right wing vote in the Hessen local elections and by the 7.1 percent national vote the Republikaner received in the June 1989 elections to the European Parliament.

The oft-proclaimed party crisis not withstanding, the "Bonn" parties in fact survived the electoral upheavals of the decade and retained their dominance of the party and political system. Taking over much of the environmental program and rhetoric of the new citizen action groups, they have proved to be far more adaptable than critics had anticipated. Although the arrival of the Greens upset the cozy tripartite party structure of the past, it had little impact on the functioning of the party state. On the contrary, the logic of the democratic party state was transforming the Greens, both in their growing readiness to work constructively within the parliamentary system and in their readiness to claim their share of the party state's privileges (signified by the formation of their own party foundation). But events in East Germany during the late summer and fall of 1989 were to present the Bonn parties with an altogether new and unanticipated challenge.

The Democratic Party State and Unification

By the end of the 1970s politicians across party lines had come to accept the permanent division of Germany (Brandt, 1988) and, like their leaders, West German citizens had accommodated themselves to the status quo. To West Germans, East Germany had become another, unknown and not very interesting country (Glaßner, 1991).

West Germany's governing and opposition parties were thus caught off-guard in 1989 by the extent and rapidity of the changes in East Germany. The combined pressures of mass exits and huge, popular demonstrations by ordinary East German citizens had successfully achieved within weeks what the West German parties had failed to bring about in four decades: the collapse of the Communist regime and the opening of the Berlin Wall.

But while the transition to democracy was initiated by East German citizen movements, West German parties soon seized control of it. Belying their image as immovable tankers incapable of responding to change, the Bonn parties were quick to seize the new political opportunities East Germany's revolutionary transformation had presented to them.

First, prodded by their West German mentors, East German parties pushed for early elections and for the right of West German parties to provide financial and other help to East German parties, although officially East Germany was still a separate country. Second, once the date for East Germany's first free parliamentary elections was set (March 18, 1990), West German parties quickly took over the electoral process. They defined the issue as unification, worked out the strategies of their East German party allies, and largely managed their campaigns. For all practical purposes, East Germany's first free election was a West German contest.

With the issue of unification settled in favor of a rapid merger, the West German governing parties pushed through the various unification treaties (social, economic, currency union and the two state treaties) mostly on West German terms. The electoral calculations of the Bonn parties determined the date for the first all-German elections, the electoral rules under which it was to be conducted, and even the date of unification. For East Germans, the party mergers prior to the all-German election, were essentially a "take-over of East German organizations by those of the West" (Naßmacher, 1994: 3). The CDU and FDP quite blatantly stacked the organizational deck against their new East German members. The SPD and the Greens were more accommodating to East German members, but the clear numerical superiority of the West German membership also meant that the parties remained largely West German organizations.

The major Bonn parties tried to maintain their electoral control in the first all-German election by insisting on a common national 5 percent threshold. Although designed to eliminate the PDS, it would have excluded the eastern democratic opposition groups (linked with the Greens in the Alliance 90/ Greens) as well. The Federal Constitutional Court ruling mandating a separate threshold for East and West Germany enabled the Alliance 90/Greens (but also the PDS) to enter the first all-German Bundestag. For the East Germans, the new party system is thus primarily a West German import under the continued hegemony of the West German parties.

Following formal unification, the West German party state was moved eastward. Five new states as well as communal governments were established along West German lines. West German politicians either headed East German state governments or controlled the key positions in the ministries. By the end of 1993, only Brandenburg still had an East German minister president, Manfred Stolpe. Despite East German resistance, the principal parties insisted on adopting West German parliamentary practices, including strict parliamentary discipline (Patzelt, 1993).

Most other practices and norms of the West German party state were also imported into the new Länder. Land and communal coalition governments quickly settled which positions in public administrations were to be filled by party members and which by public advertisement (Hoffmann et al., 1994: 382). Party book appointments in public institutions as well as party representation in all non-governmental associations were also transferred without modification to the East. So too was the West German *Filzokratie*. At times, West German networks of public and private interests *(Klüngel)* simply migrated eastward.[16] West German politicians found new opportunities in the East for self-enrichment through excessively generous salaries and other financial benefits; two East German governments

---

16. In Mecklenburg-Vorpommern, there was a Schleswig-Holstein network; in Sachsen-Anhalt, a Lower Saxony one. See *Der Spiegel* 49 (1991) and 14 (1993); for the situation in Sachsen-Anhalt see *Der Spiegel* 8 (1991). Similar networks also emerged among East Germans, the most publicized of which involved Thuringia's first Prime Minister, Josef Duchac, from the East German CDU. His lucrative hotel and highway restaurant deals with East German cronies ultimately forced his resignation (*Berliner Zeitung*, 13 July 1992; and 8 September 1992).

headed by West German CDU leaders (Mecklenburg-Vorpommern and Sachsen-Anhalt) were forced to resign for this reason.

The East German media were similarly forced into the West German party state mold. Both SPD and CDU managed to place their people into the top positions of the newly created Mid-German Radio and the East German Radio/Brandenburg: the SPD came to dominate the latter, while the CDU established its hegemony over the former. In the print media, pressure from Chancellor Kohl in 1991 helped sell several East German newspapers to West German firms with close ties to the CDU, according to *Der Spiegel*. President Weizsäcker publicly condemned these moves to remold East German media as a "power grab" by the Bonn parties (*Die Welt*, 15 January 1992; see also Hoffmann-Riem, 1991; Streul, 1993).

The structure and character of the West German party state itself was left largely untouched by unification. Instead of a broad constitutional debate, the constitutional commission (comprising an equal number of members from the Bundesrat and Bundestag and bound by strict party discipline), introduced only marginal changes in the Basic Law. Despite pleas from President Weizsäcker and Rita Süssmuth to reconsider the role and position of political parties after forty years of experience with the party state, Article 21 was left untouched. Proposals to depoliticize the civil service, to curtail party appointments in public institutions, to reconsider party financing, to allow citizen movements to participate in elections, or to give citizens a more direct voice through referenda and initiatives were similarly ignored (Voscherau, 1993; Fischer, 1993; Scholz, 1993; Guggenberger and Meier, 1994).

Despite obvious differences, there are some interesting comparisons to be made between the two democratic transformations after World War II and 1989. In both instances, external actors defined the context within which democratic institutions had to be created, the Allied occupying authorities in the first case, the West German parties in the second. Then as now, the democratic project required fundamental changes, and then as now, the same West German parties were to define and implement the new democratic system.

Yet despite the constraints imposed by Allied Occupation, the West German "licensed parties" ultimately created a democratic arrangement that reflected very much their own distinctive traditions, preferences, and objectives. By contrast, the East Germans were given no chance to work out their own democratic vision or have much impact on the constitutional order they joined. East Germans had thus much more ground for viewing the new constitutional order under which they were to live as an imposed prescribed democracy than did West Germans in 1949. The democratic party state, of course, does not repress them and it provides far more access and participation, but East Germans have inherited all its negative features without understanding their original rationale and justification.

The Party State in United Germany: Source of Crisis or Stability?

Despite efforts by West German parties to merge the two societies without altering the party and political system, unification has both reinforced old and created new electoral strains. Most of the negative electoral patterns of the pre-unification period have persisted. In the first two post-unification federal elections, the combined share of the vote for the two *Volksparteien* and the FDP not only fell below the 1987 level, but showed a slight downward trend (from to 66.9 percent in 1990, to 66.1 per cent in 1994). Non-voting, which had reached the all-time high of 16 percent in the 1987 federal election increased to 22.2 percent in 1994. In line with pre-unification trends, protest voting has continued. The real winners in 1994 were two parties outside the traditional three-party system, the Alliance Greens and the PDS. In 1994, the Greens showed they could still mobilize

West German voters disaffected with the establishment parties. In that election, the PDS, by appealing to East German disappointment with unification, received an even larger mandate than in 1990.

Public opinion polls show the addition of 18 million citizens from the former GDR has added to the number of alienated voters. A 1992 survey showed 81 percent of West German voters and 59 percent of East German voters felt the main parties did not represent their interests on key issues. In a 1994 public opinion poll, respondents in both the five new and the old Länder preferred citizen action groups and social movements seeking greater popular participation in politics over all parties, including the Alliance 90 Greens (Rattinger, 1993; Köcher, 1994; Kreikenbom, 1996; Rose and Page; 1996).

But unification has also created altogether new problems for the Federal Republic's party system. First, East German party identification is exceptionally weak; consequently, party allegiances change very rapidly and dramatically. Whereas in the West voter changes of more than 3 to 5 percent from one election to the next are exceptional, East German fluctuations have been as high as 15 to 20 percent.

Second, party membership in East German local and Land organizations have declined even more dramatically than in the West. This reflects not only disaffection with the West German-dominated party organizations, but also low levels of political involvement and engagement. One reason is that East Germans, having long been forced to participate under Communism, now find it a luxury not to do so. Most, however, are so preoccupied with adjusting to the changes that unification has brought to their lives that they find little time for political engagement. The result is that with the exception of the PDS, all parties in the East have difficulties in finding candidates for local, state, and federal offices. To use their small membership for such positions leaves no one for party work. Importing West German candidates, however, offends Eastern voters (Benzler, 1995).

Another new condition is the emergence of a stark East-West cleavage. Unification has brought together two electorates with very different experiences, outlooks, and expectations. This creates a dilemma for the western German-dominated parties. If they champion eastern German interests, they alienate their western clientele. If they ignore the much smaller eastern electorate, voters may abstain or shift to the PDS (Hürtgen et al., 1994; Schmid, Löbler, and Tiermann, 1994). Moreover, the western dominated parties now have very different social bases in the two parts of the country (Dalton and Bürklin, 1995; Schmidt, 1997).

Another post-unification problem is the continued presence and success of the PDS in the East. For East German voters, the PDS is the only authentic East German "voice" through which to protest against West German policies, insensitivities and predominance. Its core constituents are not the "losers" from unification, but rather members of the former administrative and professional class (Falter and Klein, 1994; Kleinfeld, 1995; Kreikenbom, this volume). For the all-German parties, however, the persistence of the PDS poses serious dilemmas. The West German SPD and Greens would dearly love to embrace the PDS but are opposed by their East German members and leaders, most of whom came from the democratic opposition to the Communist regime. Furthermore, such a strategy is criticized and exploited by the CDU, especially in the West (Clemens, 1995). But efforts by the CDU to isolate the PDS have produced a backlash in the East, as East German voters regard the PDS as a legitimate democratic contender. The East-CDU officeholders, in turn, must now cooperate with the PDS in many communal governments.

Finally, declining rates of participation and support for the main parties is creating the danger of weak, even minority coalitions. This, of course, was the bane of Weimar politics. In the East the choice has come down to two equally unpleasant alternatives: a coalition between the SPD and PDS or a Grand Coalition between the SPD and CDU. In the West, there have been increasing number of coalitions involving the SPD, the FDP and Greens, but these are unstable because of tensions between the environmental Greens and the business-oriented FDP. There is now increasing talk of potential CDU-Green coalitions. Whatever the mix, coalitions in united Germany are no longer simple or predictable.

The new political, social, and economic problems created by unification re-ignited and intensified the criticism of the Federal Republic's party state and major parties. But how justified are the criticisms raised against the Federal Republic's founding parties and the party state? Do recent voting and opinion trends reveal a fundamental crisis of Germany's parties and democratic party state? Have these performed as badly as their critics claim?

On the whole, the empirical indices of a party crisis are much exaggerated, especially from a comparative perspective. Despite large abstentions from voting, volatile voting patterns and significant support for the PDS, East and West Germans mostly vote for the enlarged West German parties. Moreover, in both parts of the country, citizens are fundamentally committed to the Federal Republic's political institutions and constitutional principles. Extremist voting in both parts of united Germany is low. While the PDS receives significant support, its vote is very volatile and essentially confined to the five new Länder. Radical right wing voting remains minuscule in both East and West Germany. Thus, while voters in united Germany may not like their parties, they are not looking for anti-system parties or anti-democratic solutions.

Furthermore, most of the anti-party trends before and since unification are not unique to Germany. They are found in all advanced democracies and are often more pronounced elsewhere (e.g. the U.S. or Italy). Rather than view such voter and opinion trends as indicative of a revival of Germany's anti-party culture, some analysts have traced these to increasing secularization and individualization in advanced democracies. These developments have weakened citizen attachments not only to parties but also to other formal associations, including trade unions and churches (Dalton, Flanagan and Beck, 1984). Others argue that declining levels of party attachment and support are part of a cyclical phenomenon. Voter apathy in the 1950s was followed, in the 1960s, by a long cycle of intense political engagement before moving back (since the late 1980s) to public withdrawal from politics (Erhart and Sandschneider, 1994). From a comparative perspective, fears about a party crisis or a crisis of democracy in united Germany are much exaggerated.

At the political level, critics have failed to appreciate the complexity and scale of the tasks required by unification. The Federal Republic's parties were suddenly forced to manage transformations analogous both in substance and in scale to those they had confronted after 1945. This included state and institution building, anchoring the new party system, economic reconstruction, transforming a totalitarian into a democratic political culture, and addressing the personnel and crimes of the totalitarian regime. Moreover, these challenges had to be confronted without destabilizing the economically and politically more powerful old Federal Republic or alienating two markedly different electorates. Furthermore, the post-1989 transformation had to be carried out in a rapidly changing international environment, marked by the end of the Cold War, increasing global competition, and European integration.

In view of the complexity and extent of the post-1989 transformations, it is not surprising that the main parties responded with familiar routines and recipes that had a forty-year record of success in the West. Given the pressures of the day, there was little time to work out alternative solutions, nor much room for maneuver.

Yet despite serious omissions and problems, the results of unification after six years have been largely positive. There are now five additional Länder governments, each with its own governing, legal, and administrative institutions. The restructuring of communal government has been no less impressive. Here, too, a viable political, legal, and administrative infrastructure was established in record time despite fewer resources and personnel than is available to their West German counterparts (Bullmann and Schwanegel, 1995).

While economic reconstruction is proving to be far more difficult and costly than anticipated, the five new Länder have in place those legal, banking, and administrative structures essential to a market economy. There has also been enormous progress in creating the requisite information, telecommunication, electronic, and transportation infrastructures. Levels of prosperity remain below West German standards, but compare very favorably with all other post-Communist societies.

Critics have been all too quick to condemn the eastward expansion of the Federal Republic's party state, while ignoring its positive contributions. It has become almost fashionable to attack the party state for its politicization of the Bundesrat and state administration, for its introduction of party patronage and quotas, for the pervasive presence of the parties in both governmental and societal institutions. Yet these features of the party state greatly facilitated the consolidation of democracy in the West, and may again do the same in the East.

Although the Bundesrat was originally designed to serve as a counterweight to the power of the political parties, it has in actual practice served a different but even more valuable function. The politicization of the Bundesrat has prevented its development into a bastion of state administrators and provided instead "a dual democratically legitimated federal majority" (Dyson, 1977: 15-17) By offering opportunities for the opposition parties to shape federal policies, it also prevents excessive polarization between governing and opposition parties. Since unification, the Bundesrat has given East German Länder parties and governments an arena for advancing and representing their own interests and to permits them to win concessions from the federal government. Thus the "politicized" Bundesrat has been an important arena for integrating East German Länder.

West Germany's close relationship between parties and state administration has also brought major benefits. It precluded the re-emergence of the state bureaucracy as a separate and distinctive caste. Instead it gave rise to "a new type of *Beamte*," one able to cope with the altogether different functions of public administration within a democratic political system (Dyson, 1977: 29). The presence of civil servants in the parties and parliament has also made politicians more sensitive to the administrative issues and implications of legislation and thus reduced support for populist and shoddy bills so often passed by American legislatures. Nor has party membership produced either less qualified civil servants or excessively partisan administrative behavior (Wagner, 1979).

In the East German Länder, the positive impact of this close interaction between parties and the state is not yet felt because of the predominance of West German politicians and senior administrators. Nevertheless, as qualified East Germans take their place, there is no reason to believe that the result will be any worse than it had been in the West.

Although generally condemned, party patronage and quota agreements to share patronage positions have also played a constructive role in West Germany's political development. In the early postwar years, these mechanisms helped political parties to integrate vast numbers of refugees from occupied Eastern territories by securing employment for them in state administration and the public sector (Morsey, 1977). Analogous strategies for East Germans on a sufficient scale could perform the same function. The problems so far has been the tendency to reward West rather than East Germans with patronage appointments and hence has increased East German resentments.[17]

Within the West German parties, quotas have helped to maintain party unity by rewarding various factions with important positions. While this may make dynamic policy initiatives

17. For the use of quotas as conflict regulation within the parties since the Wilhelminian period, see Kühne (1995). For comparative treatments see Lehmbruch (1967) and Lijphart (1975).

difficult, it has also prevented party splits or suicidal factional conflicts. A more aggressive strategy of placing East Germans in responsible positions in the West German party organizations would ease current East-West tensions within the main parties (Gabriel, 1991). Similarly beneficial has been the party presence in non-governmental organizations. It has helped to create and maintain strong state support for a large variety of important social activities. Because these continue to perform effectively, the active party role has prevented the type of grassroots anti-government movements which have emerged with such destructive force in the United States. Moreover, as Wolfgang Seibel points out in this volume, the presence of party representatives in non-governmental organizations, so often condemned in the old Federal Republic, has played an integrative function in the new Länder. It has facilitated the work of these organizations and thereby provided crucial material benefits and services to East Germans more efficiently than could be done by a still rudimentary administrative structure.

The Federal Republic's party state has also reduced the kind of party polarization that destroyed the Weimar Republic. Because all established Bonn parties came to share the positions and benefits of the party state, anti-systemic opposition was counterproductive. As the development of the Greens has shown, by embracing protest parties and providing concrete benefits, the party state has had a far more positive impact on reducing levels of political conflict than had they only marginalized such protest parties.

Much the same benefit follows from public financing of political parties. Although costly, this creates positive incentives for new and protest parties to play by the democratic rules, even at the price of alienating their radical constituencies. For this reason, demonizing the PDS or denying it the same privileges as those enjoyed by West German parties (e.g. rejecting public funding for a PDS party foundation) is counterproductive. Integrating the PDS into the party state is far more likely to weaken its more radical factions and to help anchor its supporters to the present party and political system.

Despite a confrontational public style, inter-party relations in parliamentary working committees are marked by moderation, cooperation, and relative objectivity (Smith, 1982b). This has been much regretted by those who long for the old milieu parties and their sharply distinguished, conflictual social and political visions. But the capacity for stability, integration, and effective governance demonstrated by the Bonn parties is clearly preferable to the hostile confrontations of the Weimar parties. As Karl Dietrich Bracher has pointed out "Even sharp criticisms of the Bonn system can't deny that nowhere is the difference between the second German democracy and the Weimar Republic clearer than in the mature and self-confident system of parties" (Bracher, 1971).

Conclusion

After World War II, a fundamental transformation occurred both in the self-conception of political parties and in their actual position in the new constitutional order. In the course of an intensive debate from 1945 to 1949, a distinctive form of democracy emerged, which in effect secured the primacy of parties in the state and in broad areas of public life. The "democratic party state" as the Federal Republic came to be called, was legitimated and reinforced by the Federal Constitutional Court and a stable system of party competition. Voter disaffection and electoral strains notwithstanding, on the eve of unification the Federal Republic's political and party system remained a stable, effective democracy.

In the face of enormous challenges created by unification, the Federal Republic's democratic party system and party state have, on balance, shown once again an impressive capacity for stability, integration, and effective governance. Certainly no other Western democracy confronted problems so immediate and on so great a scale after the collapse of Communism than did the Federal Republic after 1989. Although unification has created new strains for the all-German party and political system, on the whole the management of this extraordinary transformative process has been positive.

Yet the domestic changes created by unification, the emergence of a new, less stable international order, and the inevitable tensions accompanying European economic and monetary union will require more dramatic responses by the Federal Republic's party state and parties than "business as usual." Once again, there is a need to provide the kind of coherent political and economic vision developed after 1945.

Although it is easy to exaggerate the current anti-party mood, its persistence and growth may yet weaken the democratic foundations of the enlarged Federal Republic. Thus whereas the symbiosis between German democracy and German parties established and nurtured since 1945 has been a source of strength throughout the Federal Republic's existence, the failure of and alienation from its founding parties could become a potential threat to its survival. Whether the Berlin Republic will follow the path of Bonn or Weimar will once again be determined by the performance of Germany's political parties.

Chapter 4

UNIFICATION AND THE CHANGING FORTUNES OF GERMANY'S PARTIES OF THE FAR RIGHT

John Leslie

Introduction

Successes achieved by extreme right parties[1] in a series of elections in early 1989 cast a shadow over German unification. Amidst the turbulence and increasingly nationalistic tenor of developments in the GDR, politicians in both East and West feared events would add electoral momentum to the far right. Leaders of far right parties themselves saw things similarly and devoted considerable resources to exploit the windfall they hoped unity would bring. The initial euphoria of German unity collapsed within a year under the weight of rising unemployment in the

1. For the purposes of this paper the labels "far right" and "extreme right" are used interchangeably to refer to the Republikaner, DVU, and the NPD. The label "radical right" is reserved for those organizations and movements which German authorities have classified as "anti-constitutional."

East and rising taxes in the West, and by September 1991 the attacks of young East Germans on foreign workers in the eastern town of Hoyerswerda and the election of the far right DVU to the state parliament of Bremen confirmed the most dire predictions about growing political instability in the wake of unification. However, in little more than another year, German society and the German state drove far right parties and violence against foreigners back to the margins of society.

In considering both the emergence and the decline of far right parties, this chapter focuses on the legal and institutional parameters of parliamentary democracy in the old FRG as they shaped the electoral chances of far right parties, as well as whether and how the political environment has changed with unification. The examination is of the external constraints imposed on these parties rather than the internal organization and development of far right parties per se. Furthermore, no effort is made to compare events in Germany with similar developments elsewhere in Europe.

This investigation proceeds in three parts. The first section considers the conditions prevailing among West German institutions of parliamentary democracy in the late 1980s. A second section examines the changes in the political environment accompanying unity which explain developments after the autumn of 1991, particularly the emergence of xenophobic violence. A final section explores the extent to which, despite the transformations wrought by unification, the relatively restrictive constraints faced by far right parties have remained intact. In doing so, it asks whether the turbulence of unity, rather than assisting parties of the far right, has undermined their electoral chances.

Late 1980s – Far Right Parties and the Rules of Parliamentary Democracy

The political environment faced by far right parties at the end of the 1980s was shaped by factors independent of particular political developments or actors in Germany, in particular the economic and social transformations of the 1970s and 1980s that brought dislocations to all industrial democracies. The development of immigration and the rise of far right parties in this era is most important for this analysis.[2] Other constraints are peculiarly German, specifically the German attitudes about German identity and the proper relationship between Germans, foreigners, and public authorities. Because these attitudes exist not only in German heads but also in German laws they impose institutionalized constraints on the behavior of all political actors with regard to immigration and how its issues are brought into the public arena. Another set of limitations arising out of German history curtail the maneuverability of political actors on the far right. Although these constraints exist as attitudes, they also find expression in German law, and I initially present these factors before turning to the role played by established political parties in lifting Germany's parties of the far right over the 5 percent electoral threshold in early 1989.

Immigration: An Opportunity for Far Right Parties?

A rapidly rising number of immigrants during the 1980s created political opportunity for far right parties in the Federal Republic as well as elsewhere in Western Europe and some have even maintained xenophobic parties and violence are a "natural" reaction to the influx (Fuchs, Gerhards and Roller, 1993). These new arrivals, however, present a special problem in the

2. As a matter of political conviction or as "a kind of emphatic political denial" many German politicians affirm loudly and publicly that Germany is "not a country of immigration" (Bade, 1994). However, because a large number of the hundreds of thousands of individuals who enter the FRG every year do so with the intention of making it their permanent residence, I choose to label such individuals "immigrants" and their movements "immigration." Conflict over these labels plays a crucial role in the events being analyzed.

FRG and many politicians have claimed that "Germany is not a country of immigration." In fact, while the FRG does make legal provision for immigration (e.g. asylum, repatriation of ethnic Germans, and interstate treaties), it is not *called* immigration. Thus, the lack of explicit immigration shapes the means "immigrants" use to gain entrance to the Federal Republic, the problems associated with "immigration," and the subsequent political debates.

However, there have been openings for those seeking entrance into West Germany. The first reflects the lasting legacy of West German recruitment of guestworkers between the mid-1950s and the early 1970s. While state-guided recruitment of foreign workers ended in November 1973, piecemeal government policies have partially integrated resident aliens into German society and thereby contributing to the continued growth and changing composition of the guestworker population (Herbert, 1990: 235-37). Specifically, policies permitting the reunion of family members and dependents of resident guestworkers have contributed to an increase in both the total population of guestworkers and the number of non-working guestworkers in the FRG, though exact figures here are hard to come by.

To those who can demonstrate German ethnicity, Article 116 of the Basic Law and the 1953 Federal Expellees and Refugees Law provide a second means of entrance into the Federal Republic (Delfs, 1993). With the advent of glasnost, states in eastern Europe and Russia became more open not only to the internal flow of information, but also to the outward flow of emigrants. After 1986 a steady flow of ethnic Germans coming to the FRG began to increase rapidly. Although demonstrating German ethnicity required little more than a German name, or a parent or grandparent with a German name – and little or no understanding of the German language – these "ethnic Germans" became citizens of the FRG upon arrival.

Table 4-1 Immigration into the Federal Republic during the 1980s

Year	Ethnic Germans [Aussiedler]	East Germans [Übersiedler]	Asylum
1980	52,071	12,763	107,818
1981	69,455	13,208	49,391
1982	48,170	13,208	37,423
1983	37,925	11,343	19,737
1984	36,459	40,974	35,278
1985	38,968	24,912	73,832
1986	42,788	26,178	99,650
1987	78,523	18,958	57,379
1988	202,673	39,832	103,076
1989	377,055	343,854	121,318

Sources: For asylum applicants 1980-89 see Münch (1993: 253) and Bade (1992). For Ethnic Germans and East Germans 1985-1989 see Marshall (1992: 249) and for 1980-1984 see Mayer (1990). These figure represent new arrivals excluding dependents of resident guestworkers.

The final avenue of entrance into West German society has inspired the most controversy. Article 16 (2) of the Basic Law guarantees all those who claim they are politically persecuted a subjective inalienable right to asylum, which in practice means a right to an asylum hearing. By the end of the 1980s, the reunification of guestworker families, the liberalization of conditions for ethnic Germans in Eastern Europe, and the asylum hearing guarantee in Article 16, complemented by liberal access to judicial review of petitions, provided several hundred thousand newcomers temporary or permanent residence in the FRG each year.

With this inflow came economic, social, and fiscal problems which ensured "immigration" would find its way on to the agenda of party politics. New arrivals contributed to the general infrastructural problems of providing education and social services that are associated with immigration and created difficulties in integrating immigrants into housing and labor markets (Herbert, 1990: 235-43). The arrival of ethnic Germans and asylum applicants, however, precipitated special problems. The problem of immigration/asylum is a German one as asylees in particular serve as lightning rods (or scapegoats) for many other changes such as the loss of blue collar jobs, economic insecurity, fears about the EU, changes in welfare provisions, among others. Responsibility for the housing and support of both groups fell to state and local authorities for whom this became an increasingly large and visible fiscal and political burden. Ethnic German newcomers' privileged access, sometimes above levels granted other citizens, to occupational retraining programs, public housing, subsidized loans, and cash grants fueled existing resentments in German society over the size of fiscal outlays for "immigrants" (Marshall, 1992: 247-63; Klär et al., 1989a, 1989b). These highly visible demands on public resources presented an explosive potential for political entrepreneurs willing to combine ethnic divisions and material resentments.

Topography of Immigration Politics

Because "immigration" did not exist legally, the influx of newcomers and the problems associated with it stood open to political definition when they emerged as issues on the agenda of party politics. However, politicians seldom enjoy unrestricted freedom in choosing how to frame issues in the political arena. In the case of "immigration" a set of contradictory attitudes concerning the relations of Germans, non-Germans, and public authority, embedded in German society and institutionalized in German law, define the parameters and set the boundaries. One can call these perspectives: ethnocultural, statist/communitarian, and liberal/humanist.

The ethnocultural perspective predominated in the politics of immigration at the end of the 1980s (Brubaker, 1992). It rests not only on the belief that the nation or Volk is a constitutive entity reflected in language, culture, and history, but also that the boundaries between nations and peoples are demarcated biologically. Stated bluntly, this perspective holds that Germans are born different and special, and that the presence of non-Germans represents a dangerous dilution of that which makes German society unique. Although public expression of such attitudes has entailed the serious risk of legal censure since the end of World War II, the ethnocultural perspective remains firmly embedded in German law, reflected in the jus sanguinis regulation of citizenship, the 1913 citizenship law, and the extension of citizenship rights to "ethnic Germans" in East Europe through Article 116 of the Basic Law. The Red-Green government of Gerhard Schröder elected in 1998 pledged to make liberalizing immigration policy a major goal.

While these regulations, laws and rights reflected practical or humanitarian considerations as much as the desire to maintain the ideal of a unified, "ethnic" German nation (Prantl, 1993: 305) after defeat and division in the immediate postwar era, their persistence profoundly shaped the politics of immigration in the 1980s. By the end of the 1980s no less than 7 percent of the resident population (not including minors, prisoners, the "mentally infirm") of the FRG lived without full rights of political participation (Goltz, 1995: 5). As well as being undemocratic, this situation created incentives for politicians to engage in the divisive politics of ethnic identity. As long as foreign residents of the FRG who are not EU citizens can acquire neither citizenship nor the right to vote, politicians can engage in immigrant bashing without fear of electoral reprisal by immigrant voters, and possibly even gain support from those voters who would scapegoat immigrants.

The statist/communitarian perspective, by contrast, argues one should proceed cautiously in codifying individual rights for fear that doing so may impede a higher purpose, such as the realization of the *raison d'état* or general will. Instead, there is greater willingness to subordinate individual rights to social goals and to entrust state administrators with discretionary power to manage conflicts between individual and state or communal interests. The postwar West German attempts to regulate political asylum and guestworkers are replete with examples of legislation seeking to maximize the discretionary powers of state actors and to limit the ability of individuals to block administrative authority, particularly through judicial review (Münch, 1993: chap. 2 and 3; Herbert, 1990: chap. 5). Prominent examples are the 1965 Foreigner's Law (*Ausländergesetz*) and the 1992-93 change in the constitutional regulation of political asylum.

In the decades of rapid economic growth after the war, legislation written according to a statist/communitarian logic introduced an all-too-simple calculus into the regulation of the presence of foreign nationals in German society. Foreign labor would be managed like material factors of production: as long as they represented a net gain for the community, defined exclusively in short-term, material respects, guestworkers were tolerated. Should they become a burden they would have to leave. The growth years of the economic miracle left these assumptions unchallenged. Events in the 1970s, however, dispelled both the illusion of uninterrupted economic growth – which concealed differences of interest between guestworkers and other elements of West German society – and the belief that foreign labor could be "managed" purely as an industrial input. Persistent growth in the guestworker population, even after the end of active recruitment in 1973 raised a troubling question: with what justification and at what price could human beings be excluded from full participation in a democratic society? By the 1970s, then, statist/communitarian regulations came in conflict with the liberal/humanist perspective.

Liberals and humanists advocate strong institutional mechanisms for the protection of individual rights when faced with encroachment by either the state or social majorities. As in the constitutions of other Western parliamentary democracies, the

Basic Law contains articles guaranteeing fundamental individual rights to all residents of the FRG regardless of nationality. In the context of immigration, none has been more important than the guarantee of political asylum and the right to judicial review to those individuals who feel their rights have been violated by administrative decision.

Conceived partially in atonement for the crimes of National Socialism (and partially to provide rights that the founders of the FRG had not held themselves during the Nazi years) these articles have provided access to the physical security and material wealth of West German society to a great number of individuals. Many of these individuals were entitled to political asylum under Article 16 and many were not. However, liberal access to judicial review for all asylum applicants had by the early 1980s stretched the average length of an asylum case to more than six years (Münch, 1993: 72). During this time public resources financed not only housing and support for these individuals, but also the costs of legal proceedings themselves. As the number of applications rose, case backlogs swelled, reviews lengthened, and the asylum process became an increasingly attractive means to enter West German society. As this development became a vicious circle, resonance grew first among state and local politicians and then in the broader public for a halt to the "abuse" of Germany's asylum laws.

Because each perspective is embedded in the legal structure of the FRG, each set of attitudes represents a key topographical feature of the arena in which the presence of foreigners became politicized at the end of the 1980s. As late as the early 1980s, they coexisted tenuously without finding their way to the center of competition between the major political parties. Only undisguised appeals based on an ethnocultural vision of society were excluded from public discourse. By the mid-1980s, however, mounting pressure to solve problems associated with the rapidly rising number of "immigrants" forced politicians to search for ways to frame these developments politically. Politicization involved elevating certain interpretations of problems, along with policies to rectify them, while subordinating others. Before turning to the role of political parties in shaping the politics of immigration and opportunities for far-right parties, it is necessary to examine the powerful taboos about racism and the National Socialist past which also shape the environment of West German electoral politics.

The Past as Constraint on Extreme Right Parties

The label "extreme right" describes a diverse collection of parties, clandestine organizations, and intellectual projects in Germany sharing a cognitive orientation which rejects the principle of democratic organization in society. While programs of the Left may reject parliamentary democracy or political democracy as absurdities in the face of social inequalities, they do not share the disdain of the extreme right for the notion of equality nor do they share their eagerness to construct national, racial, and cultural hierarchies that place Germans ahead of other peoples (Backes and Jesse, 1989). In keeping with this orientation, various right extremist organizations in the FRG have supported programs to reinforce the perception of hierarchy, nationalism, and historical revisionism that would cast doubt on the legitimacy of the postwar organization of West German society. However, nowhere else in Western Europe does the weight of the past hinder such efforts more than does the Federal Republic, whether through informal social norms of formal institutionalized legal structures.

Popular attitudes measured over time reflect a growing condemnation of the Nazi past in the FRG. Public satisfaction with democratic institutions has risen as positive associations with the National Socialist past have declined, with support for the ideas and institutions of the FRG seeming to be inextricably intertwined with rejection of National Socialism. Some observers argue these developments place a psychological boundary on the electoral support available to the far right even during periods of considerable institutional change (Conradt, 1989).

Legal restrictions on the content of public messages circumscribe the room for maneuver of far-right organizations as well. Although the term "right extremism" does not exist in the Basic Law, three articles set tight legal boundaries on the behavior of extreme right political organizations. Article 18 permits the restriction of the civil rights of those who turn the freedoms of conscience, unrestricted dissemination of ideas, and association against the "basic order of freedom and democracy." Article 9 (2) grants state and federal interior ministries authority to disband associations whose purpose or activities operate contrary to law, the constitutional order, or the reconciliation of different peoples. Article 21 (2) proscribes as unconstitutional any political party that, according to the behavior of its members, seeks to undermine or eliminate the basic order of freedom and democracy or that endangers the existence of the Federal Republic (Stöss, 1989: 35-6). These limitations have been refined and extended by the rulings of the Federal Constitutional Court against extremist organizations of both the Right and Left. Conformity to the less than clear demands set forth by these regulations represents a matter of existential importance to far parties in the FRG.

Behavior of Other Political Actors as Constraint on Far Right Parties

Far right political organizations must distance themselves publicly from political violence and from unvarnished expressions of Nazi ideology as a consequence of these formal limits. Yet both violence and overt expression are regular features of neo-Nazi ghetto politics, so far right parties must navigate here with great care. Failure to do so risks near-certain legal action by state authorities exposes the party to public contempt and the threat that other political actors, and even the electorate itself, will unite against it. These imperatives suggest that far-right parties are also captive to the choices of other political actors. To escape the electoral cul-de-sac of neo-Nazi ghetto politics, far-right parties must distinguish themselves from established electoral competitors on the basis of concrete issues. Thus, the chances for far-right parties to expand their support beyond an ideologically committed core of voters, of much less than 5 percent of the electorate, are determined almost wholly by whether the major parties make room for them on an issue hospitable to interpretation by extreme right parties themselves. Given the CDU/CSU's jealous watch over the right of the political spectrum, this is a relatively rare occurrence, though the actions of the established political parties on "immigration" provided parties of the far right just such an opportunity.

"Choices" of Established Parties on Immigration

Absent legal provisions for immigration, problems arising from the annual influx of hundreds of thousands of people stood open to political definition. As the weight of numbers forced these problems onto the political agenda, it fell to elected political representatives to frame them as issues and propose solutions for them. However, immigration presented policy-makers with problems of a magnitude sufficient to defy solution by the readily available institutional means. Confronted with the problem of reforming institutions to deal with an issue, policy-makers face a dilemma in which they must either admit uncertainty or admit their dependence on other actors, including the political opposition, for finding a real solution. They can avoid this dilemma temporarily by choosing to frame the issue so as to neutralize any electoral advantage political competitors might draw from the situation.

"Immigration" confronted the CDU/CSU and SPD, with a strategic choice between recognizing the complexity of the issues involved and seeking a long-term solution involving institutional reform, with each side needing to trust the other to cooperate, or preempting the adversary and gaining an electoral advantage. While the outlines of this choice seemed clear, actors could not anticipate all the consequences of one choice or another (Bendix and Steiner, 1998).

In the second half of the 1980s elements within the CDU/CSU chose to condense the multitude of issues surrounding the influx of "immigrants" into West German society to a simple formula which explained these problems as the result of the "misuse" of the FRG's liberal regulation of political asylum. According to this interpretation, those who applied for asylum were at best economic refugees, but more likely were individuals seeking to exploit West Germany's prosperity and generous welfare provisions. The solution was therefore to change the constitutional provisions for asylum, a position originating with CSU attempts to counter attacks by the newly formed Republikaner party on "fraudulent" asylum seekers during the 1986 election to the Bavarian state parliament (Jaschke, 1993; Süddeutsche Zeitung, 22 and 28 July, 1986).

However, by attaching "misuse" to a position advocating change in the constitutional guarantee of asylum, the CSU immediately drew lines of ideological conflict between statist/communitarians and liberals. In doing so, this position raised "immigration" from a fiscal battle fought between politicians at different levels of the federal system, to an issue on the agenda of inter-party competition (Münch, 1993). The "misuse" position was also calculated to neutralize the SPD electorally, on the issue of immigration. Changing the asylum provisions in the Basic Law required a two-thirds majority and, thus, opposition support. CDU/CSU leaders calculated that their willingness to sacrifice the liberal principles contained in Article 16 would precipitate a party split within the SPD between defenders of liberal, humanist values and the more statist/communitarian-oriented social democrats. The resulting internal party deadlock would alienate those voters in urban districts, who confronted the social and fiscal consequences of immigration on a daily basis. CDU/CSU politicians assumed that they could posture themselves as the responsible party, offering a programmatic response to issues, while the obstructionist opposition had no alternatives.

The contrast between attacks on asylum applicants and the Kohl government's policy on ethnic Germans from eastern Europe demonstrates the primacy of electoral concerns over the desire to find a manageable solution to the problems of "immigration." The government's special program of August 1988 allowed ethnic Germans unrestricted entry to the FRG and access to public resources that were equal to that of average West Germans (Marshall, 1992: 256-57). The government implemented this legislation despite the fact that: 1) most Germans considered the new arrivals from East Europe – more than 80 percent of whom spoke no German – at least as foreign as most asylum applicants, and 2) in 1988, twice as many ethnic Germans entered the FRG (with the aid of government policy) as asylum-seekers (through Article 16). In 1989 the number of ethnic Germans exceeded the number of asylum applicants by a factor of three to one. However, unlike a constitutional change, legislation to control the flow of ethnic Germans or to provide resources of state and society for them, did not require a two-thirds parliamentary majority. Of course, ethnic Germans from eastern Europe tend to be religious, conservative, and hold patriarchal values that might incline them to vote for the CDU/CSU (Koller, 1993: 15).

Union efforts to focus public attention on the "misuse" of asylum produced three immediate consequences, none of which was fully intended. First, the "misuse/constitutional change" formula confused the various legal regulations granting entrance to different groups of resident foreigners with the political justification for reforming these regulations. In the public representations of politicians and media, foreign residents seldom wore labels identifying the set of legal regulations that governed their presence, but what often distinguished them in the eyes of the public were cultural and racial differences. Among the confusing multiplication of administrative labels, of Asylbewerber, Aussiedler, Umsiedler, Spätaussiedler, Fluchtling, and "Gastarbeiter," the distortion fostered by "misuse" did nothing to suppress the temptation to impose a simplifying order by using the label "foreigner."

Further, in a climate where asylum-seekers were portrayed as an undeserving burden on German society, distinctions between justifications for reforming the legal avenues of entrance into the FRG also began to erode. In their formal justifications for reform, CDU/CSU politicians emphasized West Germany's limited fiscal capacity to manage a potentially limitless "flood" of foreigners.[3] Asylum reform represented a practical necessity dictated by the problem of limited material resources. However, while arguments about the limited capacity to accept more foreigners rest on a statist/communitarian logic, the rhetoric of "misuse" injected a chauvinist element into public discussions. CDU/CSU statements presented applicants for asylum not as humans who, for whatever reasons, left their homes behind, but instead as "frauds" sapping the affluence and security created by West German society. Such statements are little different than perspectives that attribute prosperity to some superior trait found in West Germans which is lacking in other races or cultures. In short, the inflammatory rhetoric of some politicians bridged the debate of acceptable politics, from libertarian concerns for indi-

---

3. The specter of a "flood" of foreigners overwhelming the resources of the FRG is a prominent theme in the rhetoric of Union politicians and [consequently?] the media. As examples note former President of the Constitutional Court, Wolfgang Zeidler's, suggestion that "a billion Chinese would have entrance" to the FRG; former Bavarian Interior Minister, and later minister president, Edmund Stoiber's speculation about "100 million or more potential asylum applicants;" and former CSU General Secretary Erwin Huber's observation that in East Europe "millions of people" were sitting on packed suitcases "looking toward Germany." Cited in Münch (1993:106-7).

vidual constitutional rights and the needs of the state or national community, to the racial and cultural hierarchies espoused by far right groups.

A second consequence of the "misuse" campaign evolved not quite in accordance with CDU/CSU strategies, thought it did produce the expected conflict between defenders of different values within the SPD. The SPD's inability to resolve this internal controversy drove a wedge between the party and voters concerned with the problems of immigration, but despite its internal divisions, the SPD was able to damage CDU/CSU credibility on the problems of "immigration." Social Democrats assaulted the CDU/CSU for swelling numbers of ethnic Germans from East Europe, demanding a revision of Article 116. As neither side could implement such revision over the objections of the other, the West German electorate watched the spectacle of its elected representatives engage in a series of transparent electoral maneuvers that reduced the foreign residents themselves to pawns.

By creating an environment of inflamed rhetoric and political deadlock, the major parties gave the far right parties an opportunity to transcend the ghetto of radical right politics. In their defending Article 116, and in the tenor of their rhetoric, CDU/CSU politicians found themselves in the uncomfortable position of narrowing the ideological ground between themselves and parties of the extreme right, in the process giving the far right a concrete issue with which to differentiate themselves from CDU and CSU. To CDU/CSU critiques that they were the peddlers of discredited ideas from the past, far-right politicians could respond disingenuously that they were not the ones defending the legal notion of the Volk by letting in hundreds of thousands of ethnic Germans who understood neither the language nor the culture of the FRG (Lepszy, 1989). At the same time, the large parties' inability to formulate a concrete policy on immigration offered far-right parties a chance to assume a populist stance vis-à-vis not only the CDU/CSU, but the party system as a whole. Against the backdrop of legislative gridlock, far-right politicians portrayed themselves as the representatives of the concerns of common people against a cynical and corrupt political class. With a small measure of authenticity, they could claim the issue was not asylum applicants or ethnic Germans – such distinctions interested professional politicians but not common people – but rather the influx of too many foreigners. Far from offering an outlet for voters to cast an abstract or ill-defined protest vote, far-right parties focused electoral dissatisfaction on a concrete issue and the real shortcomings of the political system in dealing with "immigration."[4]

However, the presence of opportunity provided no guarantee that the far right would be prepared to exploit it. The Republikaner demonstrated their innovativeness among Germany's far-right parties by explicitly maintaining distance between themselves and statements of ideology, use of Nazi symbols, and especially any association with violence. With mixed success, the Republikaner sought to adapt right extremism to the rules of parliamentary democracy. Borrowing an innovation from the

---

4. Considerable controversy erupted in 1989 as to the origin and meaning of the electoral successes of far right parties. Researchers and politicians were divided between those who claimed success was the result of a protest vote and those who viewed voters of the far right as driven by a "closed right extremist view of life." This chapter eschews the universalizing assumptions underlying both perspectives. Several works have demonstrated that a great number of Germans (estimates run from 4 percent to 17 percent) share elements of such closed views yet on only one occasion [the 1989 election to the European Parliament] have voters in this range actually voted for far-right parties. Worldviews are insufficient to explain voting behavior, and even right extremists are to some degree motivated by the external environment. However, it is also not simply coincidence that the opportunity for the far right arose with immigration, as deadlock on almost any other issue would not have produced such an opportunity for far right parties. In essence, my perspective is that voters were registering their dissatisfaction with the major parties on a set of issues on which they often had preexisting far-right proclivities. See Pappi (1991:37-44); Klär et al. (1989a, 1989b); Falter (1994); Hennig (1991).

French *Nouvelle Droite*, objections to foreigners in German society were carefully couched in the language of culture and values, thereby skirting the stigmatizing issue of race (Jaschke, 1993: 44). To preempt official and popular suspicions about personal links between the party and other far right organizations, Paragraph 3 of the party statute excludes the functionaries of any political organization considered anti-constitutional or radical from becoming members (Stöß, 1991: 60-61). However, the dual necessity of binding committed far-right activists to the party and maintaining the appearance of public respectability demanded a nearly untenable balancing act that the party leadership performed with only limited success.

None of the far-right parties successfully claimed a segment of the West German electorate as their own, instead attracting a heterogeneous group of voters whose bonds to CDU/CSU and SPD, had been loosened by the issues around "immigration."[5] Consequently, Republikaner voters are difficult to distinguish from the electors of other parties according to demographic characteristics. While far-right supporters are overwhelmingly male, more likely to have the minimum required formal education, be a worker or self-employed, REP supporters in 1989 could not easily be differentiated from the West German electorate in terms of age, confession, income, union-membership, or home-ownership (Hofmann-Göttig, 1989; Klär et al., 1989a, 1989b; Veen, Lepszy, and Mnich, 1993; Stöß, 1993).

However, if demographic traits fail to distinguish far-right supporters, subjective orientations are more revealing. When asked to list the most important political problems of the day, Republikaner supporters responded most frequently with "asylum-

5. Klär et al. (1989a, 1989b) found that 40 percent of Republikaner voters in the 1989 European election had voted for the CDU/CSU in 1987 while 20 percent voted SPD and another 20 percent had not voted at all. Roth (1990) points out that in the 1989 Berlin election 53 percent of Republikaner voters came from the CDU/CSU camp while 21 percent came from the SPD.

seekers" (34 percent) followed by "ethnic Germans" (26 percent). The most common responses, among the sample as a whole, were "environmental protection" (33 percent) and unemployment (29 percent) (Politbarometer, August 1989). The reasons supporters listed for giving their votes in 1989 are also revealing, as 82 percent of cast their vote for the party because of dissatisfaction with the other parties (Veen, Lepszy, and Mnich, 1993: 47). Almost 90 percent of these voters saw the Republikaner as a party "that raised problems neglected by other parties (Klär et al., 1989a: 47)" Finally, 72 percent of Republikaner voters gave "Because the Republikaner advocate solutions to the 'foreigner problem'" as one of the main reasons for voting for the party. These data make clear that the problems of immigration and, specifically, the inability of the deadlocked political system to deal with them, presented far-right parties with a rare opportunity to extend their support by articulating and focusing the frustrations of voters with the established parties on a concrete issue.

In the wake of successes in three consecutive elections in the winter and spring 1989 the Republikaner, and another far right party, the NPD, seemed on the brink of transforming the West German party system.[6] The electoral opening created by immigration, the rhetoric of "misuse," and legislative gridlock presented an opportunity for far-right political entrepreneurship to collect and focus popular frustrations. The successes of far right parties, especially the Republikaner, in attracting votes outside the narrow confines of the committed far-right electorate in 1989 proclaimed West Germany's convergence with developments elsewhere in West Europe, where right extremism was attempting to "adapt and normalize" itself to the constraints

6. On January 29 the Republikaner won 7.5 percent of the vote and eleven seats in the Berlin legislature. On March 12, the NPD won 6.6 percent of the vote and representation in the Frankfurt city government. On June 18 the Republikaner obtained 7.1 percent of the vote in West Germany in the elections to the European Parliament.

of parliamentary democracy (Hennig, 1990). Unfortunately, one cannot say whether West Germany's parties of the far right would have stabilized themselves within the political system had not the events in the autumn of 1989 intervened. However, one can retrace the extent to which these events changed the political environment for far-right parties in a unified Germany. It is to this changing environment that we now turn.

Reunification – Reshuffling the Rules of Far Right Participation?

The collapse of the GDR and unification created a new political situation and a new environment for far-right politics. First, a unique political environment evolved out of the combination within a single polity of two very different societies, one transforming away from forty years of Leninist organization, and one governed by a stable set of democratic and parliamentary institutions. Second, this new environment proved hospitable to anti-foreigner violence. Before asking whether the rules of democratic participation changed for far right parties, this section considers the evolution of the world around these rules.

Collapse of Social Controls in the East

The turbulence of East German society following the collapse of the GDR represented a far different social environment than the one in which extreme right parties in the West had evolved. Unification injected into this environment the existing constellation of issues, parties, and positions of the West, including the problems of immigration and the political responses to them. In the East these issues provoked a different response than they had in the West, namely an outbreak of violence directed at foreign residents.

With the collapse of the SED party state, social control mechanisms, whether coercive in the form of police and legal systems, or integrative, as in the form of work place and community associations and even the family, underwent severe disruption and in some cases totally collapsed. At the extremes of the old system, at the political center and in local administration and production, disruption was most complete. The hundreds of thousands who fled the GDR in the summer and autumn of 1989 left unmanageable gaps in enterprises and communities behind. Centralized administrative authority flowed downward and away from the old ruling clique around Erich Honecker in response, quickly bringing about the collapse of the Honecker, Krenz, and Modrow governments in succession.

Other levels of administrative authority averted the creation of a complete political vacuum. Some elements of local government and services remained in place but with their credibility undermined by association with the old regime, particularly so in the case of the police and courts. In some cases where important social institutions collapsed or were too compromised to remain under old management, organizations from the West, particularly unions and political parties, moved in to replace them. Consequently, after the collapse of the SED many of the organizations and institutions which put controls on individual behavior in other societies, were either absent, tainted, or alien to East German society.

Rapid introduction of the West's Social Market Economy to the East disrupted many of the mechanisms which bound Easterners to society. The shock effect of inflating the exchange rate between East and West German Marks and efforts by unions to rapidly equalize eastern and western wage rates proved particularly disruptive, leading to a rapid increase in unemployment and the elimination of many welfare services. Old eastern enterprises had played a large role in the provision of public housing, consumer goods, education, and social and leisure activities for workers and their families in addition to employment. Thus closure or restructuring of these enterprises eliminated these auxiliary functions before other organizations could replace them, leaving many, especially the young, with few organized bonds to society.

"Immigration" Moves East

Unification brought the issues and debates surrounding "immigration" to the east along with the institutions of the West German Social Market Economy and parliamentary democracy. The unification treaty stipulated that the new Länder, in proportion to their population size rather than in consideration of their social conditions, host 20 percent of new asylum applicants and 20 percent of the ethnic Germans arriving from East Europe (Bade, 1992: 35). Although they represented a far smaller percentage of the resident population in the East than in the West, these foreign residents and the highly visible use of public resources to support them – particularly in light of the prevailing unemployment, housing shortages, and other unsolved problems of unification – provided a focus for dissatisfaction and resentment.

More important than either the eastward transportation of "immigration" or the material problems surrounding it, however, was the projection of the polarized and inflamed political rhetoric from the West. After the euphoria of unity subsided, public attention in both parts of Germany refocused on immigration and foreigners. Inflammatory CDU/CSU rhetoric, that the massive "misuse" of the right to asylum had overwhelmed the population's capacity for tolerance, as CDU General Secretary Rule said in September 1991, made two contributions to the development of xenophobic violence. First, it provided existing cliques of East German youths an ideal target group, an other against whom to define themselves. Second, ambiguous CDU/CSU statements about anti-foreigner violence supported the rationalizations of perpetrators that they were only enacting the will of the silent majority which politicians themselves were too hypocritical to carry out. In their failure to condemn violence without reservation, CDU/CSU politicians contributed to the appearance of social and political tolerance of xenophobia. By September 1991, after state authorities in the eastern town of Hoyerswerda removed foreign residents from the dormitories which housed them, in response to attacks by German youths, xenophobia and violence seemed to have become officially tolerated political action in Germany.

This permissive environment only needed actors with a motivation for violence to produce an explosion. Ninety percent of the incidents of xenophobic violence in East and West Germany between 1990 and 1993 were committed by groups of men under the age of twenty-five. Groups with fewer than ten members, that one could hardly call organizations, committed half of these acts (Willems, 1993: 110-13). Further, while their members overwhelmingly claim skinhead, extreme right, or xenophobic orientations, the goals of and reasons for the existence of these groups do not live up to the ambitions of far right parties or even clandestine neo-Nazi movements. Rather than organizing to seek state power or a particular political agenda, such groups build on existing social relationships: prior to the collapse of the GDR, punk, skinhead, and neo-Nazi cliques helped members exert a measure of resistance and independence vis-à-vis the homogenizing culture of "real-existing socialism" (Stock, 1994). After unification these cliques served the needs of their members for identity and orientation in a turbulent environment by dividing society into superordinate and subordinate categories. Violence, then, consolidated both the group and the boundaries between it and the surrounding environment. Because it was the group itself which serves the personal needs of individual members, and not some common group-external purpose, efforts by more traditional far-right organizations to recruit new members among these cliques or steer them for their own purposes have met with little success.

Weakening social controls, existing skinhead cliques, and the inflammatory rhetoric of "misuse" converged in the East to produce a right extremism quite different from the efforts of far-right parties to normalize and adapt themselves to parliamentary democracy before the autumn of 1989. Further, media transmission of incidents like Hoyerswerda and the appearance of an environment permissive of violence motivated an imitation of these attacks by groups of young men not only in the East but in the West as well (Ohlemacher, 1994). Premeditated and organized acts of violence were the exception: the majority of assaults on foreigners seemed more or less spontaneous incidents facilitated by alcohol, boredom, and television-mediated examples (Willems, 1993: 184). The "hedonistic" approach to action, violence, and group membership characteristic of post-unification developments represent, as one observer has suggested, right extremism not as the sanitized, parliamentary posturing of the Republikaner, but rather a kind of "post-modern neo-Nazism" (Jähner in Benz, 1994: 130-31).

Thus, political unification did not simply extend constitutional principles, institutions, and issues eastward. Nor did it produce electoral support for far-right parties in the new Länder, only one of which, the DVU in Saxony-Anhalt in March 1998, has won even 5 percent in either state or national election. Rather, the introduction of "immigration" to the East, as a physical reality and a political issue, contributed to the explosion of xenophobic violence. However, while the social environment after unification differed considerably from that of the FRG, unity did not fundamentally alter the rules according to which far-right political parties participate in the electoral system. The final section of this chapter considers the consequences of German unity, and particularly anti-foreigner violence, for the electoral chances of extreme right parties.

Continuities and Far Right Parties after Unification

After a brief electoral renaissance lasting from the autumn of 1991 until the autumn of 1992, the state, political parties, and public opinion have pushed far right parties back to the margins of German society. This development demonstrates that the rules of the game, which constrain far right parties in their pursuit of more than a marginal existence in the German party system, remained intact after unification. Specifically, the eruption of violence against foreign residents made it impossible for these parties to maintain the electoral ground they occupied prior to 1989 and again between 1991 and 1992. There are strong norms against violence and racism embedded in German law and society, making it difficult for far-right parties to maintain distance between themselves and association with these taboos. There is also continued dependence of far-right parties on the behavior of other political actors. The CDU/CSU parties used the eruption of xenophobic violence after unification to break a political deadlock on asylum and thereby eliminated the opportunity for populist demagoguery by far-right parties and helped remarginalize right extremism in German politics and society.

Overturning the "Permissive" Environment

In late autumn of 1992 the climate of public and official tolerance of violence against foreigners which had evolved after Hoyerswerda evaporated abruptly and dramatically. Although this turn came in response to an intensification of violent attacks, public and official reaction extended beyond criminal attacks to vilify other types of far-right behavior as well. Xenophobic violence and the activities of far-right parties were swept together in a universal condemnation of right extremism, partly based on a changing public perception of violence and partly on the increasingly aggressive posture of state authorities toward far right organizations of all types.

The death of two young girls and their grandmother in an attack on the home of a guestworker family in the West German city of Mölln in November 1992 precipitated a spontaneous and highly visible transformation in the public perception of violence against foreigners and xenophobia generally. The tardiness of the response by the CDU-led government, specifically chancellor Kohl's failure to go to Mölln was a powerful catalyst in the public's response. Prior to this event, some politicians excused mass assaults on dormitories housing foreign residents as understandable eruptions of social frustrations and a protest against the failure to reform asylum regulations. The fire-bombing at Mölln, on the other hand, confronted the German public with an act of premeditated murder motivated purely by racial hatred and committed by two or three individuals acting under cover of night. After such a naked transgression of taboos about violence and racism politicians could no longer deny the xenophobic nature of the wave of assaults against foreign residents.

A number of sources confirm the precipitous change in the public mood accompanying events in Mölln. In December 1992, the news magazine *Spiegel* reported that before Mölln 33 percent of Germans demonstrated understanding for right-radical tendencies in light of the "foreigner problem." After Mölln this number fell to 12 percent (Becker, 1993: 141-49). In a long-term statistical analysis of violence and public opinion, Thomas Ohlemacher (1994) demonstrated that while events in Hoyerswerda and Rostock acted as catalysts for increasing violence and popular criticisms of the "misuse" of asylum Mölln was the peak, after that acts of violence and responses critical of asylum applicants fell off precipitously. Candlelight processions with hundreds of thousands of participants took place across Germany in December 1992 and January 1993, providing the most visible indicator of the rising reaction against xenophobic violence.

The precipitous transformation of the public climate worked against far-right efforts to maintain distinctions between the various organizations and activities. Efforts by the DVU and Republikaner to maintain a distance from violence and overt racism, as well as a veneer of democratic respectability, lost their plausibility in a public mobilized against violence and xenophobia. Recognizing the opportunity presented by the change of public opinion, federal and state interior ministries under both CDU/CSU and SPD took an aggressive stance against right extremism. State authorities recognized the imperative of dispelling any appearance of official tolerance for those who challenged the state's monopoly on violence. Court decisions made clear the risks of participation in xenophobic activities through the sentences handed down in the trials of several participants in such incidents. This message was reinforced by the Federal Interior Minister's decision in 1992 to ban the neo-Nazi splinter groups Nationalistische Front, Nationale Offensive and the Deutsche Alternative in both East and West. Authorities also hoped to facilitate the narrowing of distance between the electorally-oriented far-right parties and assaults on foreigners in public perceptions. In the course of 1993, officials in the Office of Constitutional Protection and several Länder interior ministries made very public statements questioning the constitutionality of far right parties and threatened their members with exclusion from public employment (Der Spiegel 13 September 1993; Frankfurter Allgemeine 1 November 1993). Although no such actions were taken against Republikaner, DVU, or NPD, the mere suggestion served to undermine distinctions between these parties and other organizations, ensuring all would be swept away together by the turning tide of public reaction.

Strategic Dependence of Far Right Parties after Unity

The development of parliamentary politics after unification, especially on the issue of political asylum, demonstrates the continued dependence of far right parties on the behavior of other political parties in the electoral arena. In 1989 the CDU/CSU parties' "misuse" campaign, and the deadlock it created around constitutional principles, handed far-right parties a populist platform. After unification, xenophobic violence and the threat of social disorder provided CDU/CSU politicians an instrument with which to weaken the resistance of the other parties to changing Article 16 and, thereby, reclaim ground it had lost to the far right, and bring about an interparty compromise on political asylum. These developments, together with the rapid change in the public environment, pushed far right parties back to the margins of the German electorate.

In the autumn of 1991, the CDU/CSU national leaders demanded a change in Article 16, though CDU/CSU-governed Länder obstructed an initial interparty compromise reforming the process – though not the constitutional provision – of political asylum (Münch 1993: 128-29; Schäuble in Frankfurter Allgemeine 15 October 1991). Even as interparty bickering persisted, developments inside and outside the FRG increased the pressure to find a solution to the legislative deadlock on immigration. Externally, civil war in Yugoslavia and the impending collapse of the Soviet Union threatened to send a new wave of immigrants and refugees to aggravate already tense social relations in Western Europe. Inside the FRG, the electoral success of the DVU in Bremen in September 1991 and the shocking gains of the Republikaner in Baden-Württemberg and the DVU in Schleswig-Holstein in April 1992 demonstrated the vulnerability of both large parties to electoral competitors from the far right (Feist, 1992). These results and the threat to public order represented by escalating violence put enormous pressure on the major parties to end the stalemate on immigration.

That this tense situation worked to the advantage of the CDU/CSU can be attributed to their strategy of linking "misuse" with calls to change Article 16. The massive electoral losses in the spring of 1992 allowed the CDU/CSU to overcome the remaining resistance of its coalition partner, the FDP, to changing the Basic Law. Not only did this leave the SPD as the sole defender of existing constitutional provisions for asylum but it clarified the lines of conflict, as each side tried to pin blame for violence and far-right electoral successes on the other. While the CDU and CSU maintained some consistency in trumpeting the themes "asylum," "misuse," and "the boat is full," the internal division within the SPD over constitutional change rendered the party incapable of speaking with a single voice on the issue. Consequently, it offered vague, ambiguous, and, at times, contradictory formulations in response to the CDU/CSU barrage (Süddeutsche Zeitung 1 October 1991).

Recognizing they had an advantage, CDU leaders, led by then General Secretary Volker Rühe, proceeded to turn every new asylum applicant into an "SPD asylum applicant" as long as the Social Democrats resisted changing Article 16 (Süddeutsche Zeitung 25 September 1991). In this way the CDU made the SPD responsible not only for those problems directly associated with asylum seekers, but also for the rising tide of anti-foreigner violence, having already excused xenophobic violence as the eruption of frustrations in a society overburdened by the problems of asylum seekers. Since SPD intransigence on constitutional change denied the population relief from this burden, the Social Democrats bore sole responsibility for the ensuing social disorder. To the extent that this interpretation of events dominated public debate, the leadership of the SPD came under pressure from its own grass roots to move on asylum.

By the spring of 1992 the SPD leadership sought a compromise with the CDU/CSU; the problem was finding one they could present to the membership of their party. The Petersberg Program accepted the amendment of Article 16 with a list of countries declared to have no political persecution and linked it to the introduction of an immigration law. Fierce resistance to the Petersberg formula coalesced immediately in both the party executive and the larger body of active members, and was overcome only after a polarized vote at an extraordinary party congress in November. To "assist" the SPD leadership in overcoming resistance within their own party to constitutional change, CDU/CSU politicians like Theo Waigel announced that, should the SPD find itself unable to support the government's initiative, they would make asylum "the number one issue" in the 1994 Bundestag election (Süddeutsche Zeitung 14 September 1992).

Although it did not solve the FRG's immigration problem, the 1992/93 interparty compromise on asylum, based on the Petersberg Program and the introduction of lists of secure countries, did dispossess far-right parties of the single concrete issue on which they could differentiate themselves from the established parties. They could no longer demand simply that "something must be done about foreigners," as they had done while the political system remained deadlocked. Rather, they now had to offer an alternative as to what should be done, a path ending for them inevitably in the barren land of discredited ideology. Without deadlock at the political center and confronted by a public intolerant of violence against foreigners and xenophobia generally, the appeal of far right parties has receded to a marginal group of voters actively committed to an extreme right orientation.

Confined to the Margins – Declining Support for Right Extremism

Since the end of 1992 voting for far-right parties and violence against foreign residents has become restricted to those who feel themselves alienated not only from the political system but also from democratic society in the Federal Republic. Surveys conducted in early 1994 suggest those voting for far-right parties are characterized almost exclusively by a comprehensive right-extremist outlook on life. Using the most restrictive criteria, 4 percent of a representative sample of West German voters, but 51 percent of supporters of the Republikaner, demonstrated such an outlook. Using a somewhat less restrictive definition, the same survey found that the comparable numbers for the sample as a whole and Republikaner supporters were 15-17 percent and 75 percent, respectively (Falter, 1994: 149).

At the same time that an increasingly ideological orientation characterizes supporters of far-right parties, surveys show both a sharp decline and a changed background among these voters. Between the beginning of 1993 and the beginning of 1994 the number of voters reporting they would cast their ballot for a far right party fell from 6 to 3 percent. At the same time, far-right voters in 1994 were increasingly likely to have voted for a far right party previously, or not to have voted at all, but less likely to have come from the ranks of one of the major parties than were far-right voters in 1993. These developments suggest that many formerly disaffected CDU/CSU and SPD voters have been reintegrated into these parties, third parties, or have stopped voting altogether. They also point to the conclusion that, until some external motivation such as feelings of social or economic threat or frustration with the political system pushes them to it, these voters appear to remain comfortably integrated into other parties, especially the CDU/CSU (Falter, 1994: 26, 147-58).

Emotionally charged debates around "immigration" assisted some individuals inclined toward an extreme right outlook in overcoming inhibitions that stood between affect and action. Both in 1989 and in the year between the autumn of 1991 and the autumn of 1992, supporters of far-right parties represented the peak of a larger group in the German population that was most likely to spontaneously give the response "the foreigner/asylum problem" when questioned about their most pressing political concerns. Surveys demonstrate that asylum is the only issue on which voters outside the ranks of the party believe the Republikaner possess the competence to solve (Falter, 1994: 162). This issue provided a bridge between the ranks of committed far-right supporters and the larger body of the electorate. However, after the beginning of 1993, fewer and fewer voters continued to place the "foreigner issue" at the top of the political agenda and fewer still were willing to grant far-right parties a useful role in the German political system. Finally the number of voters willing to vote for far right parties declined even more rapidly. With the exception of the weakened Republikaner who returned to the state parliament of Baden-Württemberg in March 1996, and the DVU in Saxony-Anhalt in March 1998, no far right party has transcended the critical five percent threshold to win parliamentary representation since the community elections in Hessen in March 1993. None even came close to the 5 percent hurdle in the 1998 Federal elections. Had the CDU/CSU and SPD not driven emotions and expectations so high on these issues, and then left them to simmer in blatant partisanship, few voters would have found their way to the far right camp in the first place. With Mölln and the asylum compromise, frustration with the political system declined and tolerance for right-extremism evaporated. In the wake of these developments far right parties have been pushed back to a core of deeply alienated, ideological voters.

Conclusion

As in the rest of West Europe, developments at the end of the 1980s provided fertile ground for the growth of political parties on the extreme right. Explosive growth in immigration together with the creation of a disenfranchised immigrant minority generated considerable opportunity for political entrepreneurialism. However, it was the efforts of CDU/CSU politicians to exploit this opportunity for short-term electoral gains, and not their failure to do so, which opened electoral space to far-right parties. In 1989, the deadlocked and self-serving partisanship of the political center on the issue of immigration bestowed a populist platform on those far-right parties that made at least minimal efforts to abide by the rules of parliamentary democracy and sanitize themselves of violence, overt racism, historical revisionism, and association with National Socialism.

Ironically, unification proved to be a disaster for far-right parties. It was not simply that events in the autumn of 1989 and 1990 overshadowed the dramatic successes of these parties in the West German electoral system, it was also that the established parties handed them an opportunity to regain lost ground in 1991. Rather, the outbreak of xenophobic violence, which erupted as unification imposed the issues and institutions framing immigration in the west on to eastern society, destroyed the electoral prospects of even those far-right parties attempting to adapt themselves to democratic society. Violent racism provoked public and political reaction to the breaching of norms that swept up not only violent groups but far-right parties as well.

These developments point to the precarious existence of far-right parties in Germany. As long as taboos about the past and racism remain in sharp relief, there will be a difficult to reconcile tension between those on the far right who would pursue their agenda within the constraints of parliamentary democracy and those who find such efforts themselves to be in conflict with far-right principles. Nowhere else in Western Europe do electoral parties of the far right face such existential risks from the movement of members and supporters to and from clandestine organizations.

Yet while German institutions have shut out far-right parties and some German politicians have even demonstrated the capacity to learn from past events, German society only began to deal with the continuing problem of immigration with the coming of the SPD/Green coalition in 1998. The CDU/CSU's inaction in the 1990s placed this issue in a "deep freeze" and allowed administrators rather than politicians to determine policy which only started to thaw at the end of the decade (Bendix, 1990). The large and growing population of disenfranchised residents itself became a potential for alienation and resentment that a democratic society could ill-afford to ignore. Further, as long as a hierarchy of political rights divided German society only imperfect and perishable taboos about the past hindered the instrumentalization of sentiments against weak minorities for political gain. This situation prevailed regardless of whether the label used to describe this disenfranchised minority was "asylum seekers" or "illegal immigrants." The perpetuation of such differences between groups and their political exploitation ultimately undermined norms against violence and racism. In fact, in the wake of political debates on asylum, prominent internal and external observers noted that the atmosphere in Germany had become less tolerant of foreigners (Amnesty International, 1995; Bericht, 1995). Finally, while the number of such incidents had declined from a peak in 1992, violent acts committed against foreign residents occurred far more frequently in the 1990s than they did in West Germany before the autumn of 1989.

Chapter 5

GREEN TRUMPS RED?
Political Identity and Left-wing Politics in United Germany

Andrei S. Markovits and *Stephen J. Silvia*

Introduction

The world as a whole has become a much more complicated place since 1989/90 than it was in the previous forty-five years. This pertains to Europe as much as it does to Germany, where the complexities involve foreign affairs as much as they do domestic ones. Few of the pre-unification paradigms remain untouched.

This is very much the case for the Alliance Greens. On the one hand the 1990s have been an unmitigated success story for this social formation. In its incarnation as party the last five years have seen its profound (and perhaps permanent) institutionalization as the third largest electoral force in the political topography of the new Germany. By 1998 the Alliance Greens as party participated in five *Länder* governments (Bremen, Hamburg, Hessen, North Rhine-Westphalia and Schleswig-Holstein), ranked among the parliamentary opposition in six *Länder* and were a major force in local politics throughout all of western and parts of eastern Germany (N.B., the Alliance Greens are currently represented in United Berlin, all ten western *Landtage*, but hold *no* seats in the five eastern *Landtage*). Of course, the party's greatest accomplishment was joining the SPD in the first "red-green" coalition government at the Federal level after the September 1998 elections. As party, the Alliance Greens have become what many members have always wanted them to be as movement: namely, a third force between two established pillars, and a genuine alternative to the Tweedledee and Tweedledum of establishment politics as furnished by conventional capitalism and equally conventional old left Marxism, be it of the Leninist or social democratic variety. So from the conventional perspective of electoral competition, the tale of the Alliance Greens as party is an unmitigated success story.

There is yet another part of the Alliance Greens' political presence that we would gauge as an equally impressive achievement: the successful transformation of the Left as it was known in Europe and the industrial world for the last century. Whereas these developments preceded the Alliance Greens' existence as a party and have to be attributed to their predecessors and numerous tributaries among the new social movements of the late 1960s and 1970s, the ultimate and successful challenge to the old Left's institutions and values only happened with the Alliance Greens' solid ensconcing as a party in the German political landscape. *The German Left: Red, Green and Beyond* argues that the Alliance Greens began as a fundamental challenge to a century-old tradition of leftist politics and ended up transforming this left in only a decade to such a degree that it now is really a completely different political animal (Markovits and Gorski, 1993: 265-73).

One need not be a skilled dialectician to realize that some of the Alliance Greens' most pressing problems originate precisely from the party's very impressive successes. Having become a successful third force party entailed certain costs that have diminished the Alliance Greens as a third force movement. Moreover, the SPD's woes, which were a result of Green existence and Green activities, have contributed to a confusion in Alliance Green strategy that goes much deeper than the issue of coalition politics. It touches on key dimensions of Green identity.

The survival of the PDS on the political left of united Germany has triggered identity crises in both the SPD and the Alliance Greens. The endurance of the PDS, furthermore, alters the topography of German party politics on a number of essential levels. With six parties present in the Bundestag, instead of five as there were before 1990, the task of constructing a majority government has become much more arduous. Even after one excludes some alliances as implausible for either ideological or tactical reasons, the new political arithmetic alters every party's behavior. Although it is certainly premature to speak of the "Italianization" of German politics, a specter of "polarized pluralism" is increasingly likely (Almond, Powell and Mundt, 1993: 127-28).

Despite the large number of unreconstructed cadres who remain members of the PDS, the continuing presence of this post-communist party in the Bundestag has undercut the Alliance Green claim to be Germany's sole genuine progressive force and only real leftist electoral option. It is important to note that the PDS presence in the German political spectrum completes the circle of the history of the German left over the past one hundred years (Markovits and Gorski, 1993: 259-62). Its three major representatives, social democracy, communism, and a complex mixture of radical alternatives, in-betweens, third ways, and independent socialisms, are once again represented (if not united) after a nearly seventy-year hiatus from the German political scene. This, too, causes the Alliance Greens all manner of problems related to their identity and the public articulation of their political profile.

Nowhere are the western Greens' origins in the politics of the post-materialist Federal Republic of the 1960s generation clearer than in their debilitating weakness east of the Elbe. The Alliance Green successes as a party entailed transcending their milieu ghettoes of Bockenheim, Freiburg, Kreuzberg, Tübingen and various other post-materialist and decommodified centers of the former Bonn Republic. Yet their virtual absence in the East, virtually all to the benefit of the PDS, confirms a fundamental irony about the western Greens. More than any other construct of the old Bundesrepublik, this profoundly antinomian milieu, whose very identity was premised on a critique of western values and culture, was the Federal Republic's most pristine political creation. In the current politics of the German left, the Elbe continues to represent a formidable divide that will not disappear in the foreseeable future. Roughly speaking, the new left as represented by the Alliance Greens will remain anchored in the West, whereas the successor party to the old left, the PDS, will continue to occupy a substantial niche in the East.

In this chapter we discuss the problems confronting the Alliance Greens that have until very recently contributed to keeping it on the opposition benches at the federal level and have prompted periodic outbreaks of identity crises. We have organized it into three clusters. The first assesses the Alliance Greens as a political party, analyzing the Alliance Green relationship with the SPD and the PDS, as well as with the constituent parties of former chancellor Kohl's conservative coalition, FDP, CDU and CSU. The discussion here concentrates on the Alliance Greens as a political party in the changed topography of Germany's party landscape. The second cluster focuses on the impact of the Alliance Greens as a movement on the content and discourse of contemporary German politics. It assesses the trajectory of the Alliance Greens as an innovative force, using as a measuring stick the four adjectives western Greens' initially used to define their identity: ecological, socially-conscious [redistributive], grassroots democratic, and nonviolent [pacifist] (*ökologisch, sozial, basisdemokratisch, gewaltfrei*). We conclude with a discussion of policy, which attains particular salience in light of the Alliance Greens' emergence as the third electoral force in the Federal Republic and their recent acceptance of governmental responsibilities at the federal level. In other words, the importance of Green policy positions has grown with the Alliance Greens' entering the inner sanctum of German federal politics in 1998 as the junior partner in the red-green coalition. Our discussion of all three clusters concentrates exclusively on problems, which is not to say that the Alliance Greens have lacked important successes and impressive triumphs. To be sure, all three clusters are intimately related and their separation is of purely heuristic value. They constitute mere components of the changing nature of the Alliance Green identity as actors in the politics of the new Berlin Republic.

The Party Cluster

The end of the Cold War and German unification have altered the trajectory of political development by broadening the opportunities available to the Alliance Greens. Paradoxically, these developments have simultaneously increased the challenges and perils confronting them. This cluster discusses the Alliance Greens' relationship with the other political parties represented in the *Bundestag*.

Sozialdemokratische Partei Deutschlands

For over two decades, an identity crisis has bedeviled the SPD. The Keynesian and trade union wings of the SPD, traditionally the center-left core of the party, have clashed at various times with other forces on the left. One rival was the doctrinaire Marxists both inside and outside of the SPD's youth organization, the Young Socialists (*Jungsozialisten*, JUSOs), and another was the postmodern political formations within the party that challenge the SPD's defense of the welfare state and rhetorical emphasis on full employment (Braunthal, 1994: chap. 6; Silvia, 1992). These long-running internal political divides have produced a familiar pattern in German politics. During the 1990 and 1994 federal electoral cycles the SPD led in the polls at the outset of the campaign, largely owing to protest against the Kohl government, only to lose the federal election when the campaign led voters to focus on the weaknesses of the SPD as well (Silvia, 1995). The SPD turned this perception around in 1998, as much due to the shortcomings of sixteen years of Helmut Kohl in power as to a compelling message on the SPD's part.

German social democracy's identity crisis poses a serious strategic dilemma for the Alliance Greens. This new party's political identity cannot be separated from social democracy on any level of their existence, as they owe their very beginnings not only to the faults and shortcomings but also to the largesse and tolerance of social democracy. The western Greens defined themselves initially in opposition to social democracy's values and political manifestations. Yet many in the alternative movement also viewed themselves by the mid-1980s as social democracy's most reliable and fervent junior partner (at times even more faithful to the core tenets of social democracy than the SPD itself). In the nascent years of the Greens during the 1970s, both the "red" SPD and the Greens viewed a coalition between them as anathema. Yet by the late 1980s, when the pragmatic Green *Realos* finally prevailed in a decade-long internal struggle with the ideologically obstinate *Fundis*, red-green coalitions at all levels of governance had become the western Greens' core instrumental objective. By the late 1990s, the vast majority of the western German political establishment judged a red-green coalition to be acceptable. It is not clear whether the Alliance Greens' coalition desire has been detrimental for the party, but from the logic of party politics, their fixation has brought them electoral success as witnessed by the Greens becoming a junior coalition partner in the federal government in

1998. Such a clear-cut case for success is much harder to make in terms of the logic of movement politics. Suffice it to say that in the battle of the giants of political sociology, Robert Michels and his "iron law of oligarchy" (1962: 365) once again proved victorious (alas) over Frances Fox Piven and Richard Cloward (1977) or any of the other "movement" theorists.

The downside of the Alliance Greens' fixation with the SPD has been that its success as a party has come largely at the expense of the SPD. With the sturdiness and resilience of social democracy in serious doubt, evidenced by the public battle between chancellor Gerhard Schröder and former finance minister Oskar Lafontaine, the Alliance Greens may need to achieve success on their own, which might not even be the most desirable option. This quandary raises that enduring question of the left: What is to be done?

Stated briefly and following Albert Hirschman's (1970) scheme, the Alliance Greens have four options:

1. Loyalty. Try to help the SPD and social democracy in its attempts to remain a relevant force as a *Volkspartei* in Germany by serving as the loyal junior partner within a federal red-green coalition.
2. Venality. Use the new arithmetic of the German party system and play the field by forming a coalition with the party or parties offering the best prospects for implementing as much of the Alliance Green platform as possible.
3. *Rückbesinnung* or exit. Forget the importance of party politics and return to the roots as a movement with its ideologies and convictions.
4. Voice. Try to redefine the content of the political arena so that it reflects Alliance Green preferences and then coalesce with whomever is closest to these preferences. This is the hardest of the four options to achieve but also potentially the most rewarding.

The eventual reality will reflect a combination of all of these four options. Ultimately, of course, the Alliance Greens' abilities to reinvigorate social democracy are rather limited. There is only so much that can be done for a party and a movement that confronts two formidable obstacles: a steady erosion of traditional blue-collar work combined with a shift of economic policy-making competencies to a transnational level.

Partei des Demokratischen Sozialismus

From the Alliance Greens' vantage point there are three relevant components here that deserve serious consideration: the ideological, historical, and sociological sensibilities of the Alliance Greens vs. those of the PDS, the SED legacy, and the presence of the PDS as *the* party of the disaffected eastern Germans. Some eastern Germans, however, have been expressing disaffection by voting for far-right parties (Leslie, this volume).

Beginning with the first, the Alliance Greens continue to represent the historical tradition of the explicitly nonaligned expressions of the German left's "third way." To be sure: there have been plenty of dogmatic non-democratic tributaries to the contemporary Alliance Greens be they former Maoists or Trotskyites, ecological absolutists, or members of various K-groups of the early-to-mid 1970s (Hülsberg, 1988). The Alliance Greens have an ideological and historical legacy that includes much more than a compact between domesticated "spontaneous" leftists (*Spontis*) and renegade social democrats, who currently constitute the hegemonic *Realo* faction. Still, the very essence of the party as well as the movement hails predominantly from what we have come to accept as the new left. Indeed, we would argue that the German Alliance Greens are far and away the most important lasting legacy and institutional manifestation of this new left worldwide. The new left profoundly and irrevocably changed public discourse throughout the political landscape of the industrial world but it failed to attain an influential structural position and voice within national politics or even in the left wing in any major nation except for the Federal Republic.

As we know from electoral studies of the PDS, there is plenty of evidence that this party is particularly successful among young people, that is, *precisely* the western Greens' traditional clientele. Thus, while it is true that the PDS cannot be dismissed as a simple reheating of old left politics, there can be no doubt that the party's essence and legacy are much closer to the world of the old than that of the new left. The PDS's appeal and identity converge much more around old left topics such as employment, the economy and job security, rather than the classic new left icons of ecology, gender equality and other issues of empowerment and personal fulfillment. Though clearly modernized and metamorphosed, the PDS fits squarely into the tradition of the KPD and German Communism. The Greens never have. Thus these two parties represent different traditions and voices of the German left. Yet the PDS and the Alliance Greens have developed into actual competitors for the electoral support of the same clientele: the young, educated and decommodified voters who trained and employed in the public or nonprofit spheres. Why? Because both parties have "forbidden" qualities that are particularly attractive to the young.

The industrial working class in eastern Germany supported either the CDU or SPD in every federal election since the country's unification, so the PDS's votes have come from a potentially Green clientele. A notable exception, of course, is the considerable number of former SED *apparatchiki* and assorted state operatives who continue to play a major role in most facets of the PDS: electoral, organizational, personnel-related, ideological and historical. It is to the western Greens' great credit, and it most certainly behooves their new left origins and orientation, which includes important anarchist and libertarian elements, that they remained highly critical of and skeptical towards the PDS's obvious Stalinist legacy. It also speaks well of the Alliance Greens that they have opposed the

PDS's demonization by segments of the western German public and supported the PDS's right to exist as an important voice for a new, and structurally disadvantaged, segment of the German population. After all, while the West German political establishment was busily embracing the SED regime and when much of the SPD as well as the most important German trade unions were hobnobbing with the Stalinist establishment in East Germany and Eastern Europe (cf. the scandalous behavior of Willy Brandt and Helmut Schmidt on this account), the western Greens as a party took a different path. They unequivocally supported the dissidents in these Stalinist regimes, particularly because East German dissidents were particularly enfeebled and needy of West German support (Silvia, 1993: 29-32).

No West German party can claim to have pursued as steadfast an anti-Stalinist policy towards the East German regime as did the Greens: not the SPD, not the FDP, and most certainly neither the CDU nor the CSU. As a profoundly anti-Leninist party, the Greens took their anti-Stalinism very seriously, as it formed a major facet of their political identity and existence. It still does. Thus, the PDS's Stalinist legacy as well as its obvious Stalinist remnants genuinely trouble the Alliance Greens and pose problems for them in terms of embracing the PDS as another fraternal force in the progressive firmament of German politics. It is good to see that a leftist and progressive opposition to Stalinism continues in the public discourse of German politics and that the Alliance Greens are among the major voices in this opposition. Ironically, however, the PDS attracts many youthful eastern voters despite its more old-fashioned leftist platform, in large part because it has appropriated a radical chic image. The inevitable aging of the Alliance Green leadership, the rhetorical brilliance of Gregor Gysi, the clever iconoclastic advertising most notably in the 1994 and 1998 election campaigns and the now exotic Communist legacy have enabled the PDS to seize the avant-garde image from the Alliance Greens, particularly among the youth of greater Berlin. This has deprived the Alliance

Greens in eastern Germany of the political élan that sustained the Greens in the west, particularly in their early years.

Last, the PDS's continued success among the citizens of the former GDR is a daily reminder for the Alliance Greens of their own woefully inadequate presence in Germany's five eastern Länder. In April 1998, the Alliance Greens lost their last seats in any eastern Landtag when they failed to reach the 5 percent threshold in the Saxony-Anhalt election. While historically understandable, no party that claims to have a countrywide constituency and a universal appeal likes to be excluded from an entire segment of a population and region. The inability to maintain a presence in eastern Germany poses a special problem for the Alliance Greens. Since "the 1960s" never happened in East Germany, post-materialist themes, which still comprise the essence of the western Greens' political platform, have found little resonance in the five eastern Länder where all-too materialist issues such as unemployment and infrastructure predominate. The Alliance Greens, moreover, derive much of their legitimacy from their unequivocal support of the underdog, the disenfranchised and the forgotten. The eastern Germans' rejection of the Alliance Greens repudiates the party's ability to be an effective and empathetic advocate of the more disadvantaged part of Germany. The Alliance Greens' virtual disappearance in eastern Germany confirms the deeply western nature of this party. It is one of the last reminders that the Alliance Greens, despite all their success, have yet to overcome their roots as a western milieu party.

Freie Demokratische Partei

The relationship with the FDP is the only one that is actually problem-free for the Alliance Greens. First, the FDP is the "sick man" of the German party system, hence it poses virtually no threat to the Alliance Greens. To be sure, the FDP still maintains a hydrocephalic existence in Bonn as a safe alternative for those on the right dissatisfied with the CDU/CSU, thereby facilitating potential conservative coalitions in the future. However the party's traditional mandate as the representative of a genuinely liberal constituency in the German polity has all but ceased to exist in a politically meaningful manner.

The legacy of the FDP's liberalism has bifurcated with its civil dimension assumed by the Alliance Greens. On matters related to the individual's protection from excessive encroachments by the state, the Alliance Greens have attained the most vocal presence in Germany. Liberalism's economic dimensions, by contrast, have been absorbed at least in part by certain sectors of the CDU/CSU. In short, the Alliance Greens have no particular problems on account of the FDP, and in fact can continue to be the most direct beneficiaries of the FDP's demise. If the FDP were to disappear, the Alliance Greens would become the unrivaled guardians of civil and human rights on the one hand, and would become the key third force in German politics. This brings us to a discussion of the much-touted "black-green" option.

Christlich Demokratische Union/Christlich Soziale Union

Ever since the Realos triumphed unequivocally over the Fundis in the early 1990s and social democracy's all-too-persistent woes, various political pundits in Germany have floated the hitherto blasphemous idea of seeing various black-green coalitions dotting the German political landscape. Much of this speculation dissipated with the formation of the federal red-green coalition in 1998, but its resumption could easily occur should the SPD – Alliance Greens coalition begin to come apart. Foreign minister Joschka Fischer, the leader of the Realo wing, has a reputation as a brilliant strategist, superb tactician and Realpolitiker par excellence whose ambitions to become foreign minister in the federal government have been fulfilled. Many believe him pragmatic enough to consider an alliance with the CDU/CSU should the need arise. To be sure the changed nature of the country's party topography renders hitherto unthinkable combinations quite realistic. Thus, one need not hang the Alliance Greens' potential CDU/CSU option exclusively on the ambitious personalities of Joschka Fischer or Antje Vollmer. Once again structure appears to be more compelling than agency, which of course is not to say that agency is irrelevant.

Odd as it may seem, there have always been certain areas of commonality in the Greens' and the Christian Democrats' views of politics, which may render some sort of formal or even tacit alliance between these two political groupings perhaps a tad awkward but certainly far from implausible. For example, there is substantial affinity between grass-roots democracy and the politics and policy of subsidiarity in Germany as well as on the level of European affairs. For different reasons, both the CDU/CSU as well as the Alliance Greens prefer decentralized social policy to the usual *étatisme* favored by social democracy. Similarly, on certain matters of conservative values, such as preserving the traditional, rustic elements of German culture, the Greens' world is much closer to the Christian Democratic understanding than it is to social democracy. In foreign policy as well, such issues as the independence of Slovenia and Croatia in 1991, followed by events in Bosnia and in Kosovo, caused segments of the Green party to voice options and preferences that appeared to be much more compatible with the views of the CDU/CSU than those advocated by most, if not all, social democrats. Just as the topic of civil libertarianism created a strong commonality between the Alliance Greens and the FDP, so too have certain aspects of social policy, foreign affairs, and a general understanding of state-society relations fostered at least a conceptual affinity between the CDU/CSU and the Alliance Greens. To be sure, they have not even come close to rivaling the strong and traditional ties between the Alliance Greens and the SPD but, under the right political circumstances, these ties might offer the basis for a black-green dialogue that could lead to a still stigmatized but perhaps not completely unthinkable construct of a black-green coalition.

The Peculiarities of the Eastern German Party Landscape

The eastern German political landscape, to no small degree a product of pathologies resulting from a totalitarian past, the perverse excesses of the final years of Ostpolitik, the uneven pattern of resistance against the SED regime (both demographically and geographically), and the peculiarities of the absorption of the former GDR into the Federal Republic, leaves little political room for the Alliance Greens. The affinity among constituency, ideology and party differs substantially from East to West. The western Christian Democrats and the FDP (unlike the western Greens and the western SPD) merged with eastern parties that had long standing status in the former GDR as junior members of the governing "bloc of anti-fascist democratic parties," known as the National Front. The political preferences of the members of these old eastern parties differ substantially from their western counterparts, but the exigencies of organizational survival have kept the eastern and western wings of the CDU and FDP together in a marriage of convenience. Nonetheless, the regional branches of these two parties frequently espouse widely diverging political positions. Moreover, the legacy of the *relative* relations among different social formations in the former GDR have proved to be at least as powerful as ideology in determining regional party platforms. As eastern German social groups began to link up with the fixed number of available political parties, traditional foes all too often responded by forging an alliance with a rival party without considering underlying ideological incompatibilities. The result has been twofold. Ideology and policy espoused by an eastern branch of a party often differs markedly from the official position of the national party.

Ironically, the eastern SPD resembles the western Greens far more than any other party in the five new Länder (Silvia,

1993: 32-36). Unlike the western SPD, the eastern SPD is a milieu party. It arose out of a narrow segment of dissidents with strongholds in the Lutheran church, the civil rights movement, the non-sanctioned peace initiative and environmental groups who were not a part of mainstream GDR society. The eastern CDU, in contrast, has attracted a large segment of the working class vote that has traditionally gone to the SPD in western Germany. Four decades of Communism have convinced many eastern working class voters (particularly those in Saxony and Thuringia who felt particularly disadvantaged within the old GDR) never to vote for *any* variety of socialism once they have a choice. The FDP has no natural constituency in eastern Germany; Communism decimated the business classes east of the Elbe river and those interested in civil rights had already turned elsewhere.

The western Greens merged with Alliance '90 and the much smaller eastern Green movement in 1990. At first glance, this appeared to be a compatible match, but a closer analysis reveals substantial differences between the two. In particular, a large proportion of the Alliance '90 membership has political sensibilities that are far more akin to those of the western FDP than to the beliefs of the western Greens. Many Alliance '90 members maintain a strong distaste for socialism as a result of their experience under the SED regime, and have therefore been far more critical of policies that rely on government and far more sympathetic about expanding the private sphere. This stands in sharp contrast to the western Greens, most of whom maintain at least a modicum of sympathy toward new left, marxist visions. Many Alliance '90 members also believe that job creation in eastern Germany should take priority over any expansion of environmental protection. This stands in marked contrast to western Greens who saw the renovation of the eastern German economy as a golden opportunity to integrate environmental concerns directly into the production process (Strübin, 1997). These differences (along with personality clashes) help to explain why the merger talks proved so difficult and why the Brandenburg branch of Alliance '90 remains an independent splinter party.

Taken as a whole, these numerous differences between the eastern and western German political landscapes largely explain why the Alliance Greens have been unable to make significant inroads among the eastern German voters. Stubbornly high unemployment and de facto exclusion from most political and economic decision-making centers have exacerbated rather than ameliorated these political differences.

The Movement Cluster

The legacy of the Greens is substantial in the movement cluster, which is the realm outside of parliamentary politics. The presence of the Alliance Greens, as well as that of their numerous predecessors and tributaries, helped alter the form and content of the German and indeed European left to a degree virtually unimaginable barely twenty years ago. Foremost among the Alliance Greens' contributions to this transformation of the European left has been the importance accorded to ecology. Let us not forget that for both the major representatives of the traditional European left, social democracy and communism, technological progress was nothing short of a declaration of faith. Lenin extolled Taylorism, conservative social democrats praised Fordism, Ernst Bloch upheld the virtues of nuclear energy and the worst excesses of urban renewal in such places as Lichterfelde show a clear disregard for ecological concerns. Thirty years ago such concerns were not the most pressing agenda issues of the European left, be it social democratic or communist. In a matter of ten years between 1973 and 1983 the Greens and their immediate predecessors elevated ecology to one of the highest places in the left's intellectual, ideological and programmatic firmament. One simply cannot be a leftist in Europe today and disregard the issue of ecology, still less uphold a productivist credo akin to the one which characterized the old left until the mid-1970s. Despite few readily accepted common denominators among the German and European left, being pro-ecology ranks as one of the few common articles of faith.

Part of the reason for this intra-left harmony is that at least lip service to the primacy of ecology has become a consensual credo of virtually all of European politics. In other words, the Greens succeeded in forcing the entire German establishment to claim to be at least environmentally conscious (*umweltbewusst*) if not in fact environmentally friendly (*umweltfreundlich*), and a surprising percentage actually are. Germany has among the most stringent environmental protection laws in the world. Being seen as inimical to the environment is tantamount to political suicide, except perhaps if one defends the current status quo of having no speed limit on the Autobahn. Greenpeace, though international in name and headquarters, enjoys its greatest support in Germany, and Royal Dutch-Shell's 1995 Brent Spar oil platform incident in the North Sea spawned a much greater level of outrage and indignation among the German public than any of the serial massacres in the post-Yugoslav war. Indeed, the alleged and potential ecological disasters of the Gulf War caused much greater concern in Germany than anywhere else in the world, and constituted a greater worry for the German peace movement than, say, the potential gassing of Jews by virtue of Iraq's SCUD missile attacks on Israel. The Greens' success on the ecology front has been truly impressive: everybody has become "Green" on this issue. In three decades the Greens have altered the public discourse as well as behavior and attitude in Germany relating to all matters of environment and ecology, no mean feat.

Despite the swing toward environmentalism in German politics, the Alliance Greens can still propose ecological programs that the general public find beyond the pale. In early 1998, for example, the Magdeburg party conference of the Alliance Greens approved a proposal to increase taxes on gasoline until it would cost DM 5 per liter (approx. $10 per gallon). This position unleashed a torrent of criticism of the Alliance Greens from all sides of the political spectrum (Frankfurter Rundschau 28 March 1998; Spiegel 30 March 1998).

The tally is even more mixed concerning the Greens' contribution to the socially conscious part of their four-fold credo, and far less impressive, than in the realm of ecology. The Green "contagion," to use Maurice Duverger's well-worn term, has been much more limited in the social sphere, though the Alliance Greens have not surrendered their commitment to social justice and equality. It merely demonstrates three things: First, the social content of Green identity is a good deal murkier than the ecological. Second, unlike ecology, this arena of politics was long occupied prior to the Greens' arrival, making the Greens joiners (not to say Johnny-come-latelies) rather than innovators as they were in the case of ecology. Third, the resistance on the part of outside forces, especially the Alliance Greens' political rivals, was much more formidable in this social area than it was in ecological matters.

There were three major battles in which matters of social justice formed the nucleus of the debate in post-1990 German politics: the status of foreigners on German soil, Germany's competitiveness in the global economy (the "*Standort Deutschland*" controversy), and, of course, social justice and equality vis-à-vis the citizens of the former East Germany.

In the first battle, the Greens assumed by far the most radically solidaristic position: they have wanted to extend full citizenship to all foreigners currently residing in Germany who wished to become Germans. Moreover, the western Greens were major backers of an American-style immigration law that would allow people to immigrate to Germany with the clear prospect of becoming naturalized German citizens after a certain amount of time. The Alliance Greens remained unequivocal defenders of Article 16 of the Basic Law that allowed liberal access to Germany to anybody seeking asylum. Following the SPD's tactically successful (however morally questionable) retreat on this issue in 1992, the Alliance Greens' solidaristic approach toward the numerous asylum seekers and refugees populating makeshift housing in Germany remained little more than a noble moral gesture. Until 1998 it was easier to reach a political consensus in Germany to separate garbage according to four color-coded bins, evidently, than to establish a universalistic policy of inclusion vis-à-vis foreigners, immigrants and asylum seekers. The Alliance Greens' sense of social justice and equality during their years in opposition prior to 1998 had failed to generate meaningful political alliances beyond the merely symbolic creation of human chains with candles in their hands. However, the Alliance Greens participation in government forced the Social Democrats to confront this issue. While the Schröder government backed away from the Alliance Greens' full package of citizenship reform in early 1999, a more modest liberalization of the citizenship statute became law in May 1999.

Concerning the battle to liberalize certain areas of the German political economy, in particular industrial relations, as well as the introduction of greater flexibility in matters such as store closing hours, the Alliance Greens' position remains murky and contradictory. It reflects the diverse opinions expressed by the party's different constituencies, since to some, "*sozial*" denotes a full-fledged support of the unions' position. In essence, this means the unequivocal defense of the status quo: prohibiting regular work on Saturdays and Sundays, no continuous shift work, and maintaining Germany's strict closing hours. This position implies support for a certain social achievement level that from any progressive point of view, would inevitably be a step backwards. Conversely, for other Greens less committed to an alliance with organized labor, the introduction of greater flexibility constitutes less a facilitating of capitalist exploitation than it does a certain enhancement of individual choice and personal empowerment in an increasingly regulated and bureaucratized world. While retail unionists might justifiably be opposed to working additional shifts in the evenings or on weekends under the recently liberalized shop laws, working women might find such newly flexible arrangements quite convenient, perhaps even necessary. "*Sozial*" in this case means different things to different groups within the Alliance Greens.

In the effort to attain the third key social objective, a reduction of inequality, the Alliance Greens have increasingly been crowded out by the growing prominence of the PDS, which has been proclaiming itself, with some justification, the authentic voice of eastern German discontent. Here, too, the Alliance Greens have been immensely considerate of social discrepancies and rallied in support of the disadvantaged. That the party is now called Bündnis '90/DIE GRÜNEN clearly attests to the party's sensitivity to the eastern Germans' disadvantaged status, and their need to be accorded special respect. The name places the eastern segment of the party before the western one despite the overwhelming numerical predominance of western Greens as a percentage of the membership. Moreover, as is well known, eastern Germans play a major role in the Alliance Greens' leadership even though the party has been electorally very weak in the East. In a certain way, then, the party's social commitment and engagement have not been brought to bear in full in the East due to the Alliance Greens' weakness and the PDS's predominance there.

Grassroots democracy, it could be argued, fell victim to the exigencies of a modern party's effective operation in the increasingly competitive world of a liberal democracy. One of the most knowledgeable students of the Alliance Greens, Joachim Raschke (1993), argues that it has completely disappeared from the Alliance Greens' world. Once the principles of rotation were abandoned in order to safeguard leadership continuity and to foster name and face recognition of Green leaders in a television-dominated polity, a key ingredient of the movement's originally anti-Michelsian impulse and convictions disappeared. Soon after, the Greens, de facto if not de jure, abandoned the "imperative mandate," yet another mechanism by which the movement's base was trying to control the party's leadership. To be sure, important ingredients of the movement's penchant for radical democracy still remain in place, most significant of which is the continued practice of not permitting any multiple office holding among any of the Green activists. This leads to a strict separation between the holders of elective positions and the party functionaries: no other party in Germany comes even close to such a fundamentally democratic distribution of power among its leaders and elites, as it eliminates the layer of party members and *apparatchiki*, that is a major feature of all other German parties, with the possible exception of the FDP. Moreover, by continuing to have such a low membership, the Alliance Greens' base remains their voters rather than their members.

The Policy Cluster

Just as ecological stringency and environmental absolutism have formed the very core of Green identity for nearly twenty years, so too were pacifism and nonviolence crucial parts of the western Greens' self-image until the 1990s, when the party began to adjust to the post Cold War world. The western Greens traditional pacifism and non-violence assumed many dimensions. The most important were vehement opposition to NATO, strict neutralism and an anti-bloc attitude in international affairs, vocal criticism of the army, advocacy of civil defense as the best way to protect Germany and Europe from all potential enemies, severe opposition to any Great Power intervention anywhere in the world (especially by the United States), unequivocal opposition to the stationing of any nuclear weapons on German soil, and a rejection of even the possibility of any engagement by Germans in any military activity anywhere outside Germany's borders. This last point was such an implicitly understood taboo in the Green milieu that it was barely mentioned prior to the early 1990s, though even a NATO military engagement that included Germans was unthinkable for virtually all segments of German society, excepting perhaps the far right of the CDU and parts of the CSU.

The nonviolent or pacifist dimension of Green policy addresses three issues that reach well beyond the identity of the Alliance Greens as a party or a movement. First, it highlights features of the Greens' gradually changing relationship vis-à-vis the state. Second, it offers a commentary on the altered role of Germany and German politics in the new Europe. Third, it provides some insights into the interaction between power and democracy in a new Germany surrounded by a new Europe (Huelshoff, Markovits, and Reich, 1993). In other words, passionate debates within the Alliance Greens about non-violence represent not only a redefinition of their identity but also constitute an initiation into the world of the establishment, the socially acceptable, the players, as Green foreign minister Joschka Fischer can attest. If during the 1980s the western Greens' contribution to German politics, as well as the formation of their identity, lay in the realm of domestic politics, the latter half of the 1990s witnesses a similar formative struggle, but this time in the domain of foreign policy as the junior member of a governing coaltion. The changed playing field reflects the altered nature of both Germany's role and position in Europe and the Alliance Greens' identity and role in German politics.

The first rumblings of this transformation began during the Gulf War. Even though most Alliance Greens were vehemently opposed to the campaign against Iraq (having uttered nary a word about Iraq's invasion of Kuwait in August 1990), some key individuals, notably Joschka Fischer, Waltraud Schoppe and

Hubert Kleinert, the "super-*Realos*" in other words, advocated the expeditious deployment of German Army-owned Patriot missiles to Israel for its defense against Iraq's SCUD attacks. Indeed, this position attained the status of policy in the Green Party's Hessen district, traditionally one of the most realist in the Federal Republic.

The second step came in the Alliance Greens' advocacy of Slovenian and Croatian independence in mid-1991, immediately after the brief war of secession between Serb-dominated Yugoslavia and the Yugoslav National Army on the one side and Slovenia and Croatia on the other. The Alliance Greens' "super-Wilsonianism," which advocated support for any people's aspirations for self-determination and political independence, coupled with the eastern Greens' particular distaste for the Stalinist regime of Slobodan Milosevic, which transformed the party into a particularly vocal proponent of the eventual breakup of Yugoslavia.

The third step ensued in the passionate intra-German debate about the permissibility and desirability of the deployment of German troops in NATO engagements. While the Alliance Greens remained by and large true to the fundamentalist principles of their rejectionist members on this matter, there were certain discernable cracks in the Alliance Greens' previously ironclad position. Thus, while the PDS took a categorical position on this matter – German troops or military personnel were never to be deployed anywhere outside Germany under anybody's aegis, be it the United Nations, NATO, the Western European Union or anything else – the Alliance Greens upheld the possibility of participation under certain particularly compelling circumstances and with very specific limitations. German military personnel could participate in activities outside of Germany's borders according to the Alliance Greens provided that these activities occurred under the aegis of the UN (but *not* under NATO), that all German personnel were fully integrated into the UN command (that is, that they would wear "blue helmets"), and that their tasks were purely auxiliary and supportive and under no circumstances combative. Tellingly, the PDS outflanked the Alliance Greens on this matter "from the left."

The fourth step began with the publication of Joschka Fischer's letter to his party colleagues in which he implored them to rethink the Alliance Greens' hitherto sacrosanct tenet of nonviolence and pacifism in light of the massacres in Bosnia (tageszeitung 2 August 1995). Precipitated by the Bosnian Serbs' butchery of Bosnian Muslim men in Srebrenica in July 1995, Fischer basically asked the Alliance Greens to consider the following issues and existential dilemmas. Won't the German left lose its soul if it shirks its duty under whatever convenient, perhaps even partially legitimate, pretext not to intervene in what amounts to massive genocide? How is one to deal with a new fascism which mocks reason, spurns appeals for clemency, refuses to negotiate in good faith, and seems only to understand force? Life and liberty, two fundamental Green principles, seem to be irreconcilably opposed to pacifism and nonviolence, which are equally central Green principles. What is to be done? Fischer asked. His answer, though not specific, was nevertheless crystal clear: under conditions of genocide, such as had occurred repeatedly in Bosnia, it was the Alliance Greens' political *and* moral duty to support a military intervention by a multilateral force which included German military personnel engaged in combat.

The die had been cast. One of the most sacrosanct Green taboos was finally broken. The enormity of Fischer's statement could best be gauged by the complete silence preceding the storm, a silence not simply a consequence of the usually slow midsummer months on the German political scene. Instead, Fischer's words finally brought an issue to a head that had been dividing the Alliance Greens and the German left for quite some time. As expected, the criticisms of Fischer were vocal, relentless, and came from all sides of the Alliance Greens and the German left. Fischer was accused of everything from being guilty of Eurocentrism, to having become a stooge of NATO and the Americans, and from taking sides in a murky civil war in which all combatants have been guilty of war crimes, to forsaking the burdens and special responsibilities of German history that in the opinion of many automatically preclude Germany ever taking part in an armed conflict again. Many party members reminded Fischer that at a special party convention in October 1993 a vast majority of those present had made it amply clear that they wished Green policy to advocate a decisive abstention from any military engagements in Bosnia regardless of the circumstances.

That abstention still seemed to represent the wish of the Green majority became evident at a special foreign policy meeting convened by the party on 30 September 1995 in Bonn. Fischer delivered the main theses of his letter once again, to the often vehement objections and criticisms of many of the convened Green activists, but still, there were important party members and sympathizers who rallied to Fischer's side. By far the most prominent view was that it was *precisely* the burden of German history that should make leftists particularly sensitive to any renewal of fascism and genocide, especially on such a scale as in Bosnia. Especially powerful was the argument that it was simply hypocritical and profoundly ahistorical of the Alliance Greens to hide behind an absolutist interpretation of pacifism, since some of the most vocal pacifists had been ardent advocates of various Third World liberation struggles which were anything but nonviolent. Fischer's supporters argued that absolute pacifism was actually a relatively recent strain of alternative thought that superseded the earliest beliefs of the peace movement.

Fischer's supporters won the day, but failed to vanquish their opponents within the Alliance Greens. The supporters of absolute pacifism continue to wage a guerilla campaign within the Alliance Greens. For example, at the party's March 1998 Magdeburg conference, leftwing pacifists took advantage of an overconfident *Realo* majority and less than complete attendance at a late night vote on security policy to pass resolutions rejecting future participation of the German army in any peace making missions, including the ongoing effort in Bosnia (Süddeutsche Zeitung 9 March 1998). The shock from this exceptional tactical victory by the pacifist left shows the transformation that has taken place. Ten years before, the media would have judged such a result as normal rather than a stunning reversal of recent party policy.

The outbreak of the war with Yugoslavia during the early months of the Red-Green coalition greatly intensified internal tensions within the Alliance Greens. It also forced the Alliance Greens to take the last step toward full acceptance of the exigencies of power, albeit a bit sooner than they otherwise would have preferred. The war also made plain that the use of armed force remains the single most divisive issue in the party.

On 13 May 1999, a month into the "air war," the Alliance Greens held an extraordinary party convention in Bielefeld. Joschka Fischer rejected leaving the coalition, saying "I do not want to leave the government, but instead change the course of the government".

Bielefeld highlighted two things. First, the Greens' long transformation from protest movement to "responsible" party capable of governing was complete. Second, the realo-fundi divide had not softened over the course of the decade and could easily hamstring the party in the future.

Conclusion

The Alliance Greens as a party have survived many of the "childhood diseases" that were the byproduct of many of their efforts to preserve grassroots participation. This has made them far more effective and dependable as a party, but this progress has only been achieved by gradually dismantling the Greens as a movement.

Some describe this transformation as a necessary maturation; others denounce it as a sellout. The debate over the future defining contours of the post Cold War Alliance Greens has only just begun. The controversy over the use of German armed forces abroad, particularly with the Alliance Greens in government, is particularly important because it is not only a clear sign that the Green party has entered a new phase of redefining its identity. It is also an indicator that the greater significance of this redefinition extends far beyond the Green party's narrow confines. As such, Fischer's role as foreign minister represents a microcosm of the current major redefinition of German power and democracy in Europe. Although the outcome remains unclear, it is already certain that the debate on this issue within the Green party will have a substantial impact on Germany's place in Europe and the world.

Chapter 6

THE MAJOR PARTIES
Dealignment and Realignment in
Post-Cold War Germany

∽

Henry Kreikenbom

Introduction

Lipset and Rokkan (1967) created the cleavage theory as an instrument to analyze the party behavior of voters, and their theory has been discussed in Western Europe ever since. It has been further refined through discussions about the processes of dealignment and realignment, and since the 1980s we have seen declining party alignment in all West European countries (Dalton, Flanagan, and Beck, 1984).

Declining party alignment has also been evident in West Germany, where a new cleavage was created through the economic and social processes of modern industrial society that broke open the three-party system of CDU, SPD and FDP and introduced the Green Party (Dalton and Rohrschneider, 1990; Küchler, 1990; Kaase and Klingemann, 1994; Bürklin, 1994). It remains to be seen whether dealignment will be accompanied by new coalitions of voters and parties, or whether it will lead to a party system that is based on a rational choice orientation towards parties on the part of voters. Since the fall of the Berlin Wall, Germany has been faced with an additional line of conflict that has continued to influence the voting behavior of East Germans. This ideological cleavage separates those who were integrated into the GDR political system and lived according to socialist ideals, and those who could not identify with socialism and sympathized with West German lifestyles. Integrating East German citizens into the West German economic and political system therefore poses particular problems for unification.

The fusion of East and West German political cultures also raises new theoretical, empirical and methodological questions:

1. In analyzing this fusion, aggregate data analysis must be combined with individual-level data analysis, complemented by qualitative interviews. Such use of multiple methods in research is a good way to establish how people perceive social change and how they behave within the party system, and combines cleavage theory with the theory of party identification.
2. From the perspective of rational choice theory, affective party alignments can be useful in simplifying the process of understanding. As a simple way of processing information and simplifying reality, affective party alignments serve as a basis for the rational decision-making process during elections (Fuchs and Kühnel, 1994: 340). If voters persist in this affective orientation, their party preference can evolve into a voting habit, which means party alignment can be used as a comprehensive paradigm.
3. The concept of a "realigning process" (Dalton, 1986: 450) has priority within cleavage theory over the concept of dealignment. From the point of view of the individual,

new coalitions emerge between voters and parties in three stages: (1) when new issue preferences emerge and voters' values change, (2) through the transformation of basic ideological orientations during the process of realignment, and (3) in changing fundamental ideological orientations into new affective party alignments (Dalton and Rohrschneider, 1990: 297-98).

In what follows, I first describe the process of dealignment and realignment in West Germany up to 1989 in empirical terms. Then I turn to the cleavage structure in the GDR and the new Länder before addressing the possible future of the coalition between voters and parties in a united Germany.

Dealignment and Realignment in West Germany from 1945 to 1990

After World War II, the parties, and in particular the SPD, began anew with their old ideologies, much of their previous leadership, and much of their previous organizational structure. Falter (1981), in an analysis of the first federal parliamentary election in 1949, shows that the CDU/CSU had remobilized those who had supported the Zentrum and the Bayrische Volkspartei, the conservative parties of the Weimar Republic. In addition, though the CDU/CSU had enjoyed the support of catholic voters for more than forty years, it was able to create an interdenominational majority in the first years of the Federal Republic. The FDP, by contrast, was best supported in districts that had supported the Deutsche Volkspartei and the Deutsche Demokratische Partei, indicating that changes to geographic an social structures in postwar German had not destroyed the milieus that had formerly determined German cleavages (Schmitt, 1987). The traditional cleavages that arose at the end of the nineteenth century lived on, and the 1953 election did not result in a realignment. Nevertheless, the strong increase in the number of voters and the continuity in voting behavior during the next fifteen years suggests that the elections of 1953 were a "critical election" (Falter, 1981: 215).

An analysis of the social correlates in the elections from 1953 to 1980 shows that in occupational terms, farmers and the self-employed consistently heavily favored the CDU/CSU, while workers, especially those who were Protestant, favored the SPD. Catholics across all occupational categories supported the CDU/CSU, though half the catholic workers in 1969 and 1972 were willing to vote SPD. Consistent, if lower, FDP support came from salaried workers and officials (*Beamte*), as well as from those who were Protestant and self-employed. Generally, salaried workers and officials have split their vote, with the tendency of Protestants to vote SPD and Catholics to vote CDU/CSU in these groups canceling each other out (Schultze, 1983: 10).

Political behavior has changed since the end of the 1960s. Along with the revolution in political participation (Kaase, 1982), there has also been a transition from a "subject" to a "civic" culture (Almond and Verba, 1965; Barnes and Kaase, 1979; Gabriel, 1987; Berg-Schlosser, 1990; Fuchs, Klingemann, and Schöbel, 1991). The younger and better educated citizens have become politically mobilized (Schmitt, 1987, vol 2: 23-45), and changes in women's voting behavior (Lepsius, 1973b) reflect new tendencies in the political system and are themselves an outgrowth of the development of modern industrial society.

In this process, the historical cleavages have lost much of their influence on affective party alignments, though they retain residual force even into the present. One consequence of secularization, for example, has been to move away from the cleavage along confessional lines that divided Catholics from Protestants and to supplant it with a cleavage between those who are religious or church-oriented and those who are nonreligious and not church oriented (Pappi, 1985). Starting in the early 1970s, a further cleavage has arisen owing to the ecology and citizen initiative movements. The existing party system was also shaken up by the Green Party, which since the early 1990s can be considered an established party. There has also been a general reduction in party identification since the mid-1980s (Kaase and Klingemann, 1994: 390; Rattinger, 1994).

All of this leads to the conclusion that by the 1980s the Federal Republic had undergone a process of party realignment that one might have expected already at the founding of the German state in 1949.

Party Alignment in the GDR

Much as in postwar West Germany, there was continuity in party traditions and in the party-voter coalition in the Soviet Occupied Zone (Broszat and Weber, 1990: 381-93, 435-504, 544-57, 584-91; Falter, 1996). If we compare the results of the state parliament elections in 1946 with the free elections to the Volkskammer on 18 March 1990, one can discern a cleavage structure specific to the GDR. This cleavage can be characterized as a fundamental ideological conflict between those who shaped and supported the bureaucratized socialist system and those who distanced themselves from this same system and were more oriented toward West German society.

The reasons this cleavage emerged were various. In 1945, in conjunction with the Soviet military administration, the SED organized a unitary "block of antifascist democratic parties," designated as the National Front by 1950. This meant that by 1949 it was impossible to vote for different lists of party candidates, because parties were no longer separated, and thus party-specific voting was psychologically irrelevant. As a result, the conflict between those who supported bureaucratized socialism and those who would have preferred other forms of social development was no longer evident, at least not on the surface.

In terms of the party landscape, those parties that had previously represented religious and middle class milieus, such as the Liberal Democratic and Christian Democratic parties, were politically paralyzed, their connection with their traditional support base severed. To further undermine support for such parties, the SED founded the National Democratic and Democratic Farmer parties in 1948. Even within the parapolitical sector of associations, party connections to the Liberal or Christian Democrats were limited since many such associations were at least indirectly controlled by the SED. Some associations were even integrated for electoral purposes into the unified list of the National Front, meaning that the influence of these previously existing parties over groups they were otherwise closely connected to was further reduced.

In terms of property, the expropriation of industrial capital and of larger landed estates between 1945 and 1972, farm collectivization, east to west migration, with its political and economic consequences, and the centrally planned economy changed social, political and economic relationships within the population. Such sociostructural changes affected the size, internal structures and the roles of social milieus in GDR society. Middle class and religious milieus were on the decline and only continued to exist in the shadow of the GDR political system. Even the proletarian milieus declined as a result of the recruitment of workers, farmers and much of the lower middle class into the socialist service class (Solga, 1994: 532), though the development of the welfare state played a part as well. The social democratic cleavage between employer and employee decreased as well because as a sociostructural phenomenon it simply ceased to exist. In addition, the end of representing this cleavage as it was previously manifested in institutions that acted as intermediaries, and the development of a welfare state lifestyle, rendered specifically proletarian interests less important.

Finally, those whose role it was to carry out the orders of the political elite, for lack of actual political participation, adopted a strategy of output orientation. Yet the ideological cleavage between those who controlled political and economic power and those whose role it was to implement official decisions as best they could was increasing. Those who were integrated into the system had a fundamentally socialist orientation and planned their careers in accordance with the objectives of the political leadership. But those who distanced themselves from the system and had a negative opinion of socialist ideology had no opportunity until 1990 to break away from it. The closing off of GDR society from the western world forced such people to integrate themselves socially while engaged in a kind of ideological emigration: integrating themselves as much as was necessary, but distancing themselves as much as they could. In practice, this principle was lived out in various ways. One could cultivate a traditional party identification within the family or among a circle of friends, but one could also adopt a more pragmatic stance, as some younger people did. A level of political conformity with the system was necessary if one wanted a university education, so many made use of the bloc parties as a kind of niche even when it was without much ideological enthusiasm or sense of loyalty to the state. The children of religious or middle class families, and occasionally even younger people from the families of the elite or the socialist service class, began to organize themselves by the mid-1970s under the aegis of the church to discuss the problems they encountered in socialist society. This was one of several niches within the system that made it possible to avoid having to show forced loyalty to the SED state.

Most of those who distanced themselves from the system were oriented politically toward the West German parties and socially toward a West German lifestyle, though this was of course not measurable prior to 1990. After that date we could conduct retrospective surveys that asked (in Jena) about orientations toward West German parties prior to the fall of the Berlin Wall, and more than 60 percent of those asked said they had oriented themselves toward a specific West German party before 1989 (Bluck and Kreikenbom, 1991; Kreikenbom, 1992: 17).

This type of party orientation came about through both internal and external factors, and was the result of both indirect and direct socialization. Indirect socialization came partly from broadcasts of West German TV and radio that could be received in the East (Hesse, 1988), but personal contacts through relatives, as well as contacts with friends and tourists particularly during the trips to Hungary that were still possible to take for East Germans despite the division of Germany, also exerted an influence (Kreikenbom and Stapelfeld, 1994: 177-79). In addition, owing to agreements between East and West German governments, during the 1980s East Germans had more opportunities to visit the Federal Republic, and such visits made strong impressions on many East Germans.

Direct socialization was a perhaps inadvertent consequence of official propaganda on the part of the regime. The two economic and political systems were repeatedly compared in order to show the superiority of socialism, both strengthening the tendency on the part of East Germans to draw personal comparisons and leading individual East Germans to see the Federal Republic more positively than its socialist alternative. Primary socialization also took place within the family, where children learned fundamental political orientations toward party and party ideology, with the result that many learned to hold two different opinions simultaneously, one official but the other private. Finally, intra-German politics at the mesolevel allowed East Germans to learn more about West German parties and they could see what West German parties did in negotiations with the SED and the GDR government to help East Germans attain more democracy and freedom.

Contemporary Empirical Evidence of Cleavages among East Germans

In October 1994, I conducted a survey among 1000 East and 1000 West Germans over 18, dividing the East German cohort into one group that identified itself with a party and identified themselves the same way in the GDR, and into another group that began to identify themselves with a party for the first time only after 1989. I investigated these "continual" and "new" party identifiers by party orientation prior to 1989, by degree of political involvement in the GDR, and by how they formerly compared East and West German political systems.

The results indicated that about 70 percent of those who identified with the PDS in 1994 did not identify with any West German party prior to 1989, indicating a certain ideological resistance toward the West German party system by these PDS-identifiers. Of the minority remainder, the strongest identification was with the SPD (17 percent). Qualitative interviews with fifty Jena citizens in 1993 and 1994 confirmed this finding, for interviewees who identified themselves with the PDS fundamentally criticized the party system of the Federal Republic, finding it representative of the capitalist system. The social image of the SPD resulted in only weak affinities with it, though some interviewees sympathized with the Greens owing to their engagement in ecological and citizen participation issues (Kreikenbom and Stapelfeld, 1994: 171-75).

By contrast, those who had continually identified themselves with CDU or SPD were not as deeply integrated into the central organizations of the GDR. To be sure, membership in the trade union and youth organization, both official mass organizations, was relatively high (43 to 71 percent) among both new or continuing CDU or SPD identifiers. Yet depending on category, such membership was 10 to 50 percent lower than among PDS-identifiers, indicating less social and political integration into the system.

When interviewees compared the political systems of the GDR and the Federal Republic, their different perceptions became quite evident. Most of those who identified with the PDS said the opportunity to participate in governmental decision-making processes was poor, whether in the GDR or in united Germany since 1990, with about one-third evaluating it has having worsened. Nearly 70 percent of PDS-identifiers were dissatisfied as well with the opportunities to participate in local political decision-making processes, with more than half of the opinion that things were better in the GDR.

PDS-identifiers, additionally, can be broken into two subgroups. One subgroup, at the time of interview, was satisfied with the freedom to express personal opinions in the GDR but was unsatisfied with the conditions in the mid-1990s. The other subgroup was satisfied with the mid-1990s conditions but in retrospect was not satisfied with the freedoms that had been allowed in the GDR. If one examines those who continually identified themselves with the CDU/CSU, then one finds a group satisfied with political conditions in united Germany; SPD-identifiers, on the other hand, hold quite divergent opinions on the issue of participation in decision-making processes, but resemble CDU/CSU-identifiers in their strong satisfaction with the freedom to express personal opinions in the mid-1990s. Support for this assessment comes from research indicating that PDS voters agree more with socialist ideals than other voters do, with a proportionately increasing number of PDS voters among those agreeing with questions that measure socialist ideology (Falter and Klein, 1994: 32).

Table 6-1 examines the age structure and the party identification of interviewees. The largest proportion of continuous CDU/CSU-identifiers belong to the older cohort that built the GDR born in the 1920s and 1930s, while half the PDS-identifiers belong to the younger cohorts from the 1950s and 1960s that grew up under the socialist system. Only a quarter of PDS-identifiers belong to the "builders" generation. SPD-identifiers, whether continuous or newer, are more evenly spread across the generations, with a significant gain (14 percent) among the youngest cohort of new identifiers compared with the continuous SPD-identifiers (6 percent). It is also notable that among new CDU/CSU-identifiers a substantially larger proportion (27 percent) come from the first GDR generation of the 1950s and early 1960s; among the continuous CDU/CSU identifiers the percentage (14 percent) is much lower.

Table 6-1 Age Structure and Party Identification in the GDR (in percent)

Identification	continuous			new	
Party	CDU/CSU	SPD	PDS	CDU/CSU	SPD
Weimar (1900-1919)	4	4	3	5	3
GDR Builders (1920-1935)	42	28	26	32	29
Transitional (1936-1950)	27	33	21	27	30
First GDR (1951-1965)	14	30	39	27	25
Second GDR (1966-1976)	13	6	11	10	14
N	86	80	74	117	105

Source: Kreikenbom and Stapelfeld (1995: 109, 129)

If we next turn to occupational and educational levels (Table 6-2), we can see that a great many of those who identified with the PDS underwent political socialization into GDR institutions, more so than those of other party identifiers. The majority of those who continually identified with CDU/CSU or SPD belonged to the category of skilled workers, implying a low level of socialization into political institutions. If one adds unskilled workers as well, particularly among the continuous CDU/CSU-identifiers, one sees this phenomenon even more clearly. Education-level correlations with party identifications sheds some light on the social structure of the GDR. Those with less education were often put in the position of carrying out official decisions as best they could, while the better educated more often belonged to the socialist service class and to the political leadership.

Table 6-2 Occupation/Education and Party Identification in eastern Germany (in percent)

Identification	continuous			new	
Party	CDU/CSU	SPD	PDS	CDU/CSU	SPD
Unskilled Workers	16	4	1	9	11
Skilled Workers	57	57	40	68	59
Better Educated	28	31	59	23	30
N	86	80	74	110	100

Source: Kreikenbom and Stapelfeld (1995: 109, 130)

Turning to the results of the Volkskammer elections in 1990 and 1994, we can also see several cleavages in the new Länder. In terms of age groups, the CDU/CSU attracts more older than younger voters, the SPD attracts evenly across all age groups, and the smaller parties (FDP, Greens, even Republikaner) more strongly attract the youngest voters. The most striking change was the sharp increase from 1990 to 1994 in PDS support across all age groups, changing from a range of 6 to 10 percent (depending on age) to 17 to 23 percent. In terms of religion (Table 6-3), the majority of Catholics and Protestants voted for the CDU, while the majority of the nonreligious voted for the SPD and PDS. This cleavage was predetermined by the conflict between the churches and the atheistic politics pursued by the SED; GDR churches were in fact a symbol of resistance and help constitute one type of ideological cleavage. In occupational terms, workers consistently favored the CDU (1990: 50 percent; 1994: 41 percent), with the SPD profiting from the decline by raising its share from 25 to 35. Farmers (59 percent in 1994) and the independent (50 percent in 1990, 48 percent in 1994) were the strongest supporters of the CDU/CSU. Salaried workers and officials, though favoring the CDU/CSU over the SPD by about 10 percent in 1990, were close to parity by 1994. Here the most notable change was the sharp drop in FDP support between 1990 and 1994 and the equally sharp rise in PDS support in both occupational groups.

Table 6-3   Volkskammer Voting Results by Denomination, 1990 and 1994 (in percentages, rounded)

	Religion		
Parties	**Catholic**	**Protestant**	**None**
CDU/CSU			
1990	66	53	33
1994	69	53	27
SPD			
1990	12	20	29
1994	20	29	34
FDP			
1990	11	15	13
1994	3	5	3
Alliance 90/Greens			
1990	6	6	9
1994	3	5	3
PDS			
1990	2	2	13
1994	3	6	29
Others			
1990	2	2	2
1994	4	2	3

Source: Forschungsgruppe Wahlen (1990, 1994b)

The SPD has not been able to profit as much from the cleavages, as those who are SPD-identifiers can be found along a wide ideological spectrum. Many sympathize with certain socialist ideas or with the PDS, weakening their alignment with the SPD. The older social democratic cleavage was weakened in the GDR and has yet to be reestablished in united Germany.

The same is not true of the CDU/CSU or the PDS. Here the alignment is primarily due to ideological orientation, with voting motivations more often the result of affective identification. Affective identification plays a lesser role for the SPD voters. For them, issues and candidates, or situational factors, play more important roles in their voting decisions. Yet the issues raised by the SPD have evoked less sympathy among East Germans than the issues raised by other parties, and problems with individual SPD candidates has damaged the image of the party as a whole, which one could see in the particular case of the Berlin election in October 1995 (Kaase and Klingeman, 1994; Forschungsgruppe Wahlen, 1994b, 1995; Schultze, 1995; Schmitt, 1995).

Current and Future Party Alignments in East and West Germany

The legacy of the GDR has remained as an ideological cleavage in the Eastern part of united Germany, a conflict between those who criticize the market-based democratic system and those whose disappointment with socialism leads them to support the federal system of united Germany. This cleavage is reflected in the tendency for workers and the religious to vote more often CDU than PDS or SPD, and for the elderly, especially the better-educated who previously supported the GDR, as well as for many younger people, to vote PDS. The integration of the SPD into East German politics has continued to be problematic, as they have not been able to profit from this ideological cleavage.

One part of the difference here is that alignment with the CDU and PDS is stronger than that found for other parties, measurable in the congruence between party alignment and voting behavior. Compared with West Germans, individual integration within the party system is not as widespread in the East.

Among interviewees, the proportion who feel strong party alignment and the proportion who claim to sympathize with a particular party is of a similar size, but there are more who claim a "less strong" alignment to a party in the West, and more who have no party alignment at all in the East.

Party identification has long been measured in the West German population, and has been declining over time, including in the 1990s (Dalton and Rohrschneider, 1990). Party identification in the East has been measured since 1991. As one can see in Table 6-4, the number who identify with party and the subjective quality of the identification is somewhat smaller and lower in the East than in the West (Rattinger, 1993, 1994, 1995). However, there is no substantial difference in the subjective intensity of party identification. "The manner in which East Germans lean towards parties means their differences to West Germans is a matter of gradation, not of fundamental difference. Elements of party identification are in the foreground, but components of a situational preferences are more visible in the East" (Gluchowski and Zelle, 1992: 263). Those who oriented themselves toward a West German party before the Berlin Wall fell developed more of a party identification than others, illustrating the important effects of political socialization processes in the GDR. Indeed, a study done in the early 1990s indicated that those East Germans who had identified before 1989 with West German parties were twice as likely to have a fundamental identification and less than half as likely to have no identification with parties (Gluchowski and Zelle, 1992: 265).

Trends in party identification also show a change from 1993 to 1994 that is greater in the East than in the West, suggesting situational factors are at play in influencing party identification. Two parties in particular seem to have profited from this trend in the East, the CDU/CSU and the PDS.

The CDU in 1994 rebounded to its 1991 level, for which several causes may be suggested. For one, 1994 was a "super election year" which probably positively affected party identifi-

Table 6-4 Strength of Party Identification, East and West (in percent, cumulative data)

	Year				
Strength	1990	1991	1992	1993	1994
Very Strong					
West	11	10	8	6	9
East	NA	5	4	4	5
Strong					
West	28	23	20	18	23
East	NA	22	18	15	19
Medium/Weak					
West	34	36	38	38	32
East	NA	30	31	29	30
No Response/ Don't Know					
West	27	31	34	38	32
East	NA	43	47	52	46
N					
West	11,169	11,267	11,143	11,186	12,247
East	NA	9,500	11,745	11,647	12,848

Source: ZDF, Politbarometer (1991-1994)

cation. For another, changes in public sentiment increased CDU support, a likely combination of stronger party alignment and a positive reaction to CDU/CSU issues, in particular over economics, and candidates (Kaase and Klingemann, 1994; Jung and Roth, 1994; Forschungsgruppe Wahlen, 1994b; Schmitt, 1995; Schultze, 1995; Eckstein and Pappi, 1994).

PDS electoral successes at the federal level and the continued increase in identifying with the PDS are not only the result of situational factors like unemployment or frustration, however. Rather, one sees here the long-term effects of socialization among PDS-identifiers. The strongest feeling of identification among all the parties, as measured in six surveys conducted during 1993 and 1994, was among those who identified themselves with the PDS. This intensity of identification, the ideological orientation of identifiers, and the other social correlates leads one to the conclusion that the PDS enjoys a solid, milieu-anchored base in the new Länder (Schultze, 1995: 344).

In the 1994 federal election, the PDS received about 20 percent of the votes in the new Länder, a level nearly equivalent to PDS-identifier levels in 1994, but owing to the electoral rules they were not able to reach the minimum threshold. In the 1998 elections, the PDS did attain the minimum threshold with 5.1 percent of the vote. They also received majorities in several constituencies in East Berlin. In the middle term, it is likely that the PDS will become the third political force in Landtage and in the local parliaments in the new Länder. Their success at the national level depends on their successful integration into West German society, the positive public image of their candidates particularly in East Berlin, and the development of a strategy that will overcome the internal differences over aims and ideology that have erupted within the party between the leadership and various factions of party members (Lang, Moreau, and Neu, 1995: 17).

Integration rests in part on the PDS ability to influence and win the support of younger and better educated voters disillusioned by the transformation of the Greens from a radical-democratic protest party into an established and power-sharing party. Success also depends upon PDS candidates who have yet to establish a consistent basis of support, yet another reason for integration into West German society. As with the Greens in the early 1980s, PDS success rests on how the internal disputes are resolved, in this case whether the party will be able to shed its Communist ideology and transform itself into a radical-democratic one. Given the East German milieu, this may prove to be quite a political stretch.

Modern industrial society fragmented West German social structure, but despite this, both SPD and CDU/CSU still receive much of their support from older voter-party coalitions. A new political and social milieu developed by the end of the 1970s that helped the Greens to become established, indicating that there is precedent for the PDS doing the same. However, this new milieu has not been able to develop as strongly in the new Länder, and the fusion of West German Greens with the East German Bündnis 90 movement in 1993 has meant the specifically East German interests have been on the decline within the unified party (Niclauß, 1995: 99). Both of these processes have resulted in weak support for the unified party among voters in the new Länder.

The traditional FDP voters also do not exist in the East, because the GDR social and political structure undermined the non-Catholic self-employed and officials who otherwise would have been likely supporters. That has made the integration of the FDP in the new Länder problematic, along with a lack of good candidates and issues to mobilize potential voters. It was only with the support of its traditional base in West Germany that the FDP was able to reach the necessary 5 percent in the 1994 federal elections, but in what had been their best polling districts, they lost many votes to the Greens (Frankfurter Rundschau 21 October 1994).

One conclusion is that owing to its specific cleavage structure, there is a fundamental political and ideological conflict that exists in the East between CDU and PDS, whereas in the West it is between CDU/CSU and SPD. Changes in the electoral outcomes from 1990 to 1994 (Table 6-5) also show that two parties with support from specific milieus have been regionally successful: the PDS in the new Länder, and Bündnis 90/Die Grünen in West Germany. Yet only the two major parties of CDU and SPD enjoy equal support by voters in both East and West, and thus serve as a kind of political glue to hold united Germany together.

Compared with the SPD, the CDU is better positioned in East Germany due to the overlapping effects of ideological and religious cleavages, as well as the relatively good image of their candidates and the issues they have placed at the heart of their campaigns. The SPD is caught in the middle between CDU and PDS, in part because the social-democratic cleavage has an only weak effect in the new Länder. In addition, long-standing system comparisons between East and West have not made the task of political parties trying to appeal to all Germans easier, particularly not when critical opinions are being offered. In the new Länder, two processes have combined: the return to capitalism, with its effects on social structure and interest groups, and the sociostructural fragmentation that accompanies modernization. All parties in the future must face the challenges these processes create.

Table 6-5 1994 Bundestag Election Results, West and East (in percent)

	West		East	
	Percent	Difference from 1990	Percent	Difference from 1990
CDU/CSU	42.0	−2.3	38.5	−3.3
SPD	37.5	+1.8	31.5	+7.2
FDP	7.7	-2.9	3.5	−9.4
Alliance Greens	7.9	+3.1	4.3	−1.9
PDS	1.0	+0.6	19.8	+8.7
Others	3.9	−0.4	2.4	−1.3

Source: Forschungsgruppe Wahlen (1994b: A4, A5)

Chapter 7

AGENTS OF DEMOCRATIZATION AND UNIFICATION
Political Parties in the New German States

Ann L. Phillips

Introduction

Political parties are a central feature of modern liberal democracy in all of its variants and have played a pivotal role in the two democratization waves in this century.[1] The institutionalization and elaboration of party roles vary from polity to polity but core functions such as aggregating related interests, representing societal pluralism, providing a forum for political discourse, mediating between society and the state, selecting and grooming candidates for public office, and competing for power to run government institutions are common to liberal democra-

---

1. The first wave in this century occurred after World War II and the second is the current wave following the collapse of communism (Huntington, 1993: 3).

cies. Other organizations in civil society share some of these roles but, in combination, they remain unique to parties. As such, parties have provided cohesion and facilitated change, both of which are integral to the success of these systems.

In the waning years of the twentieth century, however, parties and party systems in most western democracies are under siege as are the systems in which they serve. Social and economic arrangements which became the hallmark of western democracy after World War II appear to have exhausted themselves and, therefore, face a transformation potentially as profound, albeit more subtle, as those underway in the former Soviet Union and Central and Eastern Europe. The ability of western political parties and party systems, which shaped and were shaped by the welfare state and the East-West conflict, to adapt to changing conditions and effectively perform their functions is in doubt.

Italy may first spring to mind when thinking of troubled party systems. However, the challenge confronting parties and the party system in Germany is arguably the most severe among the western liberal democracies. German parties must devise a successful course for the transformation of the two very different systems found in eastern and western Germany and integrate the two at the same time.

Although not the only actors engaged in the project, political parties bear an inordinate responsibility because of their privileged status in the Federal Republic of Germany. Their prominence was enshrined in the Basic Law that accorded them the function of mediating between state and society. Article 21 specifically entrusted the parties with participating in forming the political will of the people, and parties became the chief agents of democracy. In 1967, a new party law substantially expanded and deepened their already considerable role. First, parties were to participate in forming the political will in "all areas of public life." Second, participation in forming the political will of the people was deepened to include influencing the formation of the political will, stimulating and deepening political education, promoting the active participation of citizens in political life, and assuming responsibility for creating capable citizens (Apel, 1991: 41-42).

The parties' formidable claims on the public treasury, together with these central roles, generated the party state label which has long been attached to the Federal Republic.

The GDR was also a party state, but of quite another order. There one political party enjoyed unsurpassed authority to shape the political will, barring the special, if varying, constraints imposed by Soviet hegemony. Four other parties, known as bloc parties, did exist, however: the German Peasants Party, the National Democratic Party, the Christian Democratic Party and the Liberals. This "multiparty" system was replicated in much of Soviet dominated Central and East Europe, emblematic of their less advanced stage of socialism.[2] Bloc parties were intended to integrate residual classes and groups into the political system. The Christian Democratic and Liberal Democratic Parties were counterparts to the West German CDU and FDP, a factor that both facilitated and complicated political unification after 1990. The Social Democratic Party in the East disappeared for a second time in the twentieth century when it fused, under tremendous pressure, with the KPD to form the Socialist Unity Party in April 1946. Other groups such as the Confederation of Free German Trade Unions (FDGB), Democratic Women's Federation of Germany (DFD), Free German Youth (FDJ), and the League of Culture (KB), that had no counterpart in West Germany also participated in public life as part of the noncompetitive National Front.

2. Many elements of the political systems and the economic transformations after the establishment of Communist Party control differed from those in the Soviet Union in order to highlight the more advanced and leading position of the USSR in the bloc. The very name "Peoples' Democracies" applied to Central and Eastern Europe polities underscored their position in the first stage on the path to communism.

The rapid and largely unprepared unification in 1990 thrust these defining characteristics of the two German states onto center stage. What role the East German parties could and should play in democratization and unification became a critical and highly charged question, given the pivotal role of parties in West Germany and the existence of some sister parties in the GDR. Creating a new, legitimate party system in eastern Germany has become a key measure of success in both democratization of eastern Germany and unification of the two German states. It is central to a larger structure-agency dilemma created when West German structures and institutions were transferred wholesale to East Germany.

Structure-agency concepts, more familiar to International Relations theory,[3] are useful for our examination of German unification that has been a transition from inter-state relations to domestic politics. The concepts require some modification, however, to accommodate the unusual shift in venue. Structure here refers to political parties as institutions; agency refers to the parties as actors in the simultaneous processes of democratization of East Germany and unification with West Germany. As such, the structure-agency framework captures the tension that pervades the unification process. The purpose of this study, therefore, is to examine the transformation of political parties in east Germany as institutions since 1989 and to assess their efficacy as agents of democratization and unification.

It will do this by exploring three distinct but related aspects of the party system and political parties in the new German states. First, parties as institutions will be examined. Given the mix of "old" and "new" parties in eastern Germany, what balance between continuity and change has emerged? How has the fusion of most

3. IR scholars part company over their choice of independent variables to explain state behavior in the international system. In the starkest terms, Realists in international relations argue that the international system is decisive, while Idealists contend that the domestic politics of a state explain state behavior.

east and west German parties shaped their transformation process? Party leadership, membership, structures and organization provide some useful indicators. Second, parties as agents will be considered. This can be measured by how well parties in the new states perform traditional party functions. And finally, the salience of parties to public life in the new German states will be assessed. Here a comparison with party efficacy in western Germany and in the democratizing states of Central and Eastern Europe is helpful. Taken together, these findings allow us to draw some conclusions about the continued efficacy of political parties as key agents of German democracy which, in turn, provide one measure of the long-term prospects for system transformation and unification. The findings have important implications for the larger East-West dynamic of transformation and integration as well.

Parties as Institutions, Old and New

East Germany did not bring an unoccupied party landscape to its union with the FRG in 1990: quite the contrary. In those heady days demarcated by the collapse of the SED regime and unification, the SED began a transformation process (including its name), the bloc parties initiated their own reforms predicated upon independence from the SED, while new parties and movements proliferated.

Given this mix of participants, it is fair to ask what is old and what is new about parties in east Germany and the party system there. The answer is important in assessing (1) democratization of east German institutions and (2) the ability of parties in east Germany to further democratization and unification. The distinction implies that the new is democratic while the old represents the vestiges of the failed regime; in reality, the connection is more ambiguous.

To complicate matters further, the distinction between old and new is far from clear. One must first examine the external variables influencing party development and then establish some measures to assess the internal transformation of parties. The distinction is made for analytical purposes; the interplay of external and internal factors is assumed. Among the external variables influencing party institutions, the change in the environment within which they operate has been the most decisive. Withdrawal of Soviet support and the implosion of the SED regime fundamentally altered the options for and terms of political engagement even before unification. Subsequent union under Article 23 of the FRG's Basic Law redrew the political landscape again by extending the structures and institutions of the West German system, including the party system, to East Germany. Integral to that process but worthy of separate attention has been the internalization of the external environment via the unprecedented process of fusion of all East German parties excepting the PDS with a West German sister party. Successes and weaknesses of this fusion are addressed in the third section of the paper as a measure of democratization and unification.

Another factor, with external and internal components of another sort, is the reduction in number of parties between 1989 and 1994, altering the party system as well as the players. Early on, the number of serious competitors was reduced to five. The SED-bloc German Peasant Party and Democratic Awakening which appeared during the *Wende* joined the CDU. An amalgam of the newly established FDP-East and two SED-bloc parties, the Liberal Democrats and the National Democratic Party, formed the FDP. Newly formed Marxist splinter groups, like the *Nelken*, allied themselves with the PDS, successor to the ruling SED, for election purposes. The SPD and Bündnis '90, both established during the *Wende*, completed the list.

In the 1994 elections, the number of serious competitors declined once again, to three. As of 1997, only the CDU, SPD and PDS are strong throughout the eastern states at the local and state level. The FDP and Alliance Greens still exist but have been marginalized.

Of the five remaining parties, which are old and which are new? Two are clearly new: Bündnis '90, an umbrella organization for many of the parties and movements that sprung up during the late fall of 1989, and the SPD, which was resurrected after more than forty years, submerged within the SED.[4] The democratic character of these parties has not been questioned, although informers of the Ministry for State Security (*Stasi*) were strategically placed in virtually all of the new parties which emerged during the *Wende*.[5]

The CDU, FDP, and SED (renamed the PDS), by contrast, had all operated in the GDR. Should they, therefore, be classified as old? Here the evidence is more ambiguous. As noted above, the external environment altered the rules of the game for every party, and we need to ask whether the fusion of eastern and western parties altered internal party dynamics as well. Party leadership, membership, structures, organization, and program offer useful indicators of democratic transformation within the GDR parties.

Party Leadership

Numerous studies of east German elites, including party elites, conclude that replacement of the nomenklatura after 1989 has been thorough (Derlien, 1995; Donovan, 1995; Welsh, 1995: 46-47; Yoder, 1995: 10-14). One factor that accounts for this is the addition of new political parties as well as new members to established parties. Another factor is that resignations or expulsions of leaders from the SED-PDS and the bloc parties began during the Modrow interregnum, and produced substantial

---

4. The East German Social Democrats briefly called themselves the SDP, from the party's founding on 7 October 1989 until January 1990, but it will be referred to as the SPD-East in this chapter.
5. Ibrahim Böhme, one of a handful of founders of the SPD and leading spokesperson of the party, was exposed as an informal *Stasi* co-worker in early 1990.

internal upward mobility within party organizations so that many long-time party members held public office for the first time after 1989 (Derlien, 1995: 4-6; Welsh, 1995: 38-39).

More thoroughgoing purges followed, induced in part by ties and later fusion with West German parties. An early influx of personnel from the west also contributed to the shift. Party elites were dominated initially by westerners as a rule, the most visible of which were Kurt Biedenkopf and Bernhard Vogel, Minister Presidents of Saxony and Thuringia, respectively (Padgett, 1993: 34; Baylis, 1995: 243-62). The practice of western domination of midlevel elites was also widespread but was dropped when it backfired at the polls.

Western party functionaries were loaned to their eastern German counterparts as part of a comprehensive package to rebuild or strengthen party organization (Donovan, 1995: 5-7, 14-15). One of their tasks was to identify and groom new party leaders among east Germans once it was clear that west Germans were weak contenders.

After east Germany's Alliance Greens joined the west German Greens in 1993, the PDS was the only remaining homegrown party. Nonetheless, it too privileged west German members in high eastern party offices as well as on its candidate lists for the federal parliament. The party's top administrator, for example, who also sits on the executive board, is Wolfgang Gehrcke from Hamburg. Nine of its thirty representatives in the 1994 *Bundestag* were west Germans (*Die Zeit* 8 December 1995).

In sum, party leadership in all east German parties is new. Continuing high turnover among state legislators and in the party executive committees generates an ongoing renewal among party elites. One must be cautious, however, in equating turnover plus west German influence with an affinity for democratization and integration. In all parties, the west German presence engendered such resentment that it has been gradually reduced. In the special case of the PDS, the west German contingent hardly had a salutary effect on that party's adjustment to unification, as they injected a more radical, anti-FRG posture into leadership circles than was present initially among east German leaders. In addition, youth itself and inexperience do not necessarily bring propitious qualities to party leadership for the all-German project. In the PDS, Angela Marquardt and Sahra Wagenknecht are cases in point.[6] Both were removed from leadership positions at the 1997 party congress.

Party Membership

Bündnis 90 and SPD members are generally new participants in the political process. This might not have been true for the SPD had the party not adopted a policy prohibiting accepting SED members for one year after the system collapsed (*Tagesspiegel* 27 December 1995). Since that policy expired, decisions to accept new members are made on a case by case basis by the local party organization. No significant numbers of former SED members applying for or acquiring membership in the SPD have been reported.

The ranks of former bloc parties are filled primarily by members from the GDR days, despite the new members won either individually or through mergers with new parties in the first blush of democratization. Even then, however, new members have remained a tiny fraction of total membership.[7] The PDS also attracted some new members enchanted with its then new Chairman, Gregor Gysi, and drawn to the idea of democratic

---

6. Both are east Germans. Angela Marquardt, 23, is Vice Chair of the PDS and representative of the *Junge GenossInnen* within the party. Identified as a punk and a fundamentalist, she supports extra-parliamentary actions to overturn the system. Sahra Wagenknecht, 26, is a leader of the Communist Platform in the PDS. Class struggle remains her guiding political principle.
7. FDP data shows that only 2,000 of its total eastern German membership of 136,000 in mid-1990 were from the new dissident parties (Soe, 1995: 184). Eighty percent of east CDU members today were members of the old CDU-Ost (Donovan, 1995: 16).

socialism, but the party's profile was defined by aging SED members and by the dramatic decline in membership. The biggest drop occurred between October 1989 and early 1990 when two million of the original 2.3 million members left the party (Behrend and Meier, 1991: 10).

Since the October 1990 elections, all of the parties in eastern Germany have lost members and have found it difficult to recruit new ones. Only the two newly created parties, SPD and *Bündnis* 90, have grown, but their membership remains minuscule. Membership in the CDU and PDS has continued to decline; in the FDP, precipitously so.

Table 7-1 Party Membership in the New German States

Party	December 1990	December 1994
PDS	284,632	121,000
CDU	109,709 (Dec. 1991)	78,000
FDP	106,696	25,000
SPD	24,400	28,000
Alliance Greens	2,037	3,200

Sources: Information provided by the parties; *General Anzeiger* 27 March 1995; *Die Zeit* 8 December 1995; *Süddeutsche Zeitung*, 1 December 1995

When east and west German sister parties merged in 1990, the east German members generally constituted but a small fraction of total membership. The FDP was the anomaly: eastern membership was almost double western numbers when the parties joined forces, in 1990 at 106,696 and 66,475, respectively. The high numbers in the east had little to do with the popularity of liberalism per se. Rather, as with all bloc parties, membership offered an alternative channel for participation that smoothed the edges of some policies, protected interests, and offered significant perquisites for officeholders. By 1994, however, membership in the east had plummeted to 25,000, overtaking declining rosters in the west where the party could still muster 61,000 members. The benefits of being in the FDP in the east had disappeared and had not been replaced by any newfound conviction in the principles of liberalism. Nonetheless, in the FDP the eastern contingent remains far stronger relative to total membership than is true in the other parties. The rapid erosion reflects the absence of a traditional liberal constituency in the east and has contributed to the party's decline nationwide (Soe, 1995).

Since dwindling membership is an overriding weakness common to all of the parties in the new states, who remains in the rank and file? The question applies especially to the PDS and former bloc parties because their rosters are filled with members from the GDR days. Here, the PDS is a separate case because its members most closely identified with and were identified with the old regime. Although people joined the SED for a variety of reasons, some notion of ideological commitment was not altogether absent. Members of the bloc parties were also water carriers for the regime but without the same level of identification or responsibility. The point is that membership in the SED or one of the bloc parties actually tells us very little about an individual's political beliefs or values, nor can it provide a collective profile. The SED was a mass party that included many streams despite its monolithic public face. Together with the bloc parties, the combined memberships constituted a rough composite of GDR society: each party had its share of reformers, dedicated public servants, believers, opportunists, and scoundrels.

PDS leaders argue that opportunists were the first to abandon the party because of the stigma affixed to the party in united Germany. Many reformers also left in the first post-unification years and failed to find another political home. The rank and file, therefore, is dominated by an older generation for whom the construction of GDR socialism was a defining experience.

The liability attached to the PDS did not apply to the former bloc parties in unified Germany. Thus, even though most current members are not new, a broader cross-section of the old membership in those parties remains.

Structures and Organization

The CDU, FDP and PDS all had seasoned organizations, substantial wealth and large party memberships at the time of unification. For the CDU and the FDP this turned out to be a mixed blessing. On the one hand, it provided a ready base for west German sister parties; on the other hand, that base was tainted by decades of complicity with the GDR system. The effort of bloc parties, supported by their western counterparts, to present themselves as victims in the SED regime has been problematic.

The SPD and *Bündis* 90 Greens, by contrast, did not have much of an organization. They, too, have been subjected to the efforts of western colleagues to build organizations and recruit members, but the Greens remain more ambivalent about and are, therefore, less systematic in such matters than other parties, reflecting its origins as a grassroots movement that eschewed institutionalization and hierarchy. Nonetheless, for a time, the Greens actively tried to shore up their dwindling eastern party, but this only created the same eastern resentment found in other parties. By 1996 benign neglect seemed to be the order of the day.

By contrast, the SPD has always been a highly centralized party. Western party functionaries overwhelmed the tiny East German party with technical, administrative, and personnel assistance. As a result, the current organizational structure in the new states was established by the western SPD (Rueschemeyer, 1995).

The cost of maintaining party structures in the east with such a weak membership base has proved to be prohibitive. In the mid-1990s, the CDU subsidized its eastern branch to the tune of DM 8 million per year; while the SPD spent DM 10 million per year (Donovan, 1995: 11-12). Retrenchment is being considered by both parties and in some *Länder* has already begun.

Eastern pique toward imported party officials was exacerbated by the presence since unification of more than 20,000 West German civil servants in the upper administrative levels in the new states to facilitate system transformation. Western influence was most visible in the justice, economics and finance ministries (Derlien, 1995: 11-12; Welsh, 1995: 38; Yoder, 1995: 14-15). The pervasive pattern of elite transformation under west German guidance seemed to some altogether too reminiscent of the last system transition.

Although lacking the pressure of a west German sister party, the PDS has also undertaken substantial reform in structure, party statutes and rules. It cut the party apparatus drastically, from roughly six thousand full-time employees in SED times to fewer than 150 by January 1993 (Phillips, 1994: 507-11). The decline in apparatus was accompanied by a proliferation of committees and councils designed to democratize party life from the bottom up. Membership and party rules were completely rewritten to break with the highly centralized, top-down SED organization. The results have been mixed, and in part undercut by the rank and file.

Direct western input has been a factor in PDS reform as well. In the first years after the *Wende*, the small West German membership enjoyed disproportionate representation in top bodies as well as influence on policy. At the time, one of three vice-chairs was reserved for a west German as were a number of positions on the party executive board. Cues on matters of democratic practice, such as quotas for women in all party bodies, were taken from the western contingent. Deference to the group faded, however, when the PDS failed to gain a foothold in the west German states.

Party Program

All parties have new programs since 1990, and western sections of the party decide federal party programs in every case but the PDS. Although in full accordance with the democratic principle of majority rule, the practice is problematic for both democratization and unification. East Germans feel disenfranchised in their new state as a result. Furthermore, it reflects an underlying western assumption that expertise resides exclusively with them, reinforced by the indisputable reality of where the money is. Moreover, the imbalance underscores conflicting interests and priorities that divide eastern and western sections of individual parties.

Although hardly monolithic in their views, east German politicos parted company from their western counterparts in a number of issue areas: on compensation before restitution of expropriated property; on the level of government responsibility to provide for cultural institutions, child care, and job security; the right to abortion and the right to work (Rueschemeyer, 1995: 22-23; Soe, 1995: 163; *Die Zeit* 8 December 1995). The few East Germans in leadership positions at the federal level have been largely ineffectual in trying to shape party policy to incorporate eastern concerns (Donovan, 1995: 13-15; Soe, 1995: 186-87; *Spiegel* 21 August 1995). An example of west German indifference to the interests of party brethren in the new states comes from the SPD, but it could be duplicated in the other parties. In this particular case, a spring planning session for the 1996 SPD Party Congress abruptly dropped a forum on "Perspectives for East Germany – Opportunities for Change" from the program without explanation (*Die Zeit* 25 November 1995). Eastern members found this all too representative of the party's cavalier attitude toward their concerns.

Another, potentially more serious, division goes to the heart of the political process. Eastern Germans of all political stripes tend to favor the consociational approach to democracy, over the oppositional politics which they see in many western democracies.[8] The Round Table, pioneered by the Poles was a

---

8. Sweden's tradition of consociational democracy is a notable exception. West Germany's political practice falls between the Scandinavian model and the more confrontational Anglo-American tradition.

method of representation practiced in much of Central and Eastern Europe to guide the initial stage of democratization from Communist Party rule. Its distinguishing characteristic is the participation of all major parties and groups in the decision-making process (Welsh, 1994). The Modrow government in the GDR was pressured into accepting a similar arrangement in 1989/90, until the first free parliamentary elections were held in March 1990.

The autonomy afforded by federated party structures, which might alleviate some of this tension, has been circumscribed over the years as party organizations have become increasingly centralized. A particularly prickly case in point was the pressure brought to bear in 1994 by Bonn SPD headquarters on Harald Ringstorff, party leader in Mecklenburg-Vorpommern, to enter a grand coalition with the CDU rather than work with the PDS.

The PDS is the only party in the new states that exercises autonomy in determining its program. One of its greatest appeals, therefore, is its claim to represent east German interests. Its program has gone through many permutations since 1989 in search of the right balance between democratization in all spheres of life, including the economy, and culture, and the proper role for the state to ensure the general welfare (Phillips, 1994: 517-25).

The composite picture produced by this examination of party leadership, membership, organization, and programs of the parties in the new German states reveals that old and new do not distinguish one party from the other as much as they cut across party lines and intertwine within parties. Leadership, structures, organizations and programs are mostly new even in the parties that were part of the GDR system. Membership is the one area that qualifies as old because of the overwhelming preponderance of members from the GDR days in the PDS, CDU and FDP. But the significance of this carryover is difficult to discern. Some scholars of democratization argue that continuity in party membership should be of little concern. New party structures, programs and rules will shape democratic behavior among the apparatchiki of the old regime. Moreover, party democratization is reinforced by and anchored in the complete transfer of west German structures and rule of law to the east. The overarching structure sets the parameters within which organizations and individuals function, creating democratic behavior in both (Palma, 1993: 257-67).

As institutions, then, three of the five eastern parties incorporate elements of continuity and change but all are essentially democratic. Old and new are points along a continuum rather than distinct types. The SPD and the *Bündis* 90 Greens are new in all categories.

Parties as Agents: the Efficacy of East German Parties

System Change and Party Life-Cycles

There can be no doubt that the party system in east Germany has undergone significant change since the autumn of 1989. Giovanni Sartori (1976: 274-75) identifies two major ways in which an established party system can be transformed into another. First, endogenous transformation can occur, either through a long process or spontaneous transition, and second, discontinuity brought about by system breakdown can produce transformation of a party system. A system breakdown transpires with the removal or installation of a dictatorship. The GDR experienced system breakdown; a dictatorship was replaced by a competitive, pluralist system.

Beyond that, however, the GDR fit with Sartori's categories is problematic, for he identified the former Soviet bloc countries as single party systems. In political terms this is accurate, at least for defining issues, but structurally the GDR and other bloc countries formally had multiparty systems, though all were united in a National Front. Many of the parties survived the system collapse in some form, complicating the question of institutional change. Furthermore, unification precipitated and fashioned party system transformation, something established party theory cannot take into account. The importance of the FRG as an external actor that became an internal actor creates an independent variable not found in other country cases.

When the focus shifts from the party system to individual parties, can theory help us locate the east German parties according to type or model in the natural life cycle of a party? If so, this could tell us something about the stability or fluidity of the party system in East Germany overall.

Angelo Panebianco (1988: 6-18) identifies three phases in what he terms a party's natural life: genesis, institutionalization, and maturity. In the first phase, the party fits a so-called rational model in which it is organized to realize certain goals. The party offers collective incentives, such as ideology, in this phase to generate support. In the next phase, institutionalization, the party shifts toward the natural model in which it responds to demands and interests of its members, the "stakeholders." Here selective incentives, such as power, status and material benefits, are employed. In its mature phase, the party's primary goal is survival. The three phases are not discrete but overlapping. A party never abandons its original goals, but gradually subordinates them to organizational needs. His model of organizational evolution draws upon Robert Michels' theory that all parties move from an initial phase of system transformation according to some ideologically defined goals to one of adaptation to the system in which survival of the organization becomes the paramount goal.

Where do the east German parties fit in this framework? The answer varies from party to party. The PDS may be the most interesting case because it falls into all three phases simultaneously. It fits the rational model of the genesis phase because of its goal orientation and appeal to collective incentives. The shock of system change reinvigorated the goal orientation of this well-established party. It also elevated survival of the party, characteristic of the mature phase, to a vital component of its ideological agenda. At the same time, as the successor to the SED, the PDS also conforms to the natural model associated with institutionalization.

The other former GDR parties, the CDU and FDP, fall somewhere between institutionalization and maturity. The natural model associated with institutionalization captures the response to demands and interests of stakeholders in both the GDR (in a much more limited way) and in unified Germany. Fusion with western sister parties has reinforced this position. Priority for the FDP in both parts of Germany has become survival.

The two new parties – the SPD and *Bündis* 90 Greens – should both be in the genesis phase, but fusion with west German parties has undercut this phase. Instead of developing collective incentives to generate support and transform their environment, they are given the programs of institutionalized parties in the west. The disjuncture is more pronounced in the SPD than in the Greens because of their different life stages in the west.

A split image emerges from a life cycle examination of the eastern parties. The CDU and FDP are fairly congruent with their western partners' life stages, despite the enormous adjustments required by system change; the SPD and *Bündis* 90 Greens are not. The PDS stands apart because of the dramatic reversal in its position as a result of system change, from ruling party with a monopoly on power to the underdog in an ideologically hostile climate. As such, the intended unifying function of national parties carries the seeds of potential instability when viewed from the perspective of life stages. Only the CDU has continued in the same phase from GDR to the post-GDR system and appears to be in sync with its west German partner as well. The others have been wrenched from their normal phase by unification. Nonetheless, instability is unlikely because the overwhelming dominance of the west German branch within the national parties can effectively quell any impulse to defect. The downside is that west German dominance seems to guarantee stability at the price of real participation in the democratic process.

Party Functions

The marbling of old and new within some of the East German parties plus the fusion with west German parties has made it difficult for parties to find a constituent base in the east. This affects the ability of eastern parties to perform traditional party functions, which in turn hampers their ability to cultivate supporters.

Seymour Martin Lipset and Stein Rokkan set out six primary functions of political parties in liberal democracies (1967: 1-64). They are: political integration, democratic mediation between state and society, articulation and reconciliation of competing interests, policy formulation, coordination and control over decision-making processes, and elite recruitment. Panebianco carves out three: integration of interests, candidate selection, and participation in the public policy process (1988: 267). Sartori condenses party functions into two: articulating popular demands to the government and channeling the public's will through the formation and manipulation of public opinion (1976: 56-58).

How well do political parties in eastern Germany fulfill these functions? Not surprisingly, performance is uneven. Parties in the new states cannot effectively perform the functions of policy formulation, mediation between state and society, and coordination and control over decision-making processes at the federal level because of their weakness in the federal parties. The SPD-East and *Bündnis* 90 are simply too feeble in numerical terms to have much clout. The CDU-East is the only branch of the united parties that could theoretically carry some weight, but its leaders have been discredited and replaced. Of the original group, only Angela Merkel remains at the ministerial level. Claudia Nolte, a young CDU-East member without political experience, appointed to head the Ministry for Families, was widely regarded as a protégé of the Chancellor. Quotas for east Germans in leadership positions and decision-making bodies in the parties have been largely abandoned. The level of frustration is reflected in efforts by east German parliamentarians to establish groups within their parties, to caucus on issues, and to work with other east German parliamentarians across party lines. Parties have successfully enforced party discipline in the *Bundestag* to undercut such initiatives.

Even at the state and local levels, party effectiveness is curtailed because of a pervasive dependence upon west German parties for both structural and financial support (Padgett, 1993: 26-27; Donoval, 1995: 10-12; Rueschemeyer, 1995: 11). The parties can and do articulate competing interests but with little notable success in modifying or changing party agendas. Signs of rebellion against headquarters have been brewing at the state level, however. Harald Ringstorff, SPD party chief in Mecklenburg-Vorpommern, put Bonn on notice in 1995 that the "Social Democrats in eastern Germany know well enough how to make progress ... when advice from Bonn is not accepted, that is our right (*Die Zeit* 25 November 1995) ..." Manfred Stolpe, minister president of Brandenburg, and Reinhard Höppner, minister president of Saxony-Anhalt, joined Ringstorff to challenge SPD policy of non-collaboration with the PDS.

Similar dissatisfaction has been percolating in the CDU-East. Two "discussion" papers raised issues of thwarted east German identity within the CDU and the practical political costs to the party in the eastern states. The first paper by Eckhardt Rehberg, CDU parliamentary chair in Mecklenburg-Vorpommern, circulated in early 1996 in Schwerin, was titled "Values and Strategy Debate – CDU 2000." The other by Paul Krüger, speaker of the East-CDU members of the Bundestag, develops fourteen theses on an eastern profile in the CDU (Schmidt, 1996).

The picture of party efficacy in the east is not uniformly bleak, however. Two functions which east German parties have performed fairly well, considering the bounds created by their general weaknesses, are political integration and elite recruitment.

Ironically, the PDS may be one of the most important contributors to political integration, not in terms of aggregating individual interests so much as in keeping otherwise disaffected citizens in the process by virtue of its singular autonomy and through its system-critical politics. At the same time, although the PDS can claim autonomy in setting its program, its ability to shape politics at the federal level directly will be nil as long as the other parties continue to ostracize it. As such, the PDS role remains primarily that of a spoiler. The same cannot be said for the state level, where the party has established a strong presence. In 1997 one hundred and twenty-nine members were serving in state parliaments and unofficial cooperation with the PDS was widespread. Coalition politics in Saxony-Anhalt and Mecklenburg-Vorpommern have demonstrated the potential for official cooperation. At the local level, the PDS is even stronger: it occupied 180 mayoral posts and roughly 6000 local council seats.

Taken together, the party system, party lifecycles and efficacy in fulfilling traditional party functions reveal reinforcing disjunctures between east and west within parties. The divisions themselves are not necessarily harmful but the ancillary position of eastern parties in the new party system seriously impairs their ability to be effective agents of democratization and unification.

The Salience of Political Parties to East German Public Life

A vicious circle appears to be at work which undercuts the salience of political parties to east German public life. The general impotence of parties to translate their constituents' interests and values into policy at any level in the face of overriding west German power and priorities has contributed to small and declining party memberships in the east. Dwindling membership in the east, in turn, weakens the credibility and leverage of the parties in dealing with their western counterparts and undermines the ability of parties to do effective work in their communities.

Studies conducted at the Universities of Leipzig and Jena have measured the level of popular mistrust and alienation from political institutions, including parties, in the new states. Mistrust of political institutions is lodged in experiences under the SED regime and the perception of new institutions as imports from the west, according to the Leipzig study. Most important is the limited ability of parties and associations to solve problems which translates into low public esteem and a low level of citizen engagement. The Jena study underscores the critical appraisal of party competence to deal with political questions (Kreikenbom, this volume). Both studies conclude that the weakness of political and social integration can only be overcome if representative institutions can successfully step out of the shadow of their west German "mother institutions" to formulate eastern problems and interests (*Süddeutsche Zeitung* 1 December 1995).

East German minority status within the polity as a whole and within political parties would not be an issue if primary cleavages cut across East-West lines. The problem is not even that two distinct, but overlapping, three-party configurations emerged in east and west Germany from the "super election year" of 1994: the CDU/CSU, SPD and Greens in the West; the CDU, SPD and PDS in the East. Germany's federal system accommodates regional differences and its federalism is widely regarded as a source of strength.

The problem for political parties goes much deeper. At issue is the core relationship between institutions and culture, which scholars such as Robert Putnam (1993) have returned to center stage. Easy assumptions about the institutional and cultural wasteland that the collapse of communism was to have left in its wake have proven false throughout the former Soviet bloc. As a result, the east-west political and philosophical mismatch that Christian Soe sees as central to the German FDP is characteristic of all the parties in Germany which "married" after 1989 (1995: 163). Party labels mask substantive differences in culture, social structure, and therefore interests. The essence of the disjuncture is captured in the industrial/postindustrial divide. East Germany is still imbedded in an industrial/materialist culture shaped by 40 years of Soviet-style socialism. West Germany meanwhile has become the leading European exponent of a post-industrial/post-materialist culture. The cultural disconnect is reflected in different constituent bases for eastern and western branches within the same party (Dalton and Bürklin, 1995; Rueschemeyer, 1995: 17; Betz, 1996: 27-29).

Bündnis 90 and the Greens melded one decidedly postmaterialist party (Greens) with one that was not. The early affinity based on opposition to the status quo in their respective states has turned out to be a thin reed upon which to build a party. The CDU-East is supported primarily by the working class while the CDU-West enjoys its strongest support among the self-employed and those with a strong christian orientation. The SPD constituency is also split between the west, where the party remains based in the working class, and the east, where pastors, intellectuals, and the middle class predominate. The FDP provides the important exception in that both east and west branches draw primarily from the self-employed. Nonetheless, the FDP is divided along east-west lines by a cultural gap visible in attitudes toward the state. In the west, FDP members debate the priorities of civil liberties and market forces, while in the east there is noticeably less interest in civil liberties and greater acceptance of state engagement in all spheres of public life. The PDS has few western members; nonetheless, the culture rift is pronounced there as well. The party's constituent base in the east is primarily among salaried employees (civil servants), intellectuals, and the self-employed, and its support is particularly solid among the most highly educated and among the young.

Different social bases generate competing and at times conflicting interests and priorities which are difficult to reconcile within a party's program and agenda. Hence, east Germans feel left out in the very organizations that should be the agents to articulate and promote their interests. As a result, parties as currently constituted, other than the PDS, have found no organic base in East German society (Padgett, 1993: 23).

From this flows a divergence in party type along east-west lines. Drawing upon research by Otto Kirchheimer, Panebianco (1988: 262-74) has identified two ideal types: the mass bureaucratic party and the electoral/professional party. The strength of party membership, the role of party bureaucracy, and the importance of internal leaders are among the distinguishing characteristics. In the mass party, membership and organization are central; whereas in the electoral party, membership is low, electoral success is the sustaining ingredient, the party is run by professionals, and leadership is based on personality rather than party credentials. Parties in both east and west fail to conform to the full complement of characteristics outlined by Panebianco. Western German parties fall somewhere between, though gravitating toward the electoral type; while eastern German parties are closer to electoral parties, if only by default, though they may not qualify as "professional." The role of the media in campaigns is growing throughout Germany; the absence of strong party organizations in the new states has left a vacuum the media is eager to fill. One effect has been a heightened importance placed on personality in east German politics. As a result, the entire process of politics functions differently in east and west Germany.

Low public confidence in parties is not unique to the new states, however. A decline in west German confidence in political institutions and parties over several decades has been well documented. The convergence of parties toward the middle and the inability of the parties to develop compelling responses to contemporary problems further compounds popular disenchantment. The widespread blurring of party lines and lack of orientation has, in turn, spurred internal party conflicts over the future direction of the parties. The appearance of new and the reappearance of old fault lines within parties plagues virtually all (Phillips, 1995).

Analyses by Russell Dalton, Scott Flanagan, Peter Mair and others have demonstrated the diminishing efficacy of parties in all advanced industrialized societies. Changes in social structure lead to realignment, and a declining efficacy of parties produces dealignment (Flanagan and Dalton, 1984; Dalton and Kuechler, 1990). In response, parties have tightened their links to the state as party-society ties have weakened. Mair (1995: 42) analyzes the contradiction between weakened parties as representative agencies and strengthened parties as public and office holders. Political parties as office holders, he argues, have never been stronger which, in turn, further erodes their connection to the public. Nonetheless, political parties will not fade away even as their legitimacy diminishes, Mair concludes. The trend in party position, efficacy and legitimacy in western societies only compounds the more deep-seated weaknesses of parties in east Germany discussed above.

Parallels with Central and Eastern Europe

The background of east German disenchantment with politics stems from an historical experience that invites comparison with Central and Eastern Europe rather than west Germany.[9] The shared socialist experience shows a decline in interest and confidence in party systems across the region. Squabbling of political leaders is regarded as unseemly; parties and leaders seem more interested in self-aggrandizement than in the public good. Party membership and participation in civic associations

9. For background on the party systems in Central and Eastern Europe after 1989, see Kitschelt (1992), Ishiyama (1995), Pridham and Lewis (1996: 100-25; 229-53), and Kopecky (1995).

is very low throughout Eastern Europe. In Hungary it has been difficult to generate sufficient participation in elections at the local level to produce valid results. The longing for a different kind of democracy, as represented by the Round Tables, has been widespread.

This distinct, albeit far from homogeneous, political culture in the former Soviet bloc has produced cleavages between west and east European parties within the international party families that is reminiscent of those separating eastern and western branches within German parties (Markus, 1995). After 1989, new parties and reconstituted parties from the inter-war years blossomed in Central and Eastern Europe as they did in the GDR, and parties adopted names that were similar to western political labels. Initially many parties had "liberal" in their name even though liberal principles were largely alien to their own values and most parties scrambled to affiliate with one of the party internationals, such as the Christian Democrat International, the Liberal International, or the Socialist International. Acceptance for membership by an International would bring a coveted stamp of legitimacy as well as money, it was hoped, and both would be useful in domestic competition. The results were often disappointing for both sides: those who shared party labels found they had little else in common. Party families have had relatively little influence on party developments in Central and Eastern Europe. The situation in Germany is reversed, of course, but the disconnect between the parties is the same.

The political culture gap between East and West also accounts, in part, for the resurgence of post-communist parties throughout the region. Post-communists have been elected to govern throughout much of Central and Eastern Europe and the PDS owes much of its support to this phenomenon. As a result, it cannot aspire to govern at the federal level in Germany but it does govern at the local level and has become part of a governing coalition at the state level in eastern Germany. It has established a "cultural hegemony" in the new states beyond its own membership and electoral support in a way that the other parties cannot (*Die Zeit* 3 November and 8 December 1995). The overwhelming majority of east Germans (70 percent) regards the PDS as a democratic party like any other and feel it should be treated as such. West German public opinion shows just the reverse, according to a 1994 Politbarometer survey (25 November).

Conclusion

The structural transfer of the west German system to east Germany is virtually complete. A key element of that transfer is the party system. Today parties in east German are democratic organizations that operate within the parameters of a democratic system. As such, democratization of east German parties as institutions has been a success. However, institutional conformity in east and west Germany belies the contextual and cultural differences within which these institutions function. The fusion of eastern and western parties creates an image of unification that papers over substantial divisions, including different constituencies, replete with competing interests and priorities. The weakness of the eastern organizations puts in place a dependency on their western sisters which further erodes their ability to perform traditional party functions. The inability to perform traditional functions reduces the credibility of the parties and the willingness of citizens in the new states to become engaged. Declining memberships in the reformed GDR parties and the struggle of the two new parties to recruit members produce a level of party membership much lower than that in the west. Low membership is one indicator of the well-documented lack of trust and confidence placed in the parties. The tendency for eastern parties to begin their new lives as electoral parties further attenuates their links with society. These factors do not bode well for parties in the new states to duplicate the role parties have played as leading political actors in the FRG.

The parties have not functioned well as agents of unification: instead, the fusion of parties has underscored the differences between east and west. The federal system can in theory accommodate these differences and may do so in the future. For the time being, however, increasing centralization of party organizations and the dependence of the eastern parties on the west obviates that structural advantage. These factors together ensure the continued vitality of the PDS.

Parties will not disappear in Germany as a whole but their efficacy and, therefore, legitimacy is declining. The strong links to the state are supplanting roots in society (Mair, 1995: 42-43). Eastern Germany is in a particularly difficult position because parties there never enjoyed the status they once had in the pre-unification FRG. It remains to be seen whether intermediate organizations can fill the void (Seibel, this volume).

In an interview, Clifton Taulbert, author of *Once Upon a Time ... When We Were Colored*, spoke of the price for integration paid by the black community.

> "Integration placed a premium on the green grass on the other side of the fence, and in so doing caused our parents and grandparents to lay aside those values that sustained us. We thought that all that we had would be part and parcel of what we would find on the other side. We thought we'd get what we had and more. But the opportunity to share the best of both worlds never happened. We had no opportunity to bring within the wealth of culture we had built" (*Washington Post*, 24 January 1996).

Just as no one wants to restore the days of legal segregation and discrimination, no one advocates a return to Soviet-style socialism. But an integral part of the intangible disjuncture between eastern and western Germany is located in what the former perceive they have lost.

Chapter 8

INSTITUTIONAL ELASTICITY IN A CHANGING POLITICAL ORDER
The Eastern German Nonprofit Sector and Its Contribution to Political Integration

Wolfgang Seibel

Nonprofit Institutions and Political Integration: The German Case

Political parties are a prominent and continuous subject of scholarly attention when it comes to institutional mechanisms of political integration. Interest groups, by contrast, are a far less continuous subject of research (Lehmbruch, 1995). Nonprofit institutions hardly appear on the political science agenda at all. However, while parties and interest groups secure political legitimacy (or support in the Eastonian [1965] sense) as mere input factors of political systems, nonprofit institutions mobilize political support through both input and output functions. In terms of output, nonprofit institutions provide quasi-public goods (Weisbrod, 1988); in terms of input, they organize civil society through voluntarism and network structures (Galaskiewicz, 1986; Middleton, 1987).

Nonprofit institutions are an integral part of the German polity and are essential to political integration. The pattern of state-controlled emancipation of the ruled classes, through gradual participation at a level beneath the threshold of democratization, emerged in the 19th century (Müller, 1965; Conze, 1960). In the 1880s, state-controlled social insurance and an institutional form of self-governance established a robust pattern of input-output combination (Nipperdey, 1993:335-73; Sachße and Tennstedt, 1988:15-45). The structural interdependence of state agencies and organized civil society is one of the key elements of historical continuity in Germany, as opposed to the discontinuity of German political regimes (Lepsius, 1983). So there is good reason to look at societal continuities and discontinuities again when it comes to the role of nonprofit institutions after the recent dramatic political changes in Germany.

Today, nonprofit institutions form the institutional backbone of German social policy. In employment terms, the West German nonprofit sector in 1990 represented just 3.7 percent of total employment but 10.7 percent of employment in the culture and leisure industry, 10.9 percent of employment in research and education, 34.4 percent of employment in the health industry and 61.2 percent of employment in the field of social services, based on full-time equivalents (Anheier and Priller, 1995).

The principles of self-administration and subsidiarity as laid down in several centerpieces of German public law guarantee a stable division of labor between the public and the private nonprofit sector (Anheier and Seibel, 1997).[1] Due to their history as

1. According to Paragraph 10 of the Federal Welfare Law (BSHG), public authorities are obliged to support the peak associations of the voluntary welfare services (including the church-related Diakonisches Werk and Caritas, the German Red Cross, the social democratic Workers' Welfare Association, the German Joint Welfare Association (DPWV) and the rather small Central Welfare Office for Jews in Germany) and not to

mechanisms of state-controlled political integration, German nonprofits in general and those engaged in social service provision in particular are extremely state-centered in terms of resource mobilization. Almost 70 percent of nonprofit revenue comes from public or publicly-administered sources (Anheier and Priller, 1995).[2]

The state-centeredness of the German nonprofit sector, however, does not result in structural identity. The resource dependency of nonprofit institutions continues to account for the main difference between public authorities and nonprofit organizations. Due to what is being called the non-distribution constraint (Hansmann, 1980), nonprofit organizations are unable to mobilize monetary resources through profit-making activity or stock market engagement. Due to their legal independence, nonprofit organizations are not automatically funded through state budgets either, making their financial situation precarious.

Thus, as far as resource mobilization is concerned, the structure of civil society itself is a crucial determinant of the nonprofit sector's viability. A common pattern of resource mobilization is the use of networks of reputational and power elites (Middleton, 1987). The same holds true in western Germany, where elite networks at the local, regional and federal levels link public and nonprofit sectors through interlocking directorates. The boards of major nonprofit institutions typically include representatives from both public and private nonprofit spheres. Parties, particularly the SPD and CDU, play an important if not indispensable role in stabilizing this linkage pattern due to their influence in both spheres (Seibel, 1997).

---

    interfere where those peak associations and their subsidiaries are already engaged in service provision.

2. Public funding as shares of total revenue in selected groups of nonprofit activity: 17 percent in the nonprofit culture and leisure industry, 67 percent in nonprofit housing, 70 percent in nonprofit research and education, 84 percent in the nonprofit health sector, 83 percent in the group of social services (Anheier and Priller, 1995).

By the same token, though, nonprofit organizations provide an opportunity structure for civic engagement. Their existence and organizational density may be used as an indicator of the self-organizing capacity of civil society (Anheier and Seibel, 1996). Accordingly, nonprofit institutions, particularly voluntary associations, whether they deliver services or not, provide a dense web of civic involvement and participation. More than 50 of 100 western Germans claim membership in at least one voluntary association, a type of nonprofit institution of which some 280,000 existed in West Germany in 1990. In the same year, roughly 5.5 million West Germans were reportedly engaged in voluntary work (Anheier and Priller, 1995).

Analytically, therefore, the nonprofit sector may be thought of as both a determined and a determinant factor of political integration and political stability. On the one hand, the nonprofit sector is dependent on the resource mobilization capacity of civil society: the degree of social networking and voluntarism is crucial to the nonprofit sector's viability and vitality. On the other hand, once nonprofit institutions exist, they represent a resource of social order-building and political integration in themselves.

Restructuring the Eastern German Nonprofit Sector

The dual character of the nonprofit sector as a determined and determinant factor of social integration and political stability is also shaping its reconstruction in eastern Germany. Government action, while enhancing the legal and institutional basis of the nonprofit sector, may provide opportunity structures for civic engagement. Yet it cannot mobilize civic support directly, for as Crozier (1979) put it, one can not change society by decree. Voluntarism and private giving is beyond the control of government, and so is the reliance of nonprofit institutions on sustained personal networks.

At the same time, even if the initial impulse for such engagement may be weak, governmental action does provide opportunity structures for civic engagement. In reunifying East and West, the GDR engaged in institutional imitation,[3] so when the legal order of the FRG was transferred east, standard legal forms of nonprofit institutions became immediately available.[4] Moreover, the State Treaty of 18 May 1990 stipulated the complete transfer of the social insurance system (unemployment insurance, pension funds, health insurance, accident insurance) from west to east, and it is a system exclusively based on self-administered nonprofit institutions. The principle of subsidiarity and the privileges of the voluntary welfare services were transfered as well under Article 32 of the Unification Treaty, and the state-controlled sports system prevailing in the east was transformed according to the West German pattern of voluntary associations and self-administration (Article 35). The state constitutions of the new eastern Länder, excepting Brandenburg, once again guaranteed the privileges of the voluntary welfare services and the churches (Zimmer and Priller, 1996:215-17).

Accordingly, two different perspectives prevail regarding the future of the nonprofit sector in eastern Germany. The positive view takes the model of institutional imitation at face value: successful reconstruction of a vital nonprofit sector in eastern Germany is treated matter of factly owing to the indis-

3. As of July 1, 1990, the German Democratic Republic accepted the West German currency as well as the West German social insurance and health system on the basis of the State Treaty (*Staatsvertrag*) of May 18, 1990. On October 3, 1990, the GDR formally joined the West German Federal Republic through accession to the jurisdiction of the Basic Law on the basis of the Unification Treaty (*Einigungsvertrag*) of August 31, 1990.
4. The legal basis of German nonprofit institutions is twofold, combining an organizational type with a tax-exempt status. All legal organizations may exist in for profit and nonprofit (tax-exempt) versions. The types are the registered association (*eingetragener Verein* or e.V.) and the limited liability company (*Gesellschaft mit beschränkter Haftung* or GmbH). Tax exemption is regulated by tax law.

putable structural correspondence with the west that was created by the new legal framework (Anheier and Sokolowski, 1995; Priller, 1993). In a way, this perspective emphasizes the ouput quality while neglecting the embeddedness prerequisites on the input side. The more pessimistic view points to the weakness of civil society in East Germany deriving from the legacy of fifty-six years of totalitarianism. In this perspective, the limited self-organizing capacity of eastern German society substantially restricts civic support for nonprofit institutions (Hürtgen et al., 1994; Schmid et al., 1994). This perspective emphasizes the embeddedness prerequisites for nonprofit institutions while neglecting its output quality to provide services and, last but not least, the fabricated opportunity structures for civic involvement.

Another weakness of these conventional perspectives is that they measure eastern German reality against a western German standard. The implicit assumption is that one could reconstruct socially embedded institutions from scratch, hardly the way real societies and their political orders develop. If Crozier (1979) is right, what one may expect is a different rather than a deficient nonprofit sector in eastern Germany. To focus on the formal existence of nonprofits as such does not take into account the peculiar social embeddedness of nonprofit institutions and how that affects the way nonprofits actually function. To point to the importance of the structure of civil society as such does not specify what kind of linkage between such a structure and nonprofit institutions may occur. Moreover, both perspectives necessarily ignore the structure of civil society in pre-1989 East Germany. As a result, how these legacies shape the emergence of the eastern German nonprofit sector can not be encompassed by these approaches.

This chapter is based on a combination of some conventional premises about social order-building and state structure. First, there is good reason for acknowledging that the structure of civil society develops at a slower pace than state structures and political regimes. Second, the structure of civil society is largely beyond governmental control. Third, the organizational and legal repertoire of the state may nonetheless slow down or accelerate the reconstruction of civil society. Fourth, nonprofit institutions, due to their intermediary position between state and civil society and their double character as service-providing and socially-integrating bodies, have a high potential for mitigating the tensions between different logics of development in the statutory sphere and in the sphere of civil society. Sixth, the presumed elasticity of nonprofit institutions is crucial to political integration in times of radical change, as in eastern Germany since 1989.

> Based on these premises one can ask both descriptive and analytic questions:
>
> What types of nonprofit institutions prevail in eastern Germany today?
>
> What are the main fields of their activity?
>
> What are their significant differences relative to the western German situation?
>
> How can one explain the peculiarities of the eastern German nonprofit sector compared to its western German counterpart?
>
> What hypotheses can be suggested relative to the contribution of the eastern German nonprofit sector to the process of stable social change and political integration?

Patterns of Institutional Development: Persistent pre-1989 Institutions, "Indigenous" Post-1989 Institutions, and Expanded West German Institutions

According to Zimmer and Priller (1996) one can distinguish three types of nonprofit organizations in post-1989 eastern Germany. The distinction is drawn according to the status relative to 1989:

persisting pre-1989 organizations, post-1989 "indigenous" organizations, and post-1989 expanded West German organizations.[5]

In a literal sense, nonprofit institutions of course did not exist in the GDR, since the entire state-run economy was supposed to be not for profit. Yet voluntary associations were not unconstitutional in the GDR, and there were small-scale and large-scale voluntary associations, both service-providing and non-service-providing, whose scope of political integration and civic involvement was broader than that of the communist party and the party-controlled state apparatus. Anheier and Priller (1991: 80-81) provide the following list:

mass organizations, including the Free German Youth with 2.3 million members in the late 1980s, the Young Pioneers with 1.3 million members, the Democratic Women's Federation with 1.5 million members or the Association for German-Soviet Friendship, supposedly (!) with 6.4 million members;

cultural associations, with the Cultural Federation the largest at 260,000 members; scientific and scolarly associations, including sixty-nine medical associations; service organizations such as the German Gymnastics and Sports Federation with 3.6 million members, the German Red Cross with about 680,000 members and 130,000 volunteers, and the Peoples' Solidarity (*Volkssolidarität*), a welfare association providing services for the elderly, with 2.1 million members, and 200,000 volunteers;

---

5. Information here is derived from the Johns Hopkins Comparative Nonprofit Sector Project [Germany subproject: Anheier and Seibel; East German data collection: Priller] (Anheier and Priller, 1995, Anheier and Seibel, 1997). Qualitative information [evaluated by Zimmer and Priller under the auspices of the Kommission für die Erforschung des gesellschaftlichen und politischen Wandels in den neuen Bundesländern e.V.] was directed by the present author (Zimmer and Priller, 1996).

religious and church-related organizations, including the protestant church with 5.1 million members, the catholic church with 1 million members, and the church-related welfare service organizations (in the east, the relief organization Hilfswerk; in the west, the protestant Diakonisches Werk and the catholic Caritas which together provide about 7 percent of all hospital beds);

civic associations, especially the church-related ones with an insecure legal status that were often prosecuted by the totalitarian state, and which formed the nucleus of what became the citizens' movement of 1989/90.

Not surprisingly, most of these pre-1989 organizations did not survive the demise of the GDR. More surprising are those organizations that survived unification to become important service-providing nonprofit organizations along the West German model. The GDR Red Cross became part of the all-German Red Cross, for example, and the church-related welfare organizations Diakonisches Werk und Caritas were propped up by their western German counterparts. After initial problems, the Volkssolidarität joined the German Joint Welfare Association (Deutsche Paritätische Wohlfahrtsverband or DPWV), one of the peak associations of the voluntary welfare services.

Most sports clubs, centerpieces of GDR education and propaganda, were transformed into voluntary associations along the West German model.[6] After a sharp decline in 1990, the number of sports associations rebounded; there were more than 2,000 of them in Thuringia in 1993, for example, compared to 1,800 before 1990 (Thieß, 1994). But institutional continuity

---

6. Article 39 of the *Einigungsvertrag* of August 31, 1990, stipulated that the structure of organized sports in East Germany should be transformed according to the principle of self-governance and that public authorities are obliged to support sports associations both materially and non-materially.

prevails, for according to one representative survey, fully 77 percent of eastern German sports associations are the immediate successors of former factory sports associations, sports clubs and the like. Of the remainder, 16.5 percent are split-offs from existing or previous association and only 6 percent were newly founded (Heinemann and Schubert, 1994:63).

Another persisting type of pre-1989 organization is represented by the gardening associations. They served as an organizational setting for what was termed the "niche society" of the GDR (Gaus, 1983:156-233). Gardening associations were organized among those who possessed a "Datsche" (from the Russian dacha), a small garden house with a plot of land that was usually located on the outskirts of cities and villages, and such associations were an important element in the infrastructure needed to conduct apolitical socializing under the communist regime. According to one inquiry into the registers of associations at Frankfurt/Oder and Jena, only sports associations outrank gardening associations in frequency (Hürtgen et al., 1994).[7] A relatively successful case of a persistent but innovative pre-1989 nonprofit institution is the Universal Handicapped Association of Germany, based on the idea of independent self-help; other than in Saxony, it has resisted takeover or merger attempts by similar western German associations (Schulz, 1995).

'Indigenous' post-1989 institutions have undergone significant changes, and they are characterized by an extreme variety of tasks and organizational stability. One group consists of the remnants of the grassroots citizen action groups of 1989/90. The prevailing perception is that these groups are among the losers in the post-1989 era even though they helped trigger the key events, ironically enough (Benzler, 1995; Hampele, 1994). There

---

7. In 1992, 20 percent of all associations in Frankfurt/Oder and 17.5 percent in Jena were sports associations, 17.6 percent in Frankfurt/Oder and 15 percent in Jena were gardening associations (Hürtgen et al., 1994:60).

is some evidence that part of the old citizen action groups have been transformed into relatively stable project teams that have been active in environmental protection and in the publicly funded or second labor market and providing services (Blattert et al., 1994; Rink, 1995). Most of these new or renewed groups are heavily publicly funded (Blattert et al., 1994:407).[8]

Another group of 'indigenous' post-1989 institutions which is of extraordinary importance for social stability and political integration are the nonprofit institutions that have been created by eastern German public authorities, in a sense artificially. The typical case are Employment Associations or Associations for Occupational Promotion, Employment and Structural Development (*ABS-Gesellschaften*). Most eastern Länder have founded charitable limited liability companies (*gemeinnützige GmbH*) as quasi-nongovernmental organizations (QUANGOs); these are supposedly flexible private law institutions put in charge of organizing a publicly funded or second labor market (Bosch and Neumann, 1992; Bade, Betz, and Spies, 1993; Kaiser and Otto, 1993). The idea is to mitigate the social and political costs of mass unemployment and to save human capital through artificial jobs.[9]

---

8. Blattert et al. report a figure of 70 percent public subsidy for service-providing organizations of the citizen action groups/project team type. This would be a remarkable share given the ideology of independence and grassroot democracy that characterizes such groups.

9. According to the monthly report of the Deutsche Bundesbank, the average unemployment rate across eastern Germany was 16 percent in early 1996. In Mecklenburg-Vorpommern, it was 19.5 percent, and local rates may be still higher. In response to such figures, the Brandenburg state government in 1991 created a State Agency for (economic) Structure and Labor (*Landesagentur für Struktur und Arbeit* or LASA) in the form of a noncharitable limited liability company (GmbH). According to a 1992 survey, in practice it served as an umbrella firm for 41 limited liability companies, 35 of which were charitable, and 43 organizations, 40 of which were charitable (Wagener, 1992). However, in early 1996 LASA was involved in a scandal involving the irregular use of public funds and charges of mismanagement (Spiegel 11 March 1996).

To a significant extent, the substructure of these associations and organizations is apparently composed of the small-scale initiatives that are part of the renewed, service-oriented remnants of the citizen action groups (Kletzin and Welz, 1994). The vertically integrated network of nonprofit institutions provides an indispensable infrastructure for labor market initiatives, a publicly funded labor market which accounted for some 580,000 jobs or almost 8 percent of the eastern German workforce in 1995 (Deutsche Bundesbank, 1996 (Monatsbericht February): 60).

Finally, in the domain of expanded western German nonprofit institutions one finds interest groups which do not belong to the service-providing section of the nonprofit sector and are thus not included in the present survey. It is here, however, that West Germany's logic of a decentralized state and a centralized society (Katzenstein, 1987) implies the logic of complete institutional transfer. Since interest groups or voluntary associations indeed provide a centralized counterweight to the fragmentend state structure, they were especially suited to be completely transferred from west to east (Eichener et al., 1992; Wiesenthal, 1995).

As far as service-providing institutions are concerned, this logic applied only to the peak associations of the voluntary welfare services and similar organizations (such as the ambulance services that operate nationwide – Arbeiter-Samariterbund, Malteser Hilfsdienst, Johanniter Unfallhilfe – that have locally segmented market shares). Still, three important western German welfare associations had their GDR counterparts in the pre-1989 era, the protestant Diakonisches Werk, the catholic Caritas, and the German Red Cross, and only the smallest, the social democratic Workers' Welfare Association, did not.[10] All four have established infrastructures in the east since 1989/90, even if not

---

10. In terms of employment in 1990, based on full-time equivalent work, the Caritas had 520,000 employees, the Diakonisches Werk 420,000, and the Workers' Welfare Association 50,000.

entirely from scratch, and this is also true for the important ambulance services, the most successful of which apparently is the Arbeiter-Samariterbund (Backhaus-Maul, 1993).

The situation of the German Joint Welfare Association (DPWV) was special. The DPWV is an umbrella organization primarily composed of small-scale nonprofit organizations that provide personal social services or promote self-help initiatives. Since under the Federal Welfare Law the DPWV is an officially acknowledged peak association, membership in it is the only chance for many small-scale nonprofits to get public subsidies without abandoning their independent identity, or at least maintaining the illusion of independence. In 1990, the situation of this clientele group was particularly uncertain in East Germany, and it was unclear whether the DPWV would ever become an important institution in the eastern German nonprofit sector. At the same time, the Volkssolidarität, which in 1989 had 2.1 million members, 200,000 volunteers and 15,000 local chapters and was the most important welfare organization in the GDR, was struggling for survival. An initial attempt to join the social democratic Workers' Welfare Association failed (Tangemann, 1995), as the Volkssolidarität was run largely by former SED-members and even today remains a PDS-stronghold. Yet then, though the Volkssolidarität was atypical for the DPWV's clientele, it became a member in 1991 and literally overnight the DPWV became by far the largest and most important welfare association in eastern Germany.

Strategies of Reconstruction and Social Support of Eastern German Nonprofit Institutions

The patterns of institutional development in the nonprofit sector are the combined result of institution-building strategies and social support. One can think of the purposive actions of government and nonprofit leaders as strategies. As far as governmental action is concerned, their strategies are based on the use of two kinds of resources, regulation and money. As far as nonprofit leaders and managers are concerned, their strategies are based on the pursuit of two alternative but not mutually exclusive options, either seeking public subsidies or seeking niches in the service market. The readiness of ordinary citizens to give to, to volunteer their time for, or to join the governing boards of nonprofit institutions can be thought of as social support.

The data to investigate strategies and social support is highly uneven. Public policy vis-à-vis the nonprofit sector is well-documented and can be analyzed by subgroup, such as social service, sports, arts and culture or self-help groups (Zimmer and Priller, 1996:225-263). The strategies of nonprofit leaders can only be evaluated through indirect indicators, such as their options when there is an organizational crisis (Anheier and Sokolowski, 1995). Social support for nonprofit institutions may be measured by membership rates or the degree of private giving and volunteerism.

Governmental Action

Government, especially at the federal level, has strongly fostered the eastern German nonprofit sector through regulation and public funding. Aside from the standard support through statutory subsidies, the federal government mobilized additional funds to prop up the eastern German nonprofit sector, including six designated programs with a total budget of DM 7 billion for the period from 1990 to 1995.[11] Other programs either directly sub-

11. DM 47 million for general support of the voluntary welfare associations, DM 100 million as loan for the reconstruction of social service units, DM 32 million for *Sozialstationen*, mainly run by welfare associations, DM 183 million for the restoration of social service units, most of them run by welfare associations, DM 250 million for the restoration of day care units, and DM 6.4 billion (!) in federal and state money for investment in nursing homes for the elderly (Sozialpolitische Rundschau 385/1995).

sidized nonprofit institutions or indirectly subsidized nonprofits owing to their dominant position in the relevant social policy area.[12] Ironically, even some self-help initiatives were created and sustained by a particular program of the federal government.[13]

A similar pattern holds for arts and culture. Here federal programs did not focus especially on nonprofit institutions. Unusually for a federalist system, the Unification Treaty of 31 August 1990 stipulated the federal government's responsibility for local infrastructure in arts and culture (Article 35). Special federal programs, with a budgetary total of DM 4.2 billion, were launched as "accession-dependent culture promotion" (Ackermann, 1991), much of which was spent on nonprofit institutions that were to replace their state-run GDR predecessors in the arts and culture sector. Saxony launched a Culture Regions Law *(Kulturräumegesetz)* whose explicit purpose is to integrate public, private and nonprofit initiatives of a given region in a comprehensive public support program (Zimmer, 1995).

In the realm of sports and leisure, nonprofit sports clubs are publicly subsidized at the local level, but no precise figures are available. According to a survey by Baur, Koch, and Telschow (1995), only 15 percent of eastern German sports clubs, compared to 44 percent of their western German counterparts, own the gyms and stadiums they regularly use. According to the same source, more eastern (88 percent) than western (69 percent) sports clubs use municipal gyms and stadiums, with the same discrepancy in how many use these facilities for free (73 percent vs.

---

12. DM 50 million for the Youth Program of the Federal Government for the Expansion of Independent Organizations to Aid Youth in the New Länder *(Jugendpolitisches Programm der Bundesregierung für den Aus- und Aufbau freier Träger der Jugendhilfe in den neuen Bundesländern)* and DM 100 million for the Action Program against Aggression and Violence *(Aktionsprogramm gegen Agression und Gewalt)*.
13. The related program to Promote Social Self-Help in the New Länder *(Förderung sozialer Selbsthilfe in den neuen Bundesländer)* is financed relatively modestly at DM 10 million over 4.5 years.

55 percent). This means eastern German sports clubs remain more dependent on public infrastructure than do their western German counterparts.

Attitudes of Nonprofit Leaders and Civic Support

Eastern German nonprofit institutions are heavily state-funded, though this is not unusual: no less than 70 percent of nonprofit funding in western Germany comes directly or indirectly from public sources. One can assume this proportion is even larger in the eastern German nonprofit sector but truly comparable data is not available.

We do have comparative data, however, on the attitudinal profiles of eastern and western German nonprofit managers. According to one of the surveys conducted in the course of the Johns Hopkins Comparative Nonprofit Sector Project (Anheier and Priller, 1995; Anheier and Seibel, 1997), eastern German nonprofit managers tend to perceive public funding as normal.[14] Just 32 percent of managers of small-scale nonprofit organizations in western Germany disagree that their organizations are "too dependent" on public money, compared to 51 percent of eastern German managers. The statement "public funding has deflected (us from) our initial goals" is rejected by 79 of 100 western but by even 93 of 100 eastern German nonprofit managers. Conversely, 29 percent of the western but just 14 percent of the eastern German managers asked in the survey agreed with the statement "basically, our organization more and more resembles a private business;" 57 percent of the western but 75 percent of the eastern managers rejected the same statement.

14. In western Germany, the survey was based on a random sample drawn from publicly available registers and handbooks of nonprofit institutions (N = 520). In eastern Germany, the survey was based on a random sample from the register of associations in the capitals of the five eastern Länder: Dresden, Erfurt, Magdeburg, Postdam, Schwerin (N = 470). The survey was conducted in 1992 in both eastern and western Germany.

Apparently, eastern nonprofit leaders remain significantly more state-oriented than their already state-oriented western colleagues. Certainly such attitudinal patterns can hardly be treated as truly independent variables; after all, the affirmative stance vis-à-vis the state partly reflects the real support the state is giving to this sector. It is certainly not too daring to assume eastern nonprofit leaders do not perceive the nonprofit form as an alternative to public bureaucracy. Rather, our data support the assumption that eastern German nonprofit managers perceive their organizations as a proxy for state agencies. In fact, the boundaries between the independent nonprofit institutions, such as welfare associations, and the state-created and run nonprofit institutions, such as Employment Associations, may be almost nonexistent.

The state-centeredness of managerial attitudes is complemented by a relatively weak civic support of nonprofits in eastern Germany. Only half as many eastern (25 percent) as western (50 percent) Germans are members of at least one voluntary association. The membership rate of sports clubs reflects this as well (10 percent of eastern compared to 26 percent of western Germans).[15] Volunteerism, though, is at about the same level in both east and west: 10 percent of eastern (13 percent of western) Germans indicate they are engaged in voluntary work at least once a month, 9 percent of eastern Germans engaged in voluntary work less frequently than that (12 percent of western Germans), while 81 percent of eastern and 75 percent of western Germans report never engaging in voluntary work. That volunteerism is slightly

15. See the unpublished Allbus-Basisumfrage (survey) of 1991 for these figures (Mannheimer Zentrum für Umfragen, Methoden und Analysen). More recent data do not change this pattern. Baur et al. (1995:52) report sports club membership rates of 10.9 percent (Brandenburg), 7.8 percent (Mecklenburg-Vorpommern), 10.2 percent (Sachsen), 10.2 percent (Sachsen-Anhalt), 10.4 percent (Thüringen) in the east, compared to 41.0 percent (Saarland), 33.7 percent (Baden-Württemberg), 26.6 percent (Nordrhein-Westphalen), 36.3 percent (Rheinland-Pfalz) in the west.

less important in the east is not as remarkable as the sharp decline in the east since 1990. In that year, 17 percent of the eastern Germans said they did volunteer work at least once a month (with 10 percent doing so less frequently and 73 percent answering never).[16]

The most important feature of civic support of eastern German nonprofit institutions, however, is the low degree of church membership. As of 1993, just 30 percent of eastern Germans belonged to one of the two major Christian denominations, compared to 85 percent of western Germans. Churched Catholics are a particularly tiny minority in the east, comprising no more than 4 percent of the total population, compared to 40 percent in the west. 25 percent of eastern but 45 percent of western Germans belong to the Protestant (Lutheran) church. Amazingly enough, the decline in church membership has continued since 1990, with the Catholic church by far the most affected, losing one-third of its already meager membership base from 1990 to 1993. The most dramatic losses occurred among those aged 35 to 54 (the percentage of the unchurched rose from 67 to 72) and among those 55 and older (the percentage of the unchurched rose from 50 to 56) (Kurz-Scherf and Winkler, 1994:552-56; Terwey and McCutchon, 1995). Remarkably enough, nondenominational status decreased slightly (from 84 percent in 1990 to 82 percent in 1990) among those aged 18 to 34.

Is There Really a Nonprofit Sector in Eastern Germany?

One can offer a list of the distinctive features of the eastern German nonprofit sector in answer to the question whether a nonprofit sector really exists. In the process we find a seeming paradox that might be resolved by reformulating the question.

16. See the unpublished Socioeconomic Panel surveys of 1990 and 1994 for these figures (Mannheimer Zentrum fur Umfragen, Methoden und Analysen).

First, contrary to conventional wisdom, the eastern German nonprofit sector was not built from scratch after the demise of the totalitarian regime in 1989. Instead, there has been a remarkable persistence of pre-1989 institutions at all levels. The eastern German Red Cross, Diakonisches Werk, Caritas, Volkssolidarität, sports clubs and gardening associations all have their roots in the former GDR and its society. Today, these persisting institutions represent a broad variety of purposes, organizational forms and ideological stances.

Second, the eastern German nonprofit sector is still more state-centered, in terms of resource dependency and attitudinal profiles, than its already statist western counterpart. This is clearly indicated by the amount of money government agencies have spent and continue to spend, beyond their regular obligations, to foster and stabilize the nonprofit sector in the five new Länder. Moreover, the vast majority of eastern German nonprofit leaders, unlike their western colleagues, deny there are any risks involved, whether in terms of goal deflection or dependency on the state, in accepting the extraordinary sums of public money that are being funneled into their coffers.

Third, eastern civic support of nonprofit institutions is significantly lower in terms of membership rates but not much lower in terms of volunteerism than in western Germany.

Fourth, church affiliation is dramatically lower. With nondenominational status claimed by 70 percent of eastern Germans, nondenominationalism rather than church affiliation is the norm. This is of particular significance not only for the major churches themselves but also for the church-related welfare associations. In West Germany these have been by far the most important social service providers, not to speak of being major employers.

Fifth, post-1989 eastern Germany has witnessed a QUANGO explosion.[17] Due both to general inertia and to the particular

---

17. This metaphor has been used before (Hood 1986). QUANGOs are defined as purposefully initiated governmental split-offs.

weaknesses of public bureaucracy in the east, municipal and Land governments used the nonprofit form of charitable limited liability companies and charitable associations as a relatively readily available organizational resource. The state-centeredness of the eastern nonprofit sector has also apparently blurred the boundaries between "real" and "artificial" nonprofit institutions.

What these characteristics reveal is a paradox. If we accept the idea of an eastern German nonprofit sector, then it is one that seems to exist against all odds. It lacks civic support and ideological grounding, particularly from religion, it is highly state-centered if not quasi-public and to a large extent it is composed of organizations that date back to the totalitarian regime of the GDR.

By West German standards there is therefore no nonprofit sector in eastern Germany. Given official rhetoric from both public and nonprofit sector representatives, as well as the illusions created by institutional guarantees made to the nonprofit sector in the Unification Treaty and related articles in eastern Land constitutions, this may seem a surprising conclusion. But according to the general hypotheses concerning the importance of an organized civil society in ensuring the viability of a nonprofit sector (Anheier and Seibel, 1996), there is no eastern German nonprofit sector either. If civic support and religious grounding are both lacking, if the organizational substance dates back to the communist era and if the sector is completely dependent on public money, the conventional definition of what a nonprofit sector is hardly applies here.

But if we conclude that what we observe does not meet the conventional definition of a nonprofit sector, perhaps we are asking the wrong question. We might ask instead whether the absence of that sector would make any difference, and if so, whether that difference has anything to do with the functions the nonprofit sector has traditionally filled in the German setting. If reformulated in this manner, our answer might well be quite different and confirm that a nonprofit sector indeed exists in the east.

Political Change, Societal Continuity, and the Role of the Quasi-Nonprofit Sector

There seems to be good empirical evidence to assume the quasi-nonprofit sector in eastern Germany plays an essential role in political integration. This role is presumably based on a divergence between what the formal existence of a nonprofit milieu suggests, namely an independent institutional structure beyond state and market, and the limited viability of such independent structures in eastern German reality. This argument is based on a general hypothesis that the nonprofit sector enhances institutional coping mechanisms (Seibel, 1997). The coping itself is required by the differing speed of change in political and societal spheres. Eastern German society changes at a slower pace than its dramatically changing political environment. The quasi-nonprofit sector in eastern Germany, however insufficient it may appear by conventional standards, can be thought of as an additional ingredient of institutional elasticity through which the different speeds of political and societal change are being synchronized. The key elements of that institutional elasticity are structural continuity as well as vertical and horizontal organizational differentiation.

Structural Continuity

The most striking aspect of the quasi-nonprofit sector is its multidimensional continuity, whether in organizational structures, sociopolitical embeddedness, managerial attitudes or relationship to the state. In terms of organizational structure, major and minor associations, from the Volkssolidarität to the gardening associations, have their roots in GDR society. These persisting pre-1989 organizations vary widely in terms of purpose, size and scope of action, from large organizations like the Diakonisches Werk that provide social services throughout all the new Länder to small or medium-sized sports clubs that are locally based.

Such a diversity provides familiar organizational niches for a remarkably varied clientele.

In terms of sociopolitical embeddedness and continuity, the PDS and the CDU seem to be the most prominent. In a regional study of Saxony, Patzelt and Algasinger (1995) found that the gardening associations were a PDS stronghold while the CDU was generally well-represented in local associations, including the sports clubs. Although data is not available, one may assume the boards of gardening associations and sports clubs are partly composed if not controlled by the rank and file members of these two pre-1989 parties. The PDS is also well connected to the Volkssolidarität, a welfare association unique to eastern Germany.

Managerial attitudes in the quasi-nonprofit sector and the relationship to the state are both important elements of continuity as well. The affirmative attitude of eastern nonprofit leaders about their overwhelming dependence on the state for money and infrastructure is a traditional behavioral response in a region subjected to totalitarian rule for fifty-six years. The extreme state-centeredness on the part of such managers is certainly realistic in a situation where general civic support is weak and alternative sources of revenue are scarce to nonexistent.

Organizational Differentiation

Aside from continuity, the eastern German quasi-nonprofit sector is also characterized by organizational differentiation. In terms of formal structure, organizational differentiation takes place along a vertical and a horizontal axis.

In the horizontal dimension, the eastern German quasi-nonprofit sector provides different types of organizations according to different needs and ideological and political stances. There are small-scale organizations such as self-help initiatives, voluntary associations in the publicly funded or second labor market, and gardening associations; there are also large-scale organizations such as the charitable welfare associations Volkssolidarität, German Red Cross, Diakonisches Werk and Caritas. Medium-scale organizations, such as the sports clubs and the QUANGOs, as artificial nonprofits under the control of state and municipal government, also exist.

Moreover, political orientations of all kinds may find their interests reflected in this organizational landscape. The former citizen action groups have their stake in the project teams, the small-scale initiatives and associations active in environmental protection and the publicly funded or second labor market. The PDS, as noted, is connected to the gardening associations and to the Volkssolidarität, the SPD to the Workers' Welfare Association and the Arbeiter-Samariterbund (a first aid organization), and the CDU to the church-related welfare associations Diakonisches Werk and Caritas as well as to local associations. So despite a lack of civic support, this sector, due to its organizational diversity and to the dominant role of the party system, is politically well-embedded.

In the vertical dimension, differentiation takes place in terms of centralized and decentralized organizations and related center-periphery relationships. The welfare associations are vertically differentiated and internally integrated. Regional chapters are composed of local chapters, center-periphery relationships are based on financial support of the local chapters and on selected authoritative competencies of the regional chapters relative to local chapters. By contrast, the Volkssolidarität is a member of the DPWV, which has no authoritative competencies at all even though membership in it is a virtual prerequisite for public subsidies. Occupational and employment associations are either directly integrated into regional umbrella organizations or indirectly coupled to local or regional public authorities financially through their QUANGO subsidiaries. In the publicly funded or second labor market in particular, symbiotic relationship between QUANGOs at the central (regional) level and small-scale nonprofit organizations at the local level create a patterned division of labor and a related, if loosely coupled, vertical integration. Generally speaking, there is a relatively high degree of vertical cohesion in the eastern German quasi-nonprofit sector and a sufficient level of accessibility for small-scale local organizations to centrally distributed funds.

Institutional Elasticity and Political Integration: Concluding Thoughts

The conventional definition of elasticity refers to the stability of core structures relative to changing peripheral structures in a given biological, mechanical, economic, social or political system. The more change in the periphery that can occur without affecting the core, the more elastic is the system. My argument is that the quasi-nonprofit sector in eastern Germany substantially enhances the institutional repertoire that makes the German political system elastic in the sense described.[18] So, under the particular eastern circumstances, what does the nonprofit sector do that could not be done by the legislative and executive branches of government and the party system?

As noted at the outset, one comparative advantage of nonprofits compared to parties and interest groups is that they mobilize political support through both input and output functions. Nonprofit institutions share this dual capacity with the governmental structure, at least as manifested in parliamentary systems that combine legislative with executive functions. One very practical advantage of nonprofit institutions as opposed to government, however, is that their output function can be mobilized far more quickly. Institutions ruled by private law, such as companies with limited liability or voluntary associations, are rela-

18. The institutional component is only one of the dimensions which may contribute to the elasticity of political systems. Obviously, money, or monetary lack to be precise, is another crucial component in post-1989 Germany. Other important components are ideology, especially the idea of a social market economy, and the legal system.

tively easily created under the German legal system, but the building of regular public law authorities is a relatively time-consuming process. The urgency to enact public policies to address the social costs of unemployment, for instance, largely explains the QUANGO explosion at the Land level. Ironically, one of the most pressing problems for eastern German authorities since 1990 has been how to spend huge amounts of money in a very short time period. The rapid creation of "artificial" nonprofit organizations in the five new Länder was an appropriate response for a region where a sound public bureaucracy was still developing.

The major advantages of the nonprofit form, however, are presumably connected to the structural continuity and organizational differentiation it represents relative to the governmental structures. By its organizational continuity, sociopolitical embeddedness, managerial attitudes and relationship to the state, the quasi-nonprofit sector in post-1989 eastern Germany acts as a countervailing force to the discontinuities of the political regime. This is a familiar pattern in German history; remarkably enough, it has resurfaced since 1989. The continuity of civil society structures and of state-society relationships was crucial to the high degree of social stability which characterized the political changes of 1918/19, 1933 and 1945. The early history of the GDR was the sole exception to this rule, as it was the only case in which the political regime and the societal order completely changed at the same time. In its post-GDR manifestation, eastern Germany returns to the traditional pattern.

The structural continuity of large parts of the eastern quasi-nonprofit sector has meant that both human resources and civic support can be mobilized. For a variety of reasons, this would have been nearly impossible to do in the public or private for-profit sector. For eastern Germans, the implementation of public bureaucracy according to the western German standard as well as the adoption of the new West German legal system meant enormous challenges to mental and behavioral adaptability. But the familiar nonprofit or quasi-nonprofit institutions, though operating within the new legal structure, mitigate the stress connected to that kind of adaptation and lower the threshold for all who seek access, whether as members, staff or clients. Furthermore, personal networks from the old times (the infamous *Alte Seilschaften*) can be used as mechanisms of resource mobilization and policy making. Finally, one particular advantage of nonprofit or quasi-nonprofit institutions is that they operate below the threshold of public visibility. Thus, eastern German nonprofit or quasi-nonprofit institutions can mobilize the human capital of old professional or political elites even if they are politically implicated through their Stasi connections or previous SED-membership. Needless to say, it is here that the role of the PDS is particularly important. Due to structural continuity and relative remoteness from public attention, the classic West German linkage of nonprofit to public sector through party-controlled networks, works particularly well, ironically enough, for the PDS.

One can also assume that the interdependence of structural continuity and organizational differentiation strengthens not only the cohesion of eastern German civil society but also the cohesion of state and society. Unlike in the Weimar Republic but in a manner remarkably like that of post-1945 West Germany, no important group in society is disconnected from the democratic political system as such. This is especially important when it comes to the PDS and its clientele, and the eastern quasi-nonprofit sector presumably contributes a large share to this success in terms of political integration.

Generally speaking, the nonprofit form provides an interface which loosely but decisively connects society to the political order and the general polity. After all, it was the legal nonprofit form according to the West German standard which provided the opportunity structure that led to the richly differentiated eastern German quasi-nonprofit sector. More specifically, the sector's horizontal and vertical differentiation ultimately enhances the capacity for political integration. Since this sector is completely state-dependent, it strengthens loyalty to the democratic polity even if through nonmaterial incentives. Since every significant political group in eastern Germany is either loosely or tightly connected to the quasi-nonprofit sector, both human resources and substantial political support are being mobilized in that institutional space between state and market.

BIBLIOGRAPHY

Abelein, M. 1977. Die Rechtssprechung des Bundesverfassungsgericht. In *Um Recht und Freiheit. Festschrift für Friedrich August Freiherr von der Heydtte*, eds. Heinrich Kipp et al., vol. 2, 777-92. Berlin.

Ackermann, M. 1991. Der kulturelle Einigungsprozeß. Schwerpunkt Substanzerhaltung. *Perspektiven und Argumente* 7. Forum Deutsche Einheit. Bonn [Friedrich-Ebert-Stiftung].

Aldrich, J. 1995. *Why Parties? The Origin and Transformation of Political Parties in America*. Chicago.

Alemann, U.v. 1992. Parteien und Gesellschaft in der Bundesrepublik. In *Parteien in der Bundesrepublik Deutschland*, eds. A. Mintzel and H. Oberreuter. Opladen.

Almond, G. and S. Verba. 1965. *The Civic Culture: Political Attitudes and Democracy in Five Nations*. Boston.

Almond G., B. Powell and R. Mundt. 1993. *Comparative Politics: A Theoretical Framework*. New York.

Amnesty International. 1995. *Ausländer als Opfer. Polizeiliche Mißhandlung in der Bundesrepublik Deutschland*. ai-Index EUR-23/06/95. Bonn.

Anheier, H. and E. Priller. 1991. The Non-Profit-Sector in East Germany: Before and After Unification. *Voluntas* 2:78-94.

———. 1995. Der Non-Profit-Sektor in Deutschland. Eine sozial-ökonomische Strukturbeschreibung. Zusammenfassende Darstellung. Baltimore/Berlin [Institute for Policy Studies/

Wissenschaftszentrum Berlin für Sozialforschung]. Mimeograph.
Anheier, H. and W. Sokolowski. 1995. East is East and West is West. Isomorphic Tendencies Among German Non-Profit Organizations. Paper presented at the American Sociological Association Annual Meeting.
Anheier, H. and W. Seibel. 1996. The Non-Profit Sector and the Transformation of Eastern Europe. A Comparative Analysis. In *Public Goods and Private Action*, eds. W. Powell and E. Clemens. New Haven.
———. 1997. *Between State and Market: The Nonprofit Sector in Germany*. Manchester.
Apel, H. 1991. *Die deformierte Demokratie. Parteienherrschaft in Deutschland*. Stuttgart.
Armin, H. v. 1995. *Der Staat als Beute*. Munich.
Backes, U. and E. Jesse. 1989. *Politischer Extremismus in der Bundesrepublik Deutschland*, vol. 1. Köln.
Backhaus-Maul, H. 1993. Transformation kommunaler Sozialpolitik. Institutionelle Strukturen, soziale Aufgaben und organisierte Akteure. In *Verwaltungsintegration in den neuen Bundesländern*, ed. R. Pitschas, 143-56. Berlin.
Bade, K. 1992. *Ausländer, Aussiedler, Asyl in der Bundesrepublik Deutschland: Aktuelle-Kontroverse*, 2d ed. Hanover.
———. 1994. Immigration and Social Peace in United Germany. *Daedalus* 123 (Winter): 85-106.
Bade, H., M. Betz und B-G. Spies. 1993. Strukturerneuerung und Beschäftigungsförderung durch ABS. Erfahrungen, Erfolge, Probleme und Perspektiven aus Sicht der ostdeutschen Schiffbauindustrie. *Memo-Forum* 20:26-35.
Baker, K., R. Dalton, and K. Hildebrandt. 1981. *Germany Transformed*. Cambridge.
Barnes S. and M. Kaase, eds. 1979. *Political Action. Mass Participation in Five Western Democracies*. London.
Bauer, P. and H. Schmitt. 1990. *Die Republikaner*. Mannheim.
Baur, J., U. Koch and S. Telschow. 1995. *Sportvereine im Übergang. Die Vereinslandschaft in Ostdeutschland*. Aachen.

Baylis, T. 1995. Leadership Change in Eastern Germany: From Colonisation to Integration? In *The Federal Republic of Germany at Forty-Five: Union without Unity*, ed. P. Merkl, 243-62. New York.

Becker, H. 1993. Einstellungen zu Ausländer in der Bevolkerung der Bundesrepublik Deutschland 1992. In *Zuwanderung und Asyl in der Konkurrenz-Gesellschaft*, ed. B. Blanke, 141-49. Opladen.

Beckwith, K. 1992. Comparative Research and Electoral Systems: Lessons from France and Italy. *Women and Politics* 12 (1): 1-33.

Behrend, M. and H. Meier, eds. 1991. *Der schwere Weg der Erneuerung: von der SED zur PDS. Eine Dokumentation.* Berlin.

Belchem, J. 1991. *Class, Party, and the Political System in Britain 1867-1914.* Oxford.

Bendikat, E. 1989. Politikstile, Konfliktlinien und Lagerstrukturen im deutschen, britischen und französischen Parteiensystem des späten 19. Jahrhunderts. *Politische Vierteljahresschrift* 30 (3): 482-502.

Bendix, J. 1990. *Importing Foreign Workers: A Comparison of German and American Policy.* New York.

Bendix, J. and N. Steiner 1998. Political Asylum in Germany: International Norms and Domestic Politics *German Politics and Society* 16 (2): 32-49.

Benz, W., ed. 1979. *Bewegt von der Hoffnung aller Deutscher: Zur Geschichte des Grundgesetzes, Entwürfe und Diskussionen 1941-1949.* Munich.

———. 1994. *Rechtsextremismus in Deutschland: Vorraussetzungen, Zusammenhänge, Wirkungen.* Frankfurt a.M.

Benzler, S. 1995. Von der Bürgerbewegung zur Zivilgesellschaft. In *Deutschland Ost vor Ort: Anfänge der lokalen Politik in den neuen Bundesländern*, eds. S. Benzler, U. Bullmann, and D. Eißel, 13-48. Opladen.

Berger, M., W. Gibowski, D. Roth, and W. Schulte. 1977. Bundestagswahl 1976: Politik und Sozialstruktur. *Zeitschrift für Parlamentsfragen* 8 (2): 197-231.

Berger, M., W. Gibowski, M. Jung, D. Roth, and W. Schulte. 1990. Sieg ohne Glanz: Eine Analyse der Bundestagswahl 1987. In *Wahlen und Wähler. Analysen aus Anlaß der Bundestagswahl 1987*, eds. M. Kaase and H.-D. Klingemann. Opladen.

Berghahn, V. 1994. *Imperial Germany, 1871-1914*. Providence.

Berg-Schlosser, D. 1990. Entwicklung der Politischen Kultur in der Bundesrepublik Deutschland. *Aus Politik und Zeitgeschichte* 7:30-46.

Bericht über die Lage der Ausländer in der Bundesrepublik Deutschland. 1995. Beauftragte der Bundesregierung für die Belange der Ausländer. Document AS2-73-40.

Betz, H.-G. 1994. *Radical Right-Wing Populism in Western Europe*. New York.

———. 1996. The Social Base of German Parties. Working paper, Center for German and European Studies. University of California, Berkeley.

Betz, H.-G. and H. Welsh. 1995. The PDS in the New German Party System. *German Politics* 4 (3): 92-111.

Blattert, B., D. Rink and D. Rucht. 1994. Von den Oppositionsgruppen der DDR zu den den neuen sozialen Bewegungen in Ostdeutschland? *Politische Vierteljahresschrift* 36: 397-422.

Bluck, C. and H. Kreikenbom. 1991. Die Wähler in der DDR: Nur issue-orientiert oder auch parteigebunden? *Zeitschrift für Parlamentsfragen* 22 (3): 495-502.

Bosch, G. and H. Neumann. 1992. Beschäftigungs- und Qualifizierungsgesellschaften als Instrument zur Bewältigung der Arbeitsmarktsituation in den neuen Bundesländern. In *Systemumbruch, Arbeitslosigkeit und individuelle Bewältigung in der Ex-DDR*, ed. T. Kieselbach, 425-39. Weinheim.

Boyer, R. and D. Drache, eds. 1996. *States Against Markets*. London/New York.

Bracher, K.-D. 1955. *Die Auflösung der Weimarer Republik*. Düsseldorf.

———. 1971. Das Bonner Parteienwesen. In *Das deutsche Dilemma: Leidenwege der politischen Emanzipation*, ed. K.-D. Bracher. Munich.

Brandt, W. 1988. Wandel durch Auflehnung. *Der Tagesspiegel*, 13 September.
Braunthal, G. 1994. *The German Social Democrats since 1969: A Party in Power and Opposition*. Boulder.
Brazier, R. 1998. *Constitutional Reform: Reshaping the British Political System*, 2nd ed. Oxford.
Broszat, M. and H. Weber, eds. 1990. *SBZ-Handbuch*. Munich.
Brubaker, R. 1992. *Citizenship and Nationhood in France and Germany*. Cambridge.
Bürklin, W. 1994. Verändertes Wahlverhalten und der Wandel der Politischen Kultur. In *Das Superwahljahr 1994. Deutschland vor unkalkulierbaren Regierungsmehrheiten?* eds. W. Bürklin and D. Roth, 27-53. Köln.
Bürklin, W. and R. Dalton. 1994. Das Ergrauen der Grünen. In *Wahlen und Wähler. Analysen aus Anlaß der Bundestagswahl 1990*, eds. H.-D. Klingemann and M. Kaase. Opladen.
Bullmann, U. and W. Schwanegel. 1995. Zur Transformation territorialer Politikstrukturen. In *Deutschland Ost vor Ort: Anfänge der lokalen Politik in den neuen Bundesländern*, eds. S. Benzler, U. Bullmann, and D. Eißel. Opladen.
Butler, D. and A. Ranney, eds. 1994. *Referendums Around the World: The Growing Use of Democracy?* Washington.
Castells, M. 1996. *The Rise of the Network Society*. Cambridge.
Chandler, W. 1988. Party System Transformations in the Federal Republic of Germany. In *Parties and Party Systems in Liberal Democracies*, ed. S. Wolinetz. London.
Childers, T. 1991. The Middle Classes and National Socialism. In *The German Bourgeoisie*, eds. D. Blackbourn and R. Evans. London/New York.
Claggett, W., J. Loesch, W. Shively, and R. Snell. 1982. Political Leadership and the Development of Political Cleavages: Imperial Germany, 1871-1912. *American Journal of Political Science* 26 (4): 643-664.
Clemens, C. 1995. Second Wind or Last Gasp? Helmut Kohl's CDU/CSU and the Elections of 1994. In *Germany's New Politics*, eds. D. Conradt et al., 121-26. Providence/Oxford.

Conradt, D. 1989. Changing German Political Culture. In *The Civic Culture Revisited*, eds. G. Almond and S. Verba, 212-72. Newbury Park.
———. 1996. *The German Polity*, 6th ed. New York: Longman.
Conradt, D. and R. Dalton. 1988. The West German Electorate and the Party System: Continuity and Change in the 1980's. *The Review of Politics* 50 (1): 3-29.
Conze, W. 1960. Der Verein als Lebensform des 19. Jahrhunderts. *Innere Mission* 50:226-234.
Crepaz, M. 1996. Explaining National Variations of Welfare Expenditure: An Empirical Study of the Impact of Exclusive vs Inclusive Political Institutions. Paper presented at the Midwest Political Science Association Meetings.
Crozier, M. 1979. *On ne change pas la société par decrèt*. Paris.
Dahrendorf, R. 1967. *Society and Democracy in Germany*. New York/London.
Daley, A., ed. 1995. *The Mitterand Era: Policy Alternatives and Political Mobilization in France*. New York.
Dalton, R. 1986. Wertwandel oder Wertwende. Die Neue Politik und Parteienpolarisierung. In *Wahlen und Wähler. Analysen aus Anlaß der Bundestagswahl 1983*, eds. H.-D. Klingemann and M. Kaase, 427-54. Opladen.
———. 1992. Two German Electorates. In *Developments in German Politics*, eds. G. Smith et al. Durham.
Dalton, R. and W. Bürklin. 1995. The Two German Electorates: The Social Bases of the Vote in 1990 and 1994. *German Politics and Society* 13 (1): 79-99.
Dalton, R., S. Flanagan, and P. Beck. 1984. *Electoral Change in Advanced Industrial Democracies*. Princeton.
Dalton, R. and M. Kuechler, eds. 1990. *Challenging the Political Order*. New York.
Dalton, R. and R. Rohrschneider. 1990. Wählerwandel und die Abschwächung der Parteineigungen von 1972 bis 1987. In *Wahlen und Wähler. Analysen aus Anlaß der Bundestagswahl 1987*, eds. H.-D. Klingemann and M. Kaase, 297-324. Opladen.

Delfs, S. 1993. Heimatvertriebene, Aussiedler, und Spätaussiedler: Rechtliche und politische Aspekte der Aufnahme von Deutschstämmigen aus Osteuropa in der Bundesrepublik Deutschland. *Aus Politik und Zeitgeschichte* 48:3-11.
Derlien, H.-U. 1995. Elite Circulation and Institutional Consolidation in Eastern Germany. Paper presented at the German Studies Association Conference.
Dinse, J. 1992. *Zum Rechtsextremismus in Bremen*. Bremen.
Dogan, M. 1988. *Comparing Pluralist Democracies: Strains on Legitimacy*. Boulder.
Donovan, B. 1995. Transfer or Transformation? The Volksparteien in the Five Eastern States. Paper presented at the German Studies Association Conference.
Duverger, M. 1972. *Political Parties*, 3d ed. New York.
Dyson, K. 1977. *Party, State, and Bureaucracy in Western Germany*. Sage.
———. 1982. Party Government and Party State. In *Party Government and Political Culture in Germany*, eds. H. Döring and G. Smith. New York.
———. 1984. The Politics of Corporate Crisis in West Germany. *West European Politics* 7 (1): 24-46.
Easton, D. 1965. *A Systems Analysis of Political Life*. New York.
Ebsworth, R. 1960. *Restoring Democracy in Germany: The British Contribution*. London.
Eckstein, G. and F. Pappi. 1994. Die politischen Wahrnehmungen und die Präferenzen der Wählerschaft in Ost- und Westdeutschland: Ein Vergleich. In *Wahlen und Wähler. Analysen aus Anlaß der Bundestagswahl 1990*, eds. H.-D. Klingemann and Kaase, 397-421. Opladen.
Ehrhart, C. and E. Sandschneider. 1994. Politikverdrossenheit. Kritische Anmerkungen zur Empirie, Wahrnehmung, und Interpretation abnehmender politischer Partizipation. *Zeitschrift für Parlamentsfragen* 24 (3): 441-58.
Eichener, V. et al. 1992. *Organisierte Interessen in Ostdeutschland*. Marburg.

Falter, J. 1981. Kontinuität und Neubeginn. Die Bundestagswahl 1949 zwischen Weimar und Bonn. *Politische Vierteljahresschrift* 22 (3): 236-263.

———. 1988. Wahlen und Wählerverhalten unter besonderer Berücksichtigung des Aufstiegs der NSDAP nach 1928. In *Die Weimarer Republik 1918-1933*, 2d ed., eds. K.-D. Bracher, M. Funke, and H.-A. Jacobsen. Bonn.

———. 1990. The First German Volkspartei: The Social Foundations of the NSDAP. In *Elections, Parties and Political Traditions*, ed. K. Rohe. New York.

———. 1994. *Wer wählt rechts?* Munich.

———. 1996. Die Landtagswahlen 1946 in der Sowjetischen Besatzungszone - Eine wahlhistorische Analyse. In *Von der SBZ zur DDR*, eds. K. Möller and L. Mehringer. Göttingen.

Falter, J. and M. Klein. 1994. Die Wähler der PDS bei der Bundestagswahl 1994. Zwischen Ideologie, Nostalgie und Protest. *Aus Politik und Zeitgeschichte* 51/52: 22-34.

Falter, J. and S. Schumann. 1994. Der Nichtwähler – das unbekannte Wesen. In *Wahlen und Wähler. Analysen aus Anlaß der Bundestagswahl 1990*, eds. H.-D. Klingemann and M. Kaase, 161-213. Opladen.

Faul, E. 1964. Verfemung, Duldung und Anerkennung des Parteiwesens in der Geschichte des politischen Denkens. *Politische Vierteljahresschrift* 5:61-94.

Feist, U. 1992. Rechtsruck in Baden-Württemberg und Schleswig-Holstein. In *Protestwähler und Wahlverweigerer. Krise der Demokratie?* eds. K. Starzacher et al., 69-77. Köln.

Feist, U. and H. Krieger. 1987. Alte und neue Scheidelinien des politischen Verhaltens. *Aus Politik und Zeitgeschichte* 12.

Feist, U. and K. Liepelt. 1987. Modernisierung zu Lasten der Großen. *Journal für Sozialforschung* 27 (3/4): 277-95.

Fischer, W. 1993. Formen unmittelbarer Demokratie im Grundgesetz. *Aus Politik und Zeitgeschichte* 52/53: 16-18.

Flanagan, S. and R. Dalton. 1984. Parties Under Stress: Realignment and Dealignment in Advanced Industrial Societies. *West European Politics* 7 (1): 7-23.

Fletcher, A. 1997. The Politics of the Formulation of Telecommunications Policy in France and the United States. Ph.D. diss., University of Georgia, Athens.
Foelz-Schroeter, M. 1974. *Föderalistische Politik und Nationale Representation 1945-1947*. Stuttgart.
Forschungsgruppe Wahlen. 1990. Bundestagswahl 1990. Eine Analyse der ersten gesamtdeutschen Bundestagswahl am 2. Dezember 1990. *Berichte der FGW* 61.
———. 1994a. Gesamtdeutsche Bestätigung für die Bonner Regierungskoalition. Eine Analyse der Bundestagswahl 1990. In *Wahlen und Wähler. Analysen aus Anlaß der Bundestagswahl 1990*, eds. H.-D. Klingemann and M. Kaase. Opladen.
———. 1994b. Bundestagswahl 1994. Eine Analyse der Wahl zum 13. Deutschen Bundestag am 16. Oktober 1994. *Berichte der FGW* 76.
———. 1995. Wahlen in Berlin. Eine Analyse der Wahl zum Abgeordnetenhaus vom 22.Oktober 1995. *Berichte der FGW* 83.
———. 1996. *Wahl in Baden-Württemberg*. Mannheim.
Frotscher, W. 1985. Die parteienstaatliche Demokratiekrise – Zeichen und Zukunftsperspektiven. *Deutsches Verwaltungsblatt* 17: 917-927.
Fuchs, D., J. Gerhards and E. Roller. 1993. WIR UND DIE ANDEREN: Ethnozentrismus in den zwölf Ländern der europäischen Gemeinschaft. *Kölner Zeitschrift für Soziologie und Sozialpsychologie* 45:238-53.
Fuchs, D., H.-D. Klingemann, and C. Schöbel. 1991. Perspektiven der politischen Kultur im vereinigten Deutschland. *Aus Politik und Zeitgeschichte* 32:35-46.
Fuchs, D. and S. Kühnel. 1994. Wählen als rationales Handeln: Anmerkungen zum Nutzen des Rational-Choice-Ansatzes in der empirischen Wahlforschung. In *Wahlen und Wähler. Analysen aus Anlaß der Bundestagswahl 1990*, eds. H.-D. Klingemann and M. Kaase, 305-64. Opladen.
Gabriel, O. 1987. Demokratiezufriedenheit und demokratische Einstellungen in der Bundesrepublik Deutschland. *Aus Politik und Zeitgeschichte* 22:32-45.

———. 1991. Das lokale Parteiensystem zwischen Wettbewerbs- und Konsensdemokratie. In *Parteien und regionale politische Traditionen*, eds. D. Oberndörfer and K. Schmitt, 371-96. Berlin.
Galaskiewicz, J. 1986. *Gifts, Givers and Getters: Business Philanthropy in an Urban Setting*. San Diego.
Gans, C. 1993. Television: Political Participation's Enemy #1. *Spectrum: the Journal of State Government* 66 (2): 26-31.
Gaus, G. 1983. *Wo Deutschland liegt. Eine Ortsbestimmung*. Hamburg.
Geißler, R. 1996. *Die Sozialstruktur Deutschlands*, 2d ed. Opladen.
Geschichtliche Grundbegriffe. 1972-97, 8 vols. s.v. "Partei, Faktion."
Gibowski, W. 1995. Germany's General Election in 1994: Who Voted for Whom? In *Germany's New Politics*, eds. D. Conradt et al. Providence/Oxford.
Gibowski, W. and M. Kaase. 1991. Auf dem Weg zum politischen Alltag. Eine Analyse der ersten gesamtdeutschen Bundestagswahl vom 2. Dezember 1990. *Aus Politik und Zeitgeschichte* 11/12:3-20.
Gilbert, M. 1994. Italy Turns Rightwards. *Contemporary Review* 265:4-11.
Glaeßner, G.-J. 1991. Einheit oder Zwietracht? Bundesrepublik – DDR – deutsche Perspektiven. In *Das Ende eines Experimentes*, eds. G.-J. Glaeßner and R. Reißig. Berlin.
Gluchowski, P. and C. Zelle. 1992. Demokratisierung in Ostdeutschland. Aspekte der politischen Kultur in der Periode des Systemwechsels. In *Regimewechsel: Demokratisierung und politische Kultur in Ost-Mitteleuropa*, eds. P. Gerlich, F. Plasser and P. Ulram, 231-74. Vienna/Köln.
Golay, J. 1958. *The Founding of the Federal Republic*. Chicago.
Golz, H.-G. 1995. Wir müssen lernen, mit Fremden zu leben: Neue Daten und Fakten zur Migration. *Deutschland Archiv* 28 (1).
Guggenberger, B. and A. Meier, eds. 1994. *Der Souverän auf der Nebenbühne. Essays und Zwischenrufe zur deutschen Verfassungsdiskussion*. Opladen.

Hall, P. 1986. *Governing the Economy: The Politics of State Intervention in Britain and France*. New York.
Hamm-Brücher, H. 1991. Der freie Volksvertreter - eine Legende? Erfahrungen mit parlamentarischer Macht und Ohnmacht. Munich.
———. 1993. Wege in die und Wege aus der Politik(er)verdrossenheit. Von der Zuschauerdemokratie zur demokratischen Bürgergesellschaft. *Aus Politik und Zeitgeschichte* 31:3-6.
Hampele, A. 1994. Überlegungen zum Unabhängigen Frauenverband. Organisationslaufbahn eines frauenpolitischen Experiments im deutschen Vereinigungsprozeß. *Berliner Debatte Initial* 4:71-82.
Hansmann, H. 1980. The Role of Non-Profit Enterprise. *Yale Law Journal* 89:835-901.
Hart, J. 1992. *Proportional Representation: Critics of the British Electoral System 1820-1945*. Oxford.
Haungs, P. and E. Jesse, eds. 1987. *Parteien in der Krise?* Köln.
Heinemann, K. and M. Schubert. 1994. *Der Sportverein.* Berlin.
Hennig, E. 1990. Die REPs waren dabei: kommt der Rechtsextremismus aus der DDR? *Vorgänge* 106 (4): 79-88.
———. 1991. *Die Republikaner im Schatten Deutschlands.* Frankfurt.
Hennis, W. 1992. "Parteienstaat" des Grundgesetzes: eine gelungene Erfindung. In *Die Kontroverse: Weizsäcker Parteienkritik in der Diskussion*, eds. G. Hofman and W. Perger, 25-50. Bonn.
Herbert, U. 1990. *A History of Foreign Labor in Germany, 1880-1980.* Ann Arbor.
Hereth, M. 1969. *Die parlamentarische Opposition in der Bundesrepublik.* Munich.
Hesse, K. 1988. *Westmedien in der DDR.* Köln.
Hirschman, A. 1970. *Exit, Voice and Loyalty.* Cambridge.
Hoffmann, J. 1995. STATT Partei: Das Scheitern einer bürgerlichen Protestpartei. In *Umbruch und Wandel in westeuropäischen Parteiensystemen*, eds. W. Gellner and H. Veen. Frankfurt.

Hoffmann, R., N. Kluge, G. Linne, E. Mezger, eds. 1994. *Problemstart: Politischer und Sozialer Wandel in den neuen Bundesländern.* Köln.
Hoffmann-Riem, W. 1991. *Rundfunkneuordnung in Ostdeutschland.* Hamburg.
Hofmann, R. 1993. *Geschichte der deutschen Parteien.* Munich.
Hofmann-Göttig, J. 1989. Die Neue Rechte: Die Männerpartei. *Aus Politik und Zeitgeschichte* 41/42:21-31.
Hood, C. 1986. The Hidden Public Sector. The "Quangocratization" of the World? In *Guidance, Control, and Evaluation in the Public Sector*, eds F.-X. Kaufmann, G. Majone and V. Ostrom, 183-207. Berlin/New York.
Hülsberg, W. 1988. *The German Greens: A Social and Political Profile.* London.
Huelshoff, M., A. Markovits and S. Reich, eds. 1993. *From Bundesrepublik to Deutschland: German Politics after Unification.* Ann Arbor.
Hürtgen, R. et al. 1994. Soziopolitische Interessenvermittlungsstrukturen im Transformationsprozess. In *Politische Strukturen im Umbruch*, eds. H. Nassmacher, O. Niedermayer, and H. Wallman, 29-57. Berlin.
Humphreys, P. 1994. *Media and Media Policy in Germany: The Press and Broadcasting since 1945.* Providence.
Huntington, S. 1993. Democracy's Third Wave. In *The Global Resurgence of Democracy*, eds. L. Diamond and M. Plattner. Baltimore.
Ishiyama, J. 1995. Communist Parties in Transition. *Comparative Politics* 29 (2): 147-66.
Jagodzinski, W., J. Friedrichs, and H. Dülmer. 1995. Urban Conflict and Voting Patterns. Some Tentative Generalizations from the Last State Election in Hamburg. *Res Publica* 37 (2): 177-88.
Jaschke, H.-G. 1992. Nicht-demokratische politische Partizipation in der sozial polarisierten Stadt. In *Protestwähler und Wahlverweigerer. Krise der Demokratie?* eds. K. Starzacher et al. Köln.

———. 1993. *Die "Republikaner:" Profile einer Rechtsaußenpartei.* 2d ed. Bonn.
Jesse, E. 1992. Parteien in Deutschland. Ein Abriß der historischen Entwicklung. In *Parteien in der Bundesrepublik Deutschland*, 2d ed., eds. A. Mintzel and H. Oberreuter. Bonn.
Jung, M. and D. Roth. 1992. Politische Einstellungen in Ost- und Westdeutschland seit der Bundestagswahl 1990. *Aus Politik und Zeitgeschichte* 19:3-16.
———. 1994. Kohls knappster Sieg. Eine Analyse der Bundestagswahl 1994. *Aus Politik und Zeitgeschichte* 51/52:3-15.
Jung, O. 1993. *Grundgesetz und Volksentscheid: Gründe und Reichweite der Entscheidungen des Parlamentarischen Rats gegen Formen der Direkten Demokratie.* Opladen.
Kaack, H. 1971. *Geschichte und Struktur des deutschen Parteiensystems.* Opladen.
Kaase, M. 1982. Partizipatorische Revolution - Ende des Parteienstaates? In *Bürger und Parteien*, ed. J. Raschke, 173-81. Bonn.
Kaase, M. and H.-D. Klingemann. 1994. Der mühsame Weg zur Entwicklung von Parteiorientierungen in der "neuen" Demokratie: Das Beispiel der früheren DDR. In *Wahlen und Wähler. Analysen aus Anlaß der Bundestagswahl 1990*, eds. H.-D. Klingemann and M. Kaase, 365-96. Opladen.
Kaiser, M. and M. Otto. 1993. Was ABS-Gesellschaften bisher geleistet haben. Ergebnisse einer empirischen Trägeranalyse - neue Bundesländer. IAB WerkstattRecht 13. Nürnberg [Institut für Arbeitsmarkt- und Berufsforschung der Bundesanstalt für Arbeit].
Kaltefleiter, W. and K.-H. Naßmacher. 1994. Das Parteiengesetz 1994 – Reform der kleinen Schritte. *Zeitschrift für Parlamentsfragen* 25 (2).
Katz, R. and P. Mair. 1995. Changing Models of Party Organization and Party Democracy: The Emergence of the Cartel Party. *Party Politics* 24 (1): 5-28.
Katzenstein, P. 1987. *Policy and Politics and West Germany. The Growth of a Semi-sovereign State.* Philadelphia.

Keeler, J. and M. Schain, eds. 1996. *Mitterand's Legacy: Chirac's Challenge*. New York.
Kemp, T. 1985. *Industrialization in Nineteenth Century Europe*. 2d ed. Essex.
Kempf, U. 1984. Bürgerinitiativen – Der empirische Befund. In *Bürgerinitiativen und Repräsentatives System*, eds. B. Guggenberger and U. Kempf, 295-317. Opladen.
Kirchheimer, O. 1966. The Transformation of the Western European Party Systems. In *Political Parties and Political Development*, eds. J. LaPalombara and M. Weiner, 177-200. Princeton.
Kitschelt, H. 1990. New Social Movements and the Decline of Party Organization. In *Challenging the Political Order*, eds. R. Dalton and M. Kuechler, 179-208. Oxford.
———. 1992. The Formation of Party Systems in East-Central Europe. *Politics and Society* 20 (1): 7-50.
———. 1994. *The Transformation of European Social Democracy*. Cambridge/New York.
———. 1995. *The Radical Right in Western Europe*. Ann Arbor.
Klär, K.-H., M. Ristau, B. Schoppe, and M. Stadelmaier. 1989a. *Weder verharmlosen noch dämonisieren: Die Wähler der extremen Rechten*, vol.1. Bonn.
———. 1989b. *Sozialstruktur und Einstellungen von Wählern rechtsextremer Parteien: Die Wähler der extremen Rechten*, vol. 3. Bonn.
Klein, I. 1990. *Die Bundesrepublik als Parteienstaat: Die Mitwirkung der politischen Parteien an der Willensbildung des Volkes, 1945-1949*. Frankfurt/M.
Klein, M. and C. Caballero. 1996. Rückwärtsgewandt in die Zukunft. Die Wähler der PDS bei der Bundestagswahl 1994. *Politische Vierteljahresschrift* 37 (2): 229-47.
Kleinfeld, G. 1995. The Return of the PDS. In *Germany's New Politics*, eds. D. Conradt et al., 193-221. Providence/Oxford.
Kleinsteuber, H. 1982. *Rundfunkpolitik in der Bundesrepublik. Der Kampf um die Macht über Hörfunk und Fernsehen*. Opladen.

Kletzin, H. and P. Wels. 1994. Strategiearbeit durch Strukturgestaltung in einer Leipziger Beschäftigungsgesellschaft. In *Problemstart: politischer und sozialer Wandel in den neuen Bundesländern*, eds. R. Hoffmann and E. Mezger, 234-53. Köln.

Klingemann, H.-D. 1985. West Germany. In *Electoral Change in Western Democracies*, eds. I. Crewe and D. Denver, 230-63. New York.

Köcher, R. 1994. Auf einer Woge der Euphorie. *Aus Politik und Zeitgeschichte* 51/52:16-21.

Koller, B. 1993. Aussiedler in Deutschland: Aspekte ihrer sozialen und beruflichen Eingliederung. *Aus Politik und Zeitgeschichte* 48:12-22.

Kommers, D. 1989. *The Constitutional Jurisprudence of the Federal Republic*. Durham.

Kopecky, P. 1995. Developing Party Organizations in East-Central Europe: What Type of Party is Likely to Emerge? *Party Politics* 1 (4): 515-33.

Kreikenbom, H. 1992. Bürger und Parteien in Jena, Bürgerbefragung vom Juni 1992. Friedrich-Schiller-Universität Jena.

———. 1996. Parteiorientierungen ostdeutscher Bürger im Transformationsprozess. In *Wahlen und politische Einstellungen in westlichen Demokratien*, eds. O. Gabriel and J. Falter, 223-41. Frankfurt.

———. 1997. Einstellungen der Bürger zu den Parteien. In *Politische Orientierungen und Verhaltensweisen im vereinigten Deutschland*, ed. O. Gabriel, 167-87. Opladen.

Kreikenbom, H. and M. Stapelfeld. 1994. Steine auf dem Weg zum politischen Alltag. Vorgeprägte Orientierungen und aktuelle Erfahrungen der ehemaligen DDR-Bürger mit dem Interessenvermittlungssystem der Bundesrepublik. In *Politische Kultur in Ost- und Westdeutschland*, eds. O. Niedermayer and K. v. Beyme, 162-84. Berlin.

———. 1995. Die Transformation der politischen Kultur in den neuen Bundesländern am Beispiel der Bürgerorientierungen gegenüber den soziopolitischen Vermittlungsstrukturen und

dem politischen System in der Bundesrepublik. Forschungsbericht Teil B. Friedrich-Schiller-Universität Jena.
Krokow, C. v. and P. Lösche, eds. 1986. *Parteien in der Krise.* Munich.
Krugman, P. 1995. Growing World Trade: Causes and Consequences. *Brookings Papers on Economic Activity* 1. Washington DC.
Küchler, M. 1982. Staats-, Parteien-, oder Politikverdrossenheit? In *Bürger und Parteien*, ed. J. Raschke. Opladen.
———. 1990. Ökologie statt Ökonomie: Wählerpräferenzen im Wandel? In *Wahlen und Wähler. Analysen aus Anlaß der Bundestagswahl 1987*, eds. M. Kaase and H.-Klingemann, 419-51. Opladen.
Kühne, T. 1995. Zur Genese der deutschen Proporzkultur im wilhelminischen Preussen.*Politische Vierteljahresschrift* 36:220-42.
Kurz-Scherf, I. und G. Winkler. 1994. *Sozialreport 1994. Daten und Fakten zur sozialen Lage in den neuen Bundesländern* [Sozialwissenschaftliches Forschungszentrum Berlin-Brandenburg e.V.]. Berlin.
Lang, J., P. Moreau, and V. Neu. 1995. Auferstanden aus Ruinen ...? Die PDS nach dem Super-Wahljahr 1994. *Interne Studien* 11 [Konrad-Adenauer-Stiftung].
Lehmbruch, G. 1967. *Proporzdemokratie. Politisches System und Politische Kultur in der Schweiz und in Österreich.* Tübingen.
———. 1993. Institutionentransfer. Zur politischen Logik der Verwaltungsintegration in Deutschland. In *Verwaltungsreform und Verwaltungspolitik im Prozeß der deutschen Einigung*, eds. W. Seibel, A. Benz and H. Mäding, 41-66. Baden-Baden.
———. 1995. Die korporative Verhandlungsdemokratie in Westmitteleuropa. Universität Konstanz. Mimeograph.
Leibholz, G. 1958. *Strukturprobleme in der modernen Demokratie.* Karlsruhe.
Leonard, J. 1991. Divided Government and Dysfunctional Politics. *PS: Political Science & Politics* 24 (4): 651-54.

Lepsius, R. 1973a. Parteiensystem und Sozialstruktur: zum Problem der Demokratisierung der deutschen Gesellschaft. In *Die deutschen Parteien vor 1918*, ed. G. Ritter. Köln.

———. 1973b. Wahlverhalten, Parteien und politische Spannungen. Vermutungen zu Tendenzen und Hypothesen zur Untersuchung der Bundestagswahl 1972. *Politische Vierteljahresschrift* 5:295-313.

———. 1983. Die Bundesrepublik Deutschland in der Kontinuität und Diskontinuität historischer Entwicklungen. In *Sozialgeschichte der Bundesrepublik Deutschland*, eds. W. Conze and R. Lepsius. Stuttgart.

Lepszy, N. 1989. Die Republikaner. *Aus Politik und Zeitgeschichte* 40/41.

Liepelt, K. 1967. Anhänger der neuen Rechtspartei – Ein Beitrag zur Diskussion. Diskussion über das Wählerreservoir der NPD. *Politische Vierteljahresschrift* 8 (2): 237-71.

———. 1971. The Infra-Structure of Party Support in Germany and Austria. In *European Politics*, eds. M. Dogan and R. Rose, 183-202. Boston.

Lijphart, A. 1975. *The Politics of Accomodation. Pluralism and Democracy in the Netherlands*. Berkeley.

———. 1994. *Electoral Systems and Party Systems: A Study of Twenty-seven Democracies, 1945-1990*. New York.

Lipset, S. and S. Rokkan, eds. 1967. *Party Systems and Voter Alignments: Cross-National Perspectives*. New York.

Lorig, W. 1994. Parteipolitik und öffentlicher Dienst. *Zeitschrift für Parlamentsfragen* 25 (2): 94-106.

Loewenberg, G. 1971. The Remaking of the German Party System. In *European Politics*, eds. M. Dogan and R. Rose, 259-80. Boston.

Löwenthal, R. 1979. Bonn and Weimar: Zwei Demokratien. In *Politische Weichenstellungen im Nachkriegsdeutschland 1945-1953*, ed. H. Winkler. Göttingen.

Macridis, R. and B. Brown. 1976. *The DeGaulle Republic: Quest for Unity*. Westport.

Mair, P. 1995. Political Parties, Popular Legitimacy and Public Privilege. *West European Politics* 18 (3): 40-57.
March, J. and J. Olsen. 1989. *Rediscovering Institutions: The Organizational Basis of Politics.* New York.
Markovits, A. and C. Allen. 1984. Germany. In *Unions and Economic Crisis: Britain, West Germany and Sweden*, eds. P. Gourevitch et al. Boston.
Markovits, A. and P. Gorski. 1993. *The German Left: Red, Green and Beyond.* Oxford.
Markus, G. 1995. Reflections on the Central European Widening of Transnational Families. Budapest Papers on Democratic Transition 136. Budapest [Hungarian Center for Democracy Studies Foundation].
Marshall, B. 1992. German Migration Policies. In *Developments in German Politics*, eds. G. Smith et al., 247-63. Durham.
Matthias, E. and R. Morsey, eds. 1960. *Das Ende der Parteien 1933.* Düsseldorf.
Mayer. T. 1990. Immigration into West Germany: Historical Perspectives and Policy Implications. In *German Unification, Economic Issues*, eds. L. Lipschitz and D. McDonald. Washington.
Merritt, A and R. Merritt. 1970. *Public Opinion in Occupied Germany: The OMGUS Surveys 1945-1949.* Urbana.
Michels, R. 1962. *Political Parties: A Sociological Study of the Oligarchical Tendencies of Modern Democracy.* New York.
Middleton, M. 1987. Non-Profit Boards of Directors: Beyond the Governance Function. In *The Non-Profit Sector. A Research Handbook*, ed. W. Powell, 141-53. New Haven/London.
Molitor, U. 1992. *Wählen Frauen anders?* Baden-Baden.
Mommsen, H. 1987. Der lange Schatten der untergehenden Republik. Zur Kontinuität politischer Denkhaltungen von der späten Weimarer bis zur frühen Bundesrepublik. In *Die Weimarer Republik, 1918-1933. Politik, Wirtschaft, Gesellschaft*, eds. K.-D. Bracher, M. Funke, and H.-A. Jacobsen. Bonn.
Morlino, L. 1984. The Changing Relationship between Parties and Society in Italy. *West European Politics* 7 (4):44-66.

Morsey, R. 1977. Personal und Beamtenpolitik im Übergang von der Bizonen zur Bundesverwaltung. In *Verwaltungsgeschichte*, ed. R. Morsey. Berlin.

Müller, F. 1965. *Korporation und Assoziation. Eine Problemgeschichte der Vereinigungsfreiheit im deutschen Vormärz*. Berlin.

Münch, U. 1993. *Asylpolitik in der Bundesrepublik Deutschland: Entwicklung und Alternativen*, 2d ed. Opladen.

Nagle, J. D. 1970. *The National Democratic Party*. Berkeley/London.

Naßmacher, H. 1994. Transformationsprozesse aus regionaler und lokaler Perspektive. In *Politische Strukturen im Umbruch*, eds. H. Naßmacher, O. Niedermayer, and H.Wollman. Berlin.

Niclauß, K. 1995. *Das Parteiensystem der Bundesrepublik Deutschland. Eine Einführung*. Paderborn.

Nipperdey, T. 1980. 1933 und die Kontinuität der deutschen Geschichte. In *Die Weimarer Republik: Belagerte Civitas*, ed. M. Stürmer, 374-92. Meisenhain a. G.

———. 1993. *Deutsche Geschichte 1866-1918. Arbeitswelt und Bürgergeist*, vol. 1, 3d ed. Munich.

Ohlemacher, T. 1994. Xenophobia in the Reunified Germany. *Zeitschrift für Soziologie* 23 (3): 222-36.

Otto, V. 1971. *Das Staatsverständnis des Parlamentarischen Rats*. Düsseldorf.

Padgett, S. 1993. Party Democracy in the New German Polity. *German Politics and Society* 28: 16-38.

Padgett, S. and W. Paterson. 1994. Germany: Stagnation of the Left. In *Mapping the West European Left*, eds. P. Anderson and P. Camiller. London.

Palma, G. d. 1990. *To Craft Democracies: Reflections of Democratic Transitions and Beyond*. Berkeley.

———. 1993. Why Democracy Can Work in Eastern Europe. In *The Global Resurgence of Democracy*, eds. L. Diamond and M. Plattner, 257-67. Baltimore.

Panebianco, A. 1988. *Political Parties: Organization and Power*. Cambridge.

Pappi, F. 1973. Parteiensystem und Sozialstruktur in der Bundesrepublik. *Politische Vierteljahresschrift* 14 (2): 191-213.

———. 1977. Sozialstruktur, gesellschaftliche Wertorientierungen und Wahlabsicht. *Politische Vierteljahresschrift* 18 (2/3): 195-229.

———. 1979. Konstanz und Wandel der Hauptspannungslinien in der Bundesrepublik.In *Sozialer Wandel in Westeuropa*, ed. J. Matthes. Frankfurt.

———. 1985. Die konfessionell-religiöse Konfliktlinie in der deutschen Wählerschaft: Entstehung, Stabilität und Wandel. In *Wirtschaftlicher Wandel, religiöser Wandel und Wertwandel. Folgen für das politische Verhalten in der Bundesrepublik Deutschland*, eds. D. Oberndörfer, H. Rattinger and K. Schmitt, 263-90. Berlin.

———. 1986a. Das Wahlverhalten sozialer Gruppen bei Bundestagswahlen im Zeitvergleich. In *Wahlen und politischer Prozeß*, eds. H.-D. Klingemann and M. Kaase. Opladen.

———. 1986b. The West German Party System. In *Party Politics in Contemporary Western Europe*, eds. S. Bartolini and P. Mair. London.

———. 1990. Klassenstruktur und Wahlverhalten im sozialen Wandel. In *Wahlen und Wähler. Analysen aus Anlaß der Bundestagswahl 1987*, eds. M. Kaase and H.-D. Klingemann. Opladen.

———. 1991. Die Republikaner im Parteisystem der Bundesrepublik: Protesterscheinung oder politische Alternative? *Aus Politik und Zeitgeschichte* 21:37-44.

Pappi, F. and M. Terwey. 1982. The German Electorate: Old Cleavages and New Political Conflicts. In *Party Government and Political Culture in Western Germany*, eds. H. Döring and G. Smith, 174-96. New York.

Pappi, F. and P. Mnich. 1992. Germany (BRD). In *Electoral Change*, eds. M. Franklin et al. Cambridge.

Parlamentarische Rat 1948-49. Akten und Protokolle. 3 vols., reprint 1980-85. Boppard.

Pateman, C. 1970. *Participation and Democratic Theory*. Cambridge.

Patzelt, W. 1993. Legislators of New Parliaments: The Case of East Germany. In *Working Papers on Comparative Legislative Studies*, ed. L. Longley. Appleton.

Patzelt, W. and K. Algasinger. 1995. Strukturen politischer Interessenvermittlung in Sachsen. Technische Universität Dresden [Institut für Politikwissenschaft]. Mimeograph.

Phillips, A. 1994. Socialism with a New Face? The PDS in Search of Reform? *East European Politics and Societies* 8 (3): 507-11.

———. 1995. An Island of Stability? The German Political Party System and the Elections of 1994. *West European Politics* 18 (3): 219-29.

Piven, F. and R. Cloward. 1977. *Poor People's Movements: Why They Succeed and Why They Fail.* New York.

Prantl, H. 1993. Hysterie und Hilflosigkeit. Chronik der Asyldebatte seit der deutschen Einheit. In *Zuwanderung und Asyl in der Konkurrenzgesellschaft*, ed. B. Blanke. Opladen.

Pridham, G., ed. 1990. *Securing Democracy: Political Parties and Democratic Consolidation in Southern Europe.* London.

Pridham, G. and P. Lewis, eds. 1996. *Stabilizing Fragile Democracies.* London..

Priller, E. 1993. Zum entstehenden Nonprofit-Sektor in den neuen Bundesländern. In *Verwaltungsreform und Verwaltungspolitik im Prozeß der deutschen Einigung*, eds. W. Seibel, A. Benz and H. Mäding, 257-67. Baden-Baden.

Pütz, H., ed. 1975. *Konrad Adenauer und die CDU in der Britischen Verfassungszone.* Bonn.

Putnam, R. 1993. *Making Democracy Work: Civic Traditions in Modern Italy.* Princeton.

Rae, D. 1967. *The Political Consequences of Electoral Laws.* New Haven.

Raschke, J., ed. 1982. *Bürger und Parteien.* Opladen.

———. 1993. *Die Grünen. Was sie wurden. Was sie sind.* Köln.

Rattinger, H. 1993. Abkehr von den Parteien? Dimensionen der Parteiverdrossenheit.*Aus Politik und Zeitgeschichte* 11:24-35.

———. 1994. Parteiidentifikation in Ost- und Westdeutschland nach der Vereinigung. In *Politische Kultur in Ost- und Westdeutschland*, eds. O. Niedermayer and K. v. Beyme, 105-140. Berlin.

———. 1995. Parteineigungen in Ostdeutschland vor und nach der Wende. In *Ostdeutschland im Wandel. Lebensverhältnisse - politische Einstellungen*, ed. H. Bertram, 231-55. Opladen.
Reich, R. 1991. *The Work of Nations*. New York.
Rieger, G. 1994. "Parteienverdrossenheit" und "Parteienkritik" in der Bundesrepublik Deutschland. *Zeitschrift für Parlamentsfragen* 25 (3): 459-71.
Rinck, H.-J. 1966. Der verfassungsrechtliche Status der Politischen Parteien in der Bundesrepublik. In *Die moderne Demokratie und ihr Recht*, eds. K.-D. Bracher et al., 310-28. Tübingen.
Rink, D. 1995. Neue Bewegungen im Osten? Zur Entwicklung im ostdeutschen Bewegungssektor nach dem Ende der Bürgerbewegungen. *Forschungsjournal Neue Soziale Bewegungen* 20-26.
Ritter, G. 1990. The Social Bases of the German Political Parties, 1867-1920. In *Elections, Parties and Political Traditions. Social Foundations of Germany Parties and Party Systems, 1867-1987*, ed. K. Rohe, 27-52. New York/Oxford.
Römer, K. 1988. *Facts About Germany*. Gütersloh.
Rogers, D. 1990. The Western Allies and the Restoration of German Political Parties. Ph.D. diss., University of North Carolina, Chapel Hill.
———. 1995. *Politics after Hitler: The Western Allies and the German Party System*. New York.
Rohe, K. 1982. Wahlanalyse im historischen Kontext. Zu Kontinuität und Wandel von Wahlverhalten. *Historische Zeitschrift* 234 (3): 336-7.
———. 1992. *Wahlen und Wählertraditionen in Deutschland*. Frankfurt.
Rose, R. and E. Page. 1996. German Responses to Regime Change. *West European Politics* 19 (1): 1-27.
Ross, G. 1982. *Workers and Communists in France: From Popular Front to Eurocommunism*. Berkeley.
Roth, D. 1990. Die Wahlen zur Volkskammer in der DDR. Der Versuch einer Erklärung. *Politische Vierteljahresschrift* 31 (3): 369-93.

Rueschemeyer, M. 1995. The Social Democratic Party in Eastern Germany: Political Participation in the Former German Democratic Republic after Unification. Berlin [Wissenschaftszentrum Berlin für Sozialforschung].

Saage, R. 1983. Zum Begriff der Parteien und des Parlaments bei Carl Schmitt und Gerhard Leibholz. In *Zurück zum starken Staat?* 156-80. Frankfurt a.M.

Sachße, C. and F. Tennstedt. 1988. *Geschichte der Armenfürsorge in Deutschland. Band 2: Fürsorge und Wohlfahrtspflege 1871 bis 1929.* Stuttgart.

Sartori, G. 1976. *Parties and Party Systems: A Framework for Analysis.* Cambridge.

Scarrow, S. 1998. Party Decline at the Grassroots? A Comparative Analysis. Paper presented at the Midwest Political Science Association Meetings.

Schäfers, B. 1995. *Gesellschaftlicher Wandel in Deutschland.* 6th ed. Stuttgart.

Scheuch, E. and U. Scheuch, 1992. *Cliquen, Klüngel und Karrieren.* Reinbek.

Schmid, J., F. Löbler, and H. Tiemann. 1994. *Probleme Der Einheit: Organisationsstrukturen und Probleme von Parteien und Verbänden. Berichte aus den neuen Ländern.* Marburg.

Schmidt, U. 1996. Risse im Gefüge der vereinigten CDU. *Die neue Gesellschaft/Frankfurter Hefte* 4 (April): 303-8.

———. 1997. Die Ost-CDU im Umbruch 1989-1994. *German Studies Review* 20:105-137.

Schmitt, H. 1987. *Das Parteiensystem der Bundesrepublik Deutschland. Eine Einführung aus politik-soziologischer Perspektive.* 2 vols. Hagen.

Schmitt, K. 1990. Religious Cleavages in the West German Party System: Persistence and Change 1949-1987. In *Elections, Parties and Political Traditions. Social Foundations of German Parties and Party Systems, 1867-1987,* ed. K. Rohe. New York/Oxford.

———. 1994. Im Osten nichts Neues? Das Kernland der deutschen Arbeiterbewegung und die Zukunft der politischen

Linken. In *Das Superwahljahr*, eds. W. Bürklin and D. Roth, 185-218. Köln.
———. 1995. Die Landtagswahlen 1994 im Osten Deutschlands. Früchte des Föderalismus: Personalisierung und Regionalisierung. *Zeitschrift für Parlamentsfragen* 26 (2): 261-95.
Schmitt-Beck, R. 1994. Wählerpotentiale von Bündnis 90/Die Grünen im Ost-West Vergleich. Umfang, Struktur, politische Orientierungen. In *Kursbestimmung: Bündnis 90/Grüne Eckpunkte künftiger Politik*, ed. L. Probst. Köln.
Schmollinger, H. 1989. Die Wahl zum Abgeordnetenhaus von Berlin am 29. Januar 1989. Ein überraschender Wandel im Parteiensystem. *Zeitschrift für Parlamentsfragen* 20 (3): 309-22.
Scholz, R. 1983. *Krise der parteienstaatlichen Demokratie?* Berlin/New York.
———. 1993. Die gemeinsame Verfassungskommission: Auftrag, Verfahren, Ergebnisse. *Aus Politik und Zeitgeschichte* 52/53:3-5.
Schultze, R.-O. 1983. Wählerverhalten und Parteiensystem in der Bundesrepublik Deutschland. *Der Bürger im Staat* 1:1-18.
———. 1987. Meinungsforschung: Vom aktiven Wähler zum passiven Befragten. In *Parteien in der Krise?* eds. P. Haungs and E. Jesse, 169-74. Köln.
———. 1995. Widersprüchliches, Ungleichzeitiges und kein Ende in Sicht: Die Bundestagswahl vom 16.10.1994. *Zeitschrift für Parlamentsfragen* 26 (2): 325-52.
Schulz, M. 1995. "Für Selbstbestimmung und Würde:" Die Metamorphose des Behindertenverbandes der DDR zum allgemeinen Behindertenverband in Deutschland. Working paper AG Trap 95/1, Max-Planck-Gesellschaft zur Förderung der Wissenschaften. Berlin.
Schulze, G. 1993. *Die Erlebnisgesellschaft*. Frankfurt/New York.
Schumacher, K. 1985. *Reden, Schriften, Korrespondenzen, 1945-1952*. Berlin.
Seibel, W. 1997. *The Strength of Mediocrity. The Nonprofit Sector in German Politics and Polity*. Ann Arbor.
Sheehan, J. 1978. *German Liberalism in the Nineteenth Century*. Chicago

Silvia, S. 1992. The Forward Retreat: Labor and Social Democracy in Germany, 1982-1992. *International Journal of Political Economy* 4 (Winter): 36-52.

———. 1993. Left Behind: The Social Democratic Party in eastern Germany after Unification. *West European Politics* 16 (2): 24-48.

———. 1995. The Social Democratic Party of Germany. *German Studies Review* 18:132-44.

Smith, J., ed. 1974. *The Papers of General Lucius D. Clay: Germany 1945-1949*. Bloomington.

Smith, G. 1982a. *Democracy in Western Germany: Parties and Politics in the Federal Republic*. New York.

———. 1982b. The German Volkspartei and the Career of the Catch-all Concept. In *Party Government and Political Culture in Western Germany*, eds. H. Döring and G. Smith, 59-76. New York.

———. 1992. The "New" German Party System. In *Developments in German Politics*, eds. G. Smith et al., 77-102. Durham.

Soe, C. 1995. The Free Democratic Party: Struggle for Survival, Influence and Identity. In *Germany's New Politics*, eds. D. Conradt et al., 149-76. Providence/Oxford.

Solga, H. 1994 "Systemloyalität" als Bedingung sozialer Mobilität im Staatssozialismus, am Beispiel der DDR. *Berliner Journal für Soziologie* 4:521-42.

Staritz, D. 1987. *Die Gründung der DDR*. Munich.

Statistisches Bundesamt. 1994. *Datenreport 1994*. Bonn.

Steinkemper, B. 1974. *Klassische und Politische Bürokraten in der Ministerialverwaltung der Bundesrepublik Deutschland*. Köln.

Steinmo, S., K. Thelen and F. Longstreth. 1992. *Structuring Politics: Historical Institutionalism in Comparative Perspective*. New York.

Stock, M. 1994. Youth Culture in East Germany: from Symbolic Dropout to Politicization. *Communist and Post-Communist Studies* 27 (2): 135-43.

Stöss, R. 1990. Parteikritik und Parteiverdrossenheit. *Aus Politik und Zeitgeschichte* 21:15-24.

———. 1991. *Extreme Rechte in der Bundesrepublik*. Berlin.

———. 1993. Rechtsextremismus und Wahlen in der Bundesrepublik. *Aus Politik und Zeitgeschichte* 11: 50-61.
Stolleis, M., H. Schäfer and R. Rhinow, eds. 1986. *Parteienstaatlichkeit: Krisensymptome des demokratischen Verfassungsstaat?* Berlin/New York.
Streeck, W. 1984. Neo-Corporatist Industrial Relations and the Economic Crisis in West Germany. Working paper 97, European University Institute. Florence.
Streul, I. 1993. Die Umgestaltung des Mediensystems in Ostdeutschland. *Aus Politik und Zeitgeschichte* 40:36-46.
Strübin, M. 1997. Ecological Tax Reform in Germany. *German Politics* 6 (2).
Stürmer, M. 1983. *Das ruhelose Reich.* Berlin.
Taagepera, R. and M. Shugart. 1989. *Seats and Votes: The Effects and Determinants of Electoral Systems.* New Haven.
Tangemann, M. 1995. *Intermediäre Organisationen im deutschdeutschen Einigungsprozeß.* Konstanz.
Terwey, M. and A. McCutchon. 1995. Belief and Practice in the Unified Germanies. *ZA-Information* 34:47-69 [Zentralarchiv für empirische Sozialforschung, Köln].
Thaissen, U. 1994. The Bundesrat, the Länder, and German Federalism. Key Institutions of German Democracy 1. American Institute for Contemporary German Studies, Washington DC.
Thieß, M. 1994. Der gesellschaftliche Wandel im selbstverwalteten Sport, dargestellt am Landessportbund Thüringen. In *Organisationstrukturen und Probleme von Parteien und Verbänden. Berichte aus den neuen Ländern,* eds. J. Schmid et al. Marburg.
Veen, H.-J. and J. Hoffmann. 1992. *Die Grünen zu Beginn der neunziger Jahre.* Bonn/Berlin.
Veen, H.-J., J. Hoffmann, and P. Gluchowski. 1994. Die Anhängerschaften der Parteien vor und nach der Einheit – eine Langfristbetrachtung von 1953 bis 1993. *Zeitschrift für Parlamentsfragen* 25 (2): 165-86.
Veen, H.-J., N. Lepszy, and P. Mnich. 1993. *The Republikaner Party in Germany: Right Wing Menace or Protest Catch-All?* Westport.

Vester, M., P. v. Oertzen, H. Geiling, T. Hermann, and D. Müller. 1993. *Soziale Milieus im gesellschaftlichen Strukturwandel.* Köln.
Volkmann, U. 1992. *Politische Parteien und öffentliche Leistungen.* Berlin.
Voscherau, H. 1993. Verfassungsreform und Verfassungsdiskurs. *Aus Politik und Zeitgeschichte* 52/53:5-7.
Wagener, A. 1992. Brandenburgische Arbeitsfördergesellschaften. Ergebnisse einer Befragung. Kleinmachnow. Mimeograph.
Wagner, F. 1979. Der öffentliche Dienst im Staat der Gegenwart. *Veröffentlichungen der Vereinigung der Deutschen Staatsrechtslehrer* 37. Berlin.
Wattenberg, M. 1994. *The Decline of American Political Parties, 1952-1992.* Cambridge
Welsh, H. 1994. Political Transition Processes in Central and Eastern Europe. *Comparative Politics* 26:379-94.
———. 1995. Four Years and Several Elections Later: The Eastern German Political Landscape after Unification. In *Germany's New Politics*, eds. D. Conradt et al., 43-60. Providence/Oxford.
Weisbrod, B. 1988. *The Non-Profit-Economy.* Cambridge.
Weßels, B. 1994. Gruppenbindung und rationale Faktoren als Determinanten der Wahlentscheidung in Ost- und Westdeutschland. In *Wahlen und Wähler. Analysen aus Anlaß der Bundestagswahl 1990*, eds. H.-D. Klingemann and M. Kaase. Opladen.
Wiesendahl, E. 1992. Volksparteien im Abstieg. *Aus Politik und Zeitgeschichte* 34/35:3-25.
Wiesenthal, H. 1995. *Einheit als Interessenpolitik. Studien zur sektoralen Transformation Ostdeutschlands.* Frankfurt/New York.
Willems, H. 1993. *Fremdenfeindliche Gewalt: Einstellung, Täter, Konflikteskalation.* Opladen.
Winkler, H. 1978. From Social Protectionism to National Socialism: The German Small-Business Movement in Comparative Perspective. *Journal of Modern History* 48 (1): 1-18.

Wolf, C. 1996. Konfessionelle versus religiöse Konfliktlinie in der deutschen Wählerschaft. *Politische Vierteljahresschrift* 37 (4): 713-34.

Yoder, J. 1995. The Formation of New Political Elites in Eastern Germany: Implications for Democratization. Paper presented at the American Association for the Advancement of Slavic Studies Convention.

Ziegler, H. 1993. *Political Parties in Industrial Democracies*. Itasca.

Zimmer, A. 1995. Kultur im Transformationsprozeß. Zur Reorganisation des Museumswesens in den neuen Ländern. *Soziale Welt* 46:197-222.

Zimmer, A. and E. Priller. 1996. Intermediäre Organisationen in den neuen Bundesländern. Der Non-Profit-Sektor in Ostdeutschland. Konstanz/Halle [Kommission für die Erforschung des sozialen und politischen Wandels in den neuen Bundesländern]. Mimeograph.

Newspaper and Periodicals List

Berliner Zeitung 1992
Frankfurter Allgemeine Zeitung 1991-93
Frankfurter Rundschau 1998
Suddeutsche Zeitung 1986-98
Spiegel 1991-98
Sozialpolitische Rundschau 1995
Tageszeitung 1995-98
Welt 1992
ZDF (Politbarometer) 1994
Die Zeit 1994

INDEX

A

Adenauer, Konrad, xiii, 23, 64-65, 69-74, 80
anti-Socialist Laws, 35
Austrian *Volksparteien*, 32

B

Basic Law (*Grundgesetz*), 22-23, 71-73, 76, 84, 88, 102-103, 105, 107, 109, 111, 126, 151, 180
Bavarian Peoples Party (BVP), 40
Beamte, 95
Berlusconi, Silvio, 4, 15-16
Biedenkopf, Kurt, 186
Bismarck, Otto von, 35
Bizonal Economic Council, 70-71
Blair, Tony, 4, 7-10
Bosnia, 145, 158
Brandt, Willy, 142
British Zonal Council, 70
British Zone, xiii
Bundesrat, 73, 78, 88, 995
Bundestag, 25, 77-79, 88

C

Catholic Church, 34-35, 40, 42, 56
Center Party, 35-36, 38, 40-42

Chirac, Jacques, 15
Christian Democratic Party - Italy (DC), 16
Christian Democratic Union (CDU), xiii-xvi, 23, 25-26, 31, 40-47, 56, 59-60, 66-67, 69, 73, 77, 81, 86, 88, 91, 110-14, 116, 120, 123-27, 129-31, 136, 141-42, 144-46, 154, 160-78, 180-206, 209, 228-29
Christian Social Union (CSU), 2, 23, 26, 31, 40-47, 56, 59-60, 67, 77, 86, 110-14, 116, 120, 123, 125-27, 129-31, 136, 142, 144-46, 154, 160-78
Citizenship Law (1913), 105
"Common Program", 13
Communist Party - France (PCF), 11-14
Communist Party – Italy (PCI), 12, 15-17, 28
Consociational Democracy, 192n
Conservative Party, 6-10

D

d'Alema, Massimo, 17
de Gaulle, Charles, 11-13, 19

Index

Democratic Party, 4-6
"Democratic Party State", 24, 63, 74, 78-93, 97

E

Europeanization, xi
European Integration, xi

F

Federal Constitutional Court, 63-64, 72, 74-76, 79, 81, 97, 109
Federal Expellees and Refugees Law (1953), 102
Fifth Republic (France), 11-15
Fischer, Joschka, 144-45, 154-58
Forbes, Steven, 4
Foreigner's Law (*Ausländergesetz*) (1965), 106
Forza Italia, 4
Fourth Republic (France), 11-12
France, xii, 3-4, 10-15
Free Democratic Party (FDP), xiv-xvi, 2, 26, 31-33, 40-47, 53, 60, 66-67, 73, 77, 82, 86, 89, 92, 126, 136, 142-47, 153, 160-78, 180-206
Front National (France), 11-14
Fundis, 138

G

Gaullist Party, 11-15
Gehrke, Wolfgang, 186
German Communist Party (KPD), 66, 76n, 141, 181
German Democratic Republic (GDR), xii-xvi, 55, 58, 85-93, 118-19, 121, 143, 146-47, 161, 164-173, 181-206, 211, 214-16
German Joint Welfare Association (DPWV), 219, 229

German Peoples Union (DVU), 53-54, 99n, 100, 122, 124, 125-26, 130
Greenpeace, 149
Greens Party (Alliance Greens) xii-xvi, 26, 32, 48, 51-52, 55, 58-60, 76-77, 80, 83, 85-87, 89, 91-92, 96, 133-160, 164, 176-77, 190, 196, 201
Gysi, Gregor, 142, 187

H

Honecker, Erich, 119
Hoyerswerda, 121-24

I

Israel, 4, 15-17
Italy, xii, 3-4, 9, 32

K

Kohl, Helmut, 80n, 112, 124, 138
Kosovo, 145
Kulturkampf, 35-36

L

Labour Party, 6-10
Lafontaine, Oskar, 139
Lager, 37, 53, 59-60, 65
Länderrat, 68
Le Pen, Jean Marie, 11, 28
Liberal (Democratic) Party, 6-10
Liebholz, Gerhard, 74

M

Major, John, 10
Milosovic, Slobodan, 155
Mitterrand, FranVois, 11
Mölln, 123-24, 130

Index

N

National Assembly (France), 10-15
National Democratic Party (NPD), 53, 99n, 117, 125
National Socialist German Workers Party (NSDAP, Nazi), 37-39, 53, 59, 62, 107-109, 115
NATO, 153-57
Neo Fascist Party (MSI), 15-16
Netanyahu, Benjamin, 4

O

"Olive Tree" Coalition, 16-17
OMGUS, 69

P

Parliamentary Council, 71-72, 78
Party of Democratic Socialism (PDS), xiii-xvi, 26, 28, 32, 48, 55-58, 60, 76, 86-87, 89-92, 96-97, 135-36, 140-43, 152, 155-56, 168-78, 180-206, 219, 228, 232
Party of the Democratic Left (Italy), 16-17
Perot, Ross, 4, 15
Potsdam Conference, 66
Prodi, Romano, 17
Protestant Church, 34-35, 40, 56
Prussia, 37, 39

R

Realos, 138, 140, 144, 155, 158
"Red-Green" government, xv, 105, 131
Republican Party (France), 11-15
Republican Party (U.S.), 4-6
Republikaner (REP), 31, 48, 52-55, 76, 84, 99n, 111, 115-17, 122, 124-26, 128-29, 171

S

Schmidt, Helmut, 142
Schröder, Gerhard, 105, 139, 151
Schumacher, Kurt, xiii, 23, 64-65, 69-74, 80, 82n
Social Democratic Party of Germany (SPD), xiii-xvi, 23, 25-26, 35-36, 40-47, 55-56, 59-60, 66-67, 69, 73, 77, 80, 82, 86, 88, 91-92, 110-11, 114, 116, 125-27, 129-30, 133-159-78, 180-206, 209, 229
Social Market Economy, 119-120
Socialist Party (France), 11-15
Socialist Party (Italy), 16
Socialist Unity Party (SED), 58, 118, 140-42, 146-47, 164-67, 181, 183-85, 188-89, 219, 232
Stolpe, Manfred, 87
Süssmuth, Rita, 88
Switzerland, 19

T

Thatcher, Margaret, 7
Third Reich, 53, 65
Third Republic (France), 11

U

Unification Treaty, , 208, 221, 226
United Kingdom (Great Britain), xii, 3-4, 6-10
United Nations (UN), 156
United States, xii, 3-6, 9

V

Volksparteien, 40, 58, 75-77, 89, 139
Vogel, Bernhard, 186
Vollmer, Antje, 145

W

Weimar Republic, 24, 37-39, 53, 59, 62, 65-66, 69, 72-74, 76-77, 96-97
Weizsäcker, Richard von, 88
World War I, 37
World War II, xii, 15, 18, 37, 63, 67, 97

Y

Young Socialists (JUSOs), 137

www.ingramcontent.com/pod-product-compliance
Lightning Source LLC
Chambersburg PA
CBHW071151070526
44584CB00019B/2750